MW01503391

Angelic Physics: Why Good Eventually Triumphs Over Evil

To order additional copies of this title, or to contact the author, please e-mail: Lt.nicholas.faulkner@gmail.com

First printing January 2023
Library of Congress Cataloging-in-Publication Data

Paperback ISBN: 9798373955409
Hardcover ISBN: 9798373955676

Faulkner, Nicholas
angelic physics: why good eventually triumphs over evil / by Nicholas Faulkner

Published by AR PRESS, an American Real Publishing Company

Roger L. Brooks, Publisher
roger@incubatemedia.us
americanrealpublishing.com

Edited by Claire Gault
Interior Design by Eva Myrick

Visit: angelicphysics.org

Printed in the U.S.A.
.

ANGELIC PHYSICS
WHY GOOD EVENTUALLY TRIUMPHS OVER EVIL

NICHOLAS FAULKNER

Table of Contents

Caveat:

I recall sitting on my back porch about eight years ago reading the caveat for Dr. David Hawkins' book *Eye of the Eye,* in which he states that the information contained in this book may be better bypassed by some.

If one is comfortable and happy within the confines of current scientific dogma or the rather restrictive spiritual box that some religions offer, then the information contained within is better bypassed. The universe has us all evolving in the proper place and skipping grades isn't always a good thing.

The social turbulence we now see is evidence of a human race rapidly evolving, as people try to step out of the traditional boxes that worked relatively well in the past. Unfortunately, people trying to step out of the box society laid out for them are finding no safe higher next step.

This book is the Angelic kingdom's attempt to reconcile traditional science, current technological thinking, and time-tested religion to create a safe next step. Only when played together perfectly do these three elements sound harmonic and create a higher octave sound.

Years ago reading Dr. David Hawkins' warning, I felt ready for an evolutionary jump, so I went forward with the reading, having no clue the infinite grandness of the reality that awaited me. In retrospect, the decision to keep reading was made in haste. Life has never been the same since.

I urge the reader to consider their current reality and relationship with God and gauge if one wants to move forward. The evolution of souls tends to be a slow process but as I'll say in this book, Earth is where souls come for fast-tracked evolution. Fast-tracked evolution may sound appealing to some, but in reality, this means karma and personal flaws rapidly coming to the surface to be healed. This will likely show up as turbulence in one's life, not unlike the turbulence one feels on a plane rising in altitude.

This book is for those who really feel the 'need for speed' in their evolution.

If one enjoys their current box then this book is better bypassed. The Angelic kingdom will love you equally whatever decision you make. God bless everyone!

Forward:

Angelic Takeaway: In this book I'll summarize every chapter very briefly at the beginning in an 'Angelic Takeaway.' One can skip areas they are not interested in, and it helps those of you too lazy to read an entire book.

I'm writing this book to deliver the good news. As nothing happens by accident, if you are reading this book I'm here to tell you nothing is wrong and there is nothing to fear; you simply are in an Angel-evolving Simulation. At the time of the writing of this book, approximately 1.7% of humans on Earth have graduated from the animal stages of evolution and entered the Angelic stages of evolution. We can expect to see this number rise exponentially from here on out as the human species continues to evolve.

This Simulation is clearly not heavenly and clearly not hellish, though it contains pockets of both. The Simulation is purgatorial by divine design. By having such a wide variety of energies coexisting together on this planet, there are virtually infinite choices for a soul to make. This maximizes the speed of the soul's evolution towards the Angelic kingdom, but gives the Simulation a 'school of hard-knocks' kind of feel.

One may wish this Simulation was a dance in some celestial garden, where one's most difficult choice was whether or not to pet the unicorn, but this would mean extremely slow evolution. This Simulation is where souls come who are on God's fast-tracked evolutionary path.

In this Simulation we are all bound by a very basic rule set, known to the world as physics. This Simulation has seven levels stacked on top of each other which interact. This allows souls of different levels of evolution to interact with each other for learning and evolution purposes. These levels of the Simulation have been known to humanity for about 3000 years as the seven chakras.

The more evolved or the further along a soul is in evolution, the more access it generally has to the higher levels of the Simulation, which are less bound by the time-based physics rule-set. The majority of earth's human occupants currently occupy the lower three levels primarily.

Souls occupy bodies in the Simulation. While in the Simulation, any energy projected onto another soul must eventually be experienced. This is widely understood in the Eastern world as the Law of Karma. The Western world is most familiar with the concept via the biblical golden rule, "In everything, do to others what you have them do to you" (Mathew 7:12). The physics of the western world also points to this concept, which shows that everything in the universe must eventually be balanced.

Over lifetimes in many bodies, souls slowly evolve by experiencing the effects of their own energy from different perspectives. In order for the Simulation to seem real and its lessons to take hold, the effects of one's energy must be experienced as coming from outside oneself from an unrelated source. However, this is always simply the ripples of one's own energy returning to them. Forgiving something apparently outside yourself relieves your personal karma. This is why earthly memory is normally reset between lifetimes to give the appearance of randomness. Details of previous lives in other bodies becomes increasingly recallable in the higher levels of the Simulation.

In this Simulation, only one power source ultimately exists. This power source has unlimited power and is infinitely loving. The most common word for this power source is 'God.'

A main point of the Simulation is for players to learn to access this power source and use its power wisely, which is the role of Angels in the universe. The higher a level the soul is on, the more of this divine power the soul has access to. This, however, increases the potential for its misuse, which can have devastating karmic consequences for both the individual and the collective. This is why evolving up through the levels of the Simulation takes many lifetimes and is a slow controlled process which requires faith.

In the Simulation, there are two major teams playing. Players switch teams on a fairly regular basis without realizing it, and many of the lower-level players don't even realize they are playing for a team.

One team is the Angelic, which is rallied around and draws from the only power source in the Simulation. They tend to encourage other players to follow the way of truth and love which ultimately pulls them into the higher, more powerful levels of the Simulation closer to God, love and happiness.

The other team is the demonic; they lack any real power and only obtain a semblance of power by encouraging other players to move down into the lower levels of the Simulation, where less power is available and more restrictions apply so that they can be controlled. This team tries to keep you in the Simulation, oftentimes long after it stops being fun.

Given the descriptions of these two teams, one may wonder why anyone would choose to play for the demonic instead of the Angelic. The short answer is no one would voluntarily if they fully understood the rules of the Simulation and the long-term consequences. This is why a characteristic of demonic energy is extreme complexity and confusion. A main purpose of this book is to explain the rules of the Simulation as clearly as possible.

Another question one could pose is, *Why would an infinitely powerful loving god even allow the demonic team to exist?* Again, the short answer is that in order for souls to evolve and learn, unfavorable options and choices must exist in the Simulation so that the consequences of these actions can be lived out and lessons learned. Oftentimes it's the demonic presenting these unfavorable options, so even the demonic serves divinity in a roundabout way. Also, certain lessons can only be learned by temporarily being tricked into playing out an evil role and living out a difficult lesson through karma. I HIGHLY recommend trying one's best to avoid this path, as the suffering is severe.

Once the rules of the Simulation are understood, progress becomes increasingly enjoyable, happy, and Angelic as the individual player continuously melts back into oneness with the universe, and ultimately out of the drama of the Simulation.

Some of the greatest Angelic players in recorded history such as Jesus, Buddha, and Lord Krishna have explained the rules of the Simulation in a language appropriate for their time and audience.

I describe the rules of the Simulation in a different language and style than these previous great players, but want to emphasize that I do not disagree with any of the direct observations of these aforementioned great players.

I was born in 1980, educated in the fields of Physics, Mathematics, Computers, and Engineering. I also have a condition known as autism, which presented difficulties in this lifetime but allowed me to sense quantum vibrations (someone's vibe) extremely well. This helped make this book happen. Someone's vibe feels very different, depending on whether they are playing for the Angelic or demonic team and what level of the Simulation they are playing in.

As nothing happens by accident, if you are reading this book, you are probably already a higher-level player or are ready for a giant quantum leap in evolution up in the Simulation. You are also probably playing on the Angelic team, as the energy of this book is repulsive to the other team.

This book simply sets out to explain the rules of the Simulation and unscramble basic truth. Once one understands the rules, one can know what direction one is headed and life gets progressively calmer and more enjoyable. As previously stated, the Angelic team ultimately has all the real power and any appearance of demonic power is an illusion. This leads to the best news of all, which is that despite appearances, the Angelic team always wins in the end and the demonic always loses. Good always eventually triumphs over evil, even if it takes centuries. A matter of fact, any appearance of competition between the two teams is an illusion.

Light does not battle darkness but simply nullifies darkness wherever it goes.

Gloria in Excelsis Deo (Glory be to God in the highest).

How This Book is Written:

Angelic Takeaway: This book was written by the Angelic kingdom with me as a low-paid translator. Fans with dyslexia will rejoice that the order this book is read is of a bit less importance than a normal book, as absorbing the book's energy is actually more important than the details. These Angelic Takeaways are written to facilitate moving quickly to the parts of the book that one is intuitively attracted to. One should take what resonates and leave the rest.

In December of 2019 I was blessed with an Angelic experience which initiated a rapid rise through the levels of the Simulation, and began to cleanse the remnants my personal karma.

This process largely occurred concurrently with COVID-19 pandemic, which was simply karma being rapidly cleansed on a collective level. On both an individual and collective level, karma from the lower levels must be repaid before a higher level can be achieved. One cannot move onto the next level of a video game without beating the previous one and learning its lessons.

The recent chaos in the collective consciousness of humanity is simply all of us balancing our karma in our own way. Humanity is now set for a momentous leap in evolution, and this book is a tiny part of it.

This book was not as much written by me, but was downloaded and translated through me. The download was holistic and complete from the Angelic field, and then my limited earthly mind has done its best to translate it into human language, relating to the fields of nerdy knowledge previously learned in this life.

Most books are written by an author who claims to have written it, while some spiritual books claim to be channeled from some higher source and the author claims no credit. This book was written with a process in the middle of those two extremes. It came from a higher source, but the personal self of the author was involved.

The order of presentation presented a challenge, as the download was holistic but had to be divided into linear parts to be presented in human language. Because of this, the order it is read is relatively unimportant, but some basic information from parts of the book are necessary to understand other parts. I sometimes repeat important points to facilitate the reading in different orders and place further emphasis on them.

I've included humor in this book, even though it is not common in the spiritual literature of the world. It is a very useful tool as it transmits essence quickly and is able to resolve paradoxes that cold logic simply cannot. It also dispels any nasty rumors that the Angelic kingdom does not have a sense of humor, and may help you resist breaking into the booze cabinet while reading this thing.

An upside of this book is that it is truly multi-dimensional and written to capture reality holistically, not just from a single perspective. A downside is one will notice the language and style changes from section to section. Great efforts were taken to minimize this, however one may feel like they are reading a book written by multiple authors with different writing styles, which may annoy those of you that prefer consistency.

As I advise with all things: take what resonates with you about this book and consider what does not resonate with you, but don't get bogged down by it. As this book is written from multiple perspectives and levels of the Simulation, very few people will agree with everything.

My Angelic guides have encouraged me to trim this first book down to a bare minimum to hopefully provide a fun, basic read. Some chapters in this book will eventually be turned into books unto themselves, but "Rome was not built in a day."

In this book I go into a lot of areas of knowledge that have been widely written about, such as autism, Quantum Mechanics, chakras, Simulation theory, and Angels. I've read a bit of the pre-existing literature on each of these topics, but am admittedly not well-read on any of them. I've found that my observations generally agree with the pre-existing literature, but not completely. When one of my personal observations has disagreed with pre-existing literature I've stuck by my personal observation. This is in line with proper scientific thinking in that one should draw conclusions based on their experiential observations rather than draw conclusions to fit pre-existing data or someone else's theory. Effort has been placed to avoid confirmation bias in this book, which is simply setting out to prove a pre-existing belief system.

I also use a process called calibration, which involves a pendulum and communication with the Angelic universe. If one sees "(tested true)" at the end of the statement it simply means that the previous statement was at least double checked using this process. All the information in this book was tested with the process to some extent. Belief in this process is not necessary to enjoy the book, and a later chapter discusses the process in more detail.

Numbers are also used in this book more often than is typical in spiritual texts. As numbers point to reality but cannot encapsulate ultimate reality, one should take them with a grain of salt. The Quantum Mechanics concept of 'fuzzy numbers' can be researched for information on how the numbers in this book should be interpreted.

Virtually no book is without errors and I'm quite sure this book will contain errors, but one can read this book confident that it is an original work not restricted by pre-existing dogma. If errors are found in the future, I'll happily correct them.

Wave-Particle Duality:

Angelic Takeaway: Quantum Mechanics nerds figured out a long time ago that everything, including ourselves, can be described mathematically as both a wave or a particle. YOU are a soul (wave) playing the temporary role of body (particle) inside this nutty Angel training video game.

A common concept in Quantum Mechanics is "wave-particle duality." Google (at the time of the writing) describes it as "the concept in quantum mechanics that every quantum entity may be described as either a **particle** or a **wave**." Basically everything is a particle and a wave. Not one or the other, but both at the same time.

Newtonian Physics tends to describe the particle universe. Religion and spirituality tend to describe the wave universe. In certain circles, arguments occur over which of these realities is correct. Both are correct within their own paradigm and actually don't conflict with each other if properly contextualized (tested true).

Quantum Mechanics is the mathematical science which connects the two. A main goal of this book is to connect up the wavy world of spiritual reality with the partically world physical reality. It should be noted, however, that they are not actually separate realities, but our limited senses tend to interpret it that way.

Our English language reflects this wave-particle duality, as throughout history humans have intuited two sides of our particle/wave reality with the following word-pairs:

Physical vs. Spiritual

Newtonian vs. Quantum

Time Domain vs. Frequency Domain

Linear vs. Non-Linear

Objective vs. Subjective

Explicit vs. Implicit

Unfolded vs. Folded

Concrete vs. Abstract

Body vs. Soul

Materialistic vs. Philosophical

Physical vs. Metaphysical

Dark vs. Light

Content vs. Context

Western vs. Eastern

External vs. Internal

Wild vs. Civilized

Demonic vs. Angelic

Evolution vs. Creation

Two words I'll be using in this book are 'wavy' and 'partically.' Broadly, I'll use wavy to mean spiritual and partically to describe physical. I do this, because in my forty-two years of life I've watched the world of spirituality and science grow further and further apart. A primary goal of this book is to describe wavy reality in such a way that it connects up to partically reality better, using basic physics and engineering concepts.

I've noticed that the English language that this book was originally written in lacks words and phrases for certain high-level spiritual concepts, which makes even the best English translations of Hindu and Buddhist texts clunky. However, the English language has recently gained many technological words and phrases to describe computers, technology, and video games. These new words provide an excellent opportunity to describe these Eastern spiritual concepts to technologically proficient westerners (tested true). This is why my Angels guided me to educate myself and work as an engineer (even though it's a profession I'm not particularly well-suited for) so this book could come into existence (tested true).

I hope to create a context where people viewing life more from the wavy/spiritual context can understand the people viewing life more from the partically/physical context a bit better and vice-versa. They aren't actually separate realities but simply reflections of each other.

If you are not familiar with Quantum Mechanics and science, substituting the word 'energy' for 'waves' or 'energetic' for wavy may make you more comfortable. The essence of this book can be comprehended in those terms even if it is a bit of an oversimplification.

Albert Einstein's famous equation $E=mc^2$ (Energy = Mass time the speed of light squared) points to the concept of wave-particle duality in traditional Newtonian scientific terms. Mass and energy are not separate realities, but simply different aspects of the same reality vibrating at a different frequency, much like particles and waves.

Broadly here is a brief description of the wavy universe and the partically universe. Humans experience both, with most humans experiencing the partically universe primarily, due to our current stage of evolution.

Wavy Universe	Partically Universe
All exist as a unified reality. Any energy radiated out from any source eventually returns to it (karma). This universe exists outside the construct of time so a feeling of patience, bliss, and immortality exists here as life is experienced forever. There is infinite freedom. Infinite love and protection is experienced from an immense power some choose to call God. There is no separation from this power source but there is an understanding that all power in the universe flows from this source. Traditional religions seem to point to this universe using terms such as 'Heaven,' 'Paradise' or 'Lotus Land.' If technologically inclined, one can think of the wavy universe as the electricity	This universe is subject to and inside the construct of time, run by a tight set of laws much like a computer simulation is. Newton's three laws learned in any traditional physics course are an excellent primer of these rules and the basic functioning of the partically universe. The primary rule of this universe is that everything must eventually balance. Traditional science is always in the process of attaining a better understanding of the precise details of these laws. Entities experience themselves not 'as one with each other' but as individual entities separate from one another. All motion, forces, and doing play out in this universe. However if one focuses too primarily on this universe,

that runs a computer, and the partically Simulation as the computer itself, which has no power unless powered by the electricity.	one begins to feel alone or cut off from one's true source.

The wavy world is fundamental and the partically world is a time-delayed copy. This time delay between the wavy world and its partically play-out increases exponentially as one falls down into the lower levels of the Simulation (tested true).

This book is written to intersect these two paradigms. Humans experience the world from both paradigms simultaneously, but it is extremely important to note, and in-line with the great spiritual literature of the world, that one's true self is a 'wave' or 'soul' and not a 'particle' or 'body' (tested true). The particle aspect of you is your physical body and could be likened to a character you are temporarily playing in a video game.

Perhaps the biggest crossover between the wavy universe and the partically universe besides Quantum Mechanics is the placebo effect. The placebo effect occurs when a drug or treatment has an effect on a patient that cannot be attributed to any inherent physical properties of the drug or treatment itself. This effect is the Achilles heel of partically scientists, who insist that only what their partically senses pick up is real.

The pharmaceutical industry must take this into account in their trials, as even a sugar pill will tend to heal a person if they truly believe that it will do so. Oftentimes things of this world have effect on us greater than of the physical properties of thing itself. This is because at the end of the day, our powerful wavy souls assign meaning, value, power, and effects to the various things in our lives.

In the next chapter I will discuss the seven levels of the Simulation, often referred to as levels of consciousness or development on similar scales. The top levels represent the experience of life from a wavy perspective, and the bottom levels represent the experience of life from a partically perspective.

The Seven Levels of the Simulation:

Angelic Takeaway: This Simulation has seven major levels that correspond to classic chakra system of the east. The higher levels are more spiritual, wavy, peaceful, and powerful and the lower levels are more physical, partically, competitive, and subject to time. No level is strictly better than any other. However, since all energy flows from the higher levels down to the lower levels, the lower levels of the Simulation are always subject to the higher levels.

Imagine you are making a documentary on the human experience and you've decided to use your film's budget to find seven different people, talk deeply to them about the human experience, and try to find commonalities and wisdom in their diverse experiences.

If the purpose of your documentary is truly to see the human experience, two things would be very important. You would want to interview very different people and you would want to hear about their experience in a raw, untainted way. This would mean interviewing them with no preconceived agenda and not trying to prove any existing idea. As Quantum Mechanics and the scientific process teaches us, any investigation with an agenda to 'prove' something tends to do just that, whether what you were trying to prove is true or not (tested true).

Let's say you design your documentary to be centered around seven walks of life. You have $1000 in your budget for each of your seven interviewees to give them in exchange for their time.

You start your interviews with a homeless person sitting on the side of the street. By talking to him, you discover that he had a troubled childhood and fell into substance abuse. He has a very pessimistic and fatalistic view on reality. He is only interested in continuing the interview because you offered him $1000. At the conclusion of the interview you give him $1000, which in the follow-up interview you find out was used to buy drugs.

Next you talk to a waitress who works in a restaurant in a very ethnocentric area. She agrees to the interview for the $1000 but is very hesitant, as you don't look or act quite like the people in her local environment. However after the interview gets rolling, she lights up when given an opportunity to talk about her family and the local culture of her people, but then gets angry when she begins to talk about another group of people moving into her neighborhood. At the conclusion of the interview you give her $1000, which you find out in the follow-up interview was used to help a family member with legal issues.

Next, you find a construction worker to interview. He runs a martial arts dojo on the side and has won a few individual martial arts competitions. During the interview, you find out that the man believes in standing up for both oneself and others and doing what is right. Despite a strong work ethic, he has been through a few divorces and struggles with personal and legal issues. At the conclusion of the interview you give him $1000. In the follow-up interview you learn was used to upgrade his martial arts dojo.

Now you decide to interview a teacher from a small town. She loves the idea of your documentary and agrees to do the interview before any talk of money. During the interview, you find her positive energy infectious and find out in the interview that she is very active in her school and local church.

The interview is going wonderfully until the subject of an opposing political party comes up, whom she blames for the problems in her community. At the conclusion of the interview you give her $1000, which in the follow-up interview you learn she used to buy supplies for her school.

Next you find a computer engineer who works for a reputable software company. He agrees to your interview, despite obviously being very busy. During the interview you find out the man has a master's degree, makes very good money, and has a stable family life at home. The man reads profusely and is very well-informed about a wide range of societal issues. We learn that the man wrote a piece of software that his 'stupid boss' rejected and is now thinking of starting his own business. At the conclusion of the interview you give him $1000, which in a follow-up interview you learn was used as seed money for the new business.

Next you go a bit off the beaten path to a retired physician who runs a holistic healing center in a rural area. She agrees to the interview, claiming nothing happens by accident. In the interview, you find out she has had to curtail the growth of her healing center and stop advertising because of her remarkable results. She views life holistically, and thinks of the universe as a single organism and herself as a cell in that organism. Before the interview is over you find yourself receiving a free healing treatment, as she sees something in your aura. At the conclusion of the interview you give her $1000, which she is completely uninterested in. You find out in the follow-up interview that she used it to pay past-due bills for her healing center, which was in financial dire straits.

Finally, you hear of a man who lives by himself and is known to be very friendly, but a bit eccentric. The man is difficult to contact, but after getting ahold of him he agrees to your interview. In the interview the man displays a delightful sense of humor and you find out that the man has had many jobs in many walks of life. His interests are very diverse and though he is not an expert in any particular one of them, he shows aptitude in many and enjoys talking about how they relate to one another. The man is very positive and has a deep faith in God. He seems to anticipate the direction of your energy in the interview and displays a 'live and let live' attitude towards life, though he expresses some frustration at not being understood. At the conclusion of the interview, he blesses you as you give him the $1000. It does not seem to excite him much, but you learn in the follow-up interview that he used money to invest in a new hobby, which miraculously already seems to be making some income.

In making this documentary, most would have chosen to pick their seven interviews based on some traditional way of dividing people up, like income, race, religion or country of origin. However I believe the seven people chosen here would give a better cross-sectional view of the human experience than any of the other traditional ways. These interviews were with seven people operating from the seven levels of the Simulation we find ourselves in. Most people reading this probably saw aspects of themselves in multiple levels of the Simulation, which is normal.

The following chart summarizes the seven levels of the Simulation that I will reference in this book.

Simulation Level/Chakra Name	% of Human Population with Consistent Access	Responsibility in the Simulation	Rough Dr. Hawkin's Number Scale Correspondent	Rough Spiral Dynamics Color Scale Correspondent

Crown	1%	Channel/dire ct/angle divine energy	600+	2nd Tier Colors
Third Eye	3%	Distinguish and read truth	500s	Green
Throat	10%	Learn, hold, and promulgate knowledge	400s	Orange
Heart	27%	Promote enthusiasm and positivity	300s	Blue
Solar Plexus	71%	Enforce and promote integrity	200s	Red
Sacral	90%	Maintain tribal and pack structures	100s	Purple
Root	100%	Ground in being and promote survivability	0s	Beige

I will primarily use the classic chakra system in this book, however the numbered scale of consciousness Dr. David Hawkins used in his work and the color-based scale of consciousness presented in the Spiral Dynamic system all point to the same fundamental reality. Earlier versions of this book used the Spiral Dynamic system and Dr. David Hawkins'

Number scale primarily, but I finally settled on using the chakra system, as it's been around by far the longest; it has been greater refined and is most familiar to the human race. Abundant literature is available on the chakra system, and those already somewhat familiar with the chakra system will find understanding this book a bit easier.

Below is a picture of the classic chakra system using their classic names—which I use in this book—along with some names I've given them, which may transmit their meaning better to a scientifically-literate western mind.

Crown/Divine Connection

3rd Eye/Bullshit Detector

Throat/Nerdy Animal

Heart/Loving Animal

Solar Plexus/Ambitious Animal

Sacral/Social Animal

Root/Survival Animal

The lower chakras are more associated with the physical/partically animal world and view the world in terms of individual things. The upper chakras are more associated with the wavy/spiritual world and view the world as a unified whole. The middle Heart chakra is associated with individual love, which bonds individual things together tightly and acts as a 'go-between' for the disconnected partically world and the connected wavy world.

Each chakra corresponds to functioning in one of the seven levels of the Simulation. Generally as a soul matures and evolves, increased access and control is granted to higher chakras. More power is available in the higher levels of the Simulation, so access becomes more restricted to maintain the health of the entire Simulation.

One could also lay out the levels like the picture drawing below:

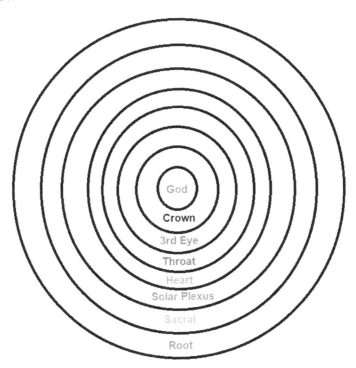

This actually gives a better vibrational map of things, as God is the central power source of the universe. The levels of the Simulation at their core just represent vibrational nearness or farness from this power source (tested true).

Souls over great eons of time journey vibrationally out from God in order to explore the lower levels of Simulation, and then begin a journey back home when their learning is done and need rest (tested true). Power increases exponentially the closer one vibrates to God, and suffering increases exponentially the further one vibrates from God (tested true).

As life evolves, it slowly gains access to more levels of the Simulation. For example reptile life is almost completely contained within the first Root chakra level of the Simulation. This is also the case of some very young souls in human bodies. The soul is completely concerned with survival and is run by the pleasure and pain inputs of the nervous system. The higher levels of the Simulation would present too much complexity for these souls to have the proper learning experiences.

When animals became evolved enough to begin functioning in packs and working together, they began operating in the Sacral level of the Simulation as well. Over many lifetimes the soul of a being operates from more and more levels of the Simulation simultaneously, which presents more and more complex lessons and situations for the soul to evolve into the Angelic realm (tested true).

Due to the limitations of language, I'll have to write about humans operating from levels of the Simulation like they are completely discrete levels, even though they blend together in reality. Souls also operate from multiple levels of the Simulation at once. For example, an academic might operate mostly from his Throat chakra when in the midst of his academic field, but would still need to occasionally concern himself with other levels of the Simulation. For the survival of his physical body, he would need to at least temporarily operate from the Root chakra level of the Simulation, and he may operate in the Sacral and Heart levels while with his family.

In this book I'll refer to this academic as operating from his Throat chakra even though the reality is far more complex. This linguistic shortcut is the result of having to squeeze holistic vibrational knowledge into limited linear language. Readers of this book will likely notice aspects of themselves in different levels of the Simulation, which is actually quite normal.

The vibration one gets from reading this book is more important than intellectual comprehension, which will come when the time is right.

The consciousness distribution of beings on this planet have the vast majority in the lower levels of the Simulation, with exponentially less at each higher level (tested true).

However, this is counterbalanced by the fact that the few beings in the higher levels have exponentially greater power in managing the Simulation, even though this power isn't personal in the way many would be tempted to understand it. Their power flows directly from divinity (tested true).

These two factors make this Simulation purgatorial. Our planet is clearly not heavenly or hellish, but contains all the variants in between, so souls are given the maximum amount of variation to experience and choices in which to evolve optimally. This Simulation is where you come for fast-tracked evolution (tested true).

This book comes out the following levels of the Simulation by percentage:

These percentages were arrived at by my calibration process, and not some sort of logical analysis of the book itself.

Level of the Simulation	Percentage of this book written from
Crown	8%
Third Eye	12%
Throat	30%
Heart	17%
Solar Plexus	11%
Sacral	11%
Root	11%

Therefore, this book is truly multidimensional and not written from a single perspective or level of the Simulation. There is a bit of energy from all the levels of the Simulation in order to give a holistic view. The largest component is from the Throat chakra because this is the level of science and the level of the Simulation where knowledge is most efficiently absorbed and transmitted through language.

My personal experience in this life allowed this multidimensional energy to come through. This is documented later in 'my vibrational swimming lesson' where my Angelic guides planned a nice tour of the different levels of the Simulation in a single lifetime. I do not recommend this Angelic roller coaster, and next life I hope to stay on a bench eating nachos with grandma and the little kids.

The Angels tell me that the book is aimed at people operating from the Heart and Throat levels of the Simulation, which are the fourth and fifth levels of Simulation respectively. A main purpose of this book is to facilitate these soul's evolution up into the sixth Third Eye level of the Simulation, and finally the seventh Crown level of the Simulation. This is very important to our collective evolution at this time, and it is why I was tasked to write this book (tested true).

Autism:

Angelic Takeaway: Autistic people like me have part of their sensory system tuned to something outside the typical frequency band humans perceive with their physical senses. This gives us insight/perceptions of the world that most humans do not have access to. However, as only so much water can be added to a cup, we are a bit less tuned to the normal wavelengths that most people experience. Though we have special insight, we have a harder time operating in the world of conventional endeavor and acting normal at parties.

An early reader of this book said, "You need to explain why you know what you know." I mention that I'm autistic not to claim special or victim status, but to describe how I was able to arrive at the conclusions in this book as it seems an integral part. I'd also love to perhaps shed some more understanding onto the condition, which in my opinion is neither good nor bad, just different.

Autistic people are people who perceive the world in a non-typical frequency band (tested true). Most people's sensory systems are almost 100% rooted in the partically world. Autistic people have some percentage of themselves rooted in the wavy, less concrete world.

I get by calibration that 5% of my sensory system was tuned to the wavy/spiritual world as a child. This seems to be about the threshold where autism gets formally diagnosed. This allowed me to go forty years being able to pass as normal, though most people who knew me closely suspected something was a bit different.

The graphic below demonstrates this in simple terms:

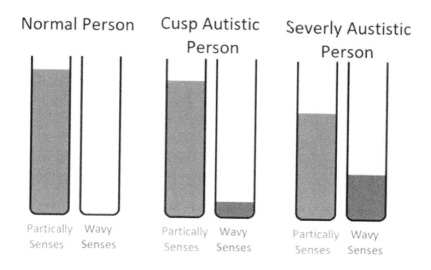

As you can only have so much water in a cup, logic tells us that the wavy insight into the non-physical, non-typical frequency bands that autistic people enjoy comes at the cost of having bit less perception in the conventional frequency bands that most of the world perceives in. A common observation of autistic people is they find certain tasks difficult that the world considers easy and certain tasks easy that the world considers difficult. This is the result of the trade off between wavy and partically perception (tested true).

My particular brand of autism came with a clear downside but also a huge upside, which when combined with my education in physics and engineering allowed this book to come through me.

At the time of my birth, my chakras had the following energy levels. These numbers were derived from my calibration process but were not surprising given my characteristics as a child. The numerical scale which has not yet been discussed goes roughly from 0-1000 with 200 being a neutral/average point. These energy levels changed drastically throughout my life, but this level at birth is useful to explain the autistic condition.

Level of Simulation	Nicholas Faulkner at Birth
Root	80
Sacral	80
Solar Plexus	80
Heart	20
Throat	40
Third Eye	440
Crown	440

How and why I ended up with chakras of these energies goes beyond the scope of this book but the two major reasons were past-life karma and my soul-mission for this particular lifetime.

One can see that the two top chakras came into this life relatively energized, while all my lower physical chakras were under-energized. This gave rise to my autistic condition.

With the energized Third Eye chakra, I always had an unusual tendency to notice when something was wrong and manage to avoid severe trouble despite bad decisions often putting me in its path. It was also normally obvious when I was being lied to, and I've noted how often people didn't even know when they are lying, as they were simultaneously lying to themselves.

The developed Crown chakra gave me what would appear to the external world as luck. However, in reality, it was divine assistance (tested true). Although being agnostic as a youth would cause this chakra to slowly de-energize over the years, and would eventually lead to total spiritual despair at the age of twenty-eight when it had been drained of virtually all energy.

The wavy/spiritual gifts that came from these two energized higher chakras came at a cost in my ability to function in the conventional world.

The broad tendencies were observed particularly early in life due to my autistic condition and underdeveloped lower chakras:

- Below average ability to manipulate mechanical objects and technology

- Below average athletic ability

- Below average language ability and a stutter

- Missing certain social nuances

- Below average physical sexuality

-Trouble navigating complex bureaucracies

Autistic people are often referred to as being on a spectrum. Some autistic people far out of the spectrum need help simply to survive in the physical world, but have a truly divine gift if they can connect to it.

This is brilliantly portrayed in the classic film *Rain Man,* where the character ingeniously portrayed by Dustin Hoffman needs help just to survive in the physical world but displays a divine gift with numbers.

My particular autistic condition is in many ways a much lighter version than portrayed in *Rain Man*. Many autistic people like myself are closer to the norm, and with a bit of effort can blend in and act normal, even though they have a bit of insight into a world most do not comprehend. A good friend and fellow teacher who helped greatly in the development of the ideas behind this book shares a similar 'cusp' autistic condition.

During my early years of school, my mother and father were insistent that I was never labeled or pigeonholed and that I interface with the normal classroom environment. Luckily the universe clearly knew what it was doing, as this turned out to be a hidden gift (not to imply diagnosing a youth with autism and helping a child adapt is at all a bad thing).

Because I was never labeled autistic, I never fell in with the autistic crowd. A downside of this is that I'm not particularly well-read on autism and may have missed out on a number of coping strategies that could have helped early in life. However, the upside is that I may have avoided the dogma in the field and can look at autism through a lens unclouded by preconceived notions and bias.

The relatively small of literature I've read on autism seems to have fallen into three broad categories:

> #1: Literature that seemed to correlate with my experience. Ironically, after reading just a bit of this research I'd almost immediately lose interest. A dog has no interest in reading about what it's like being a dog, and a cat has no interest in reading about what it's like to be a cat.

#2: Literature that seemed to promote autism as a disability. This tended to rub me the wrong way. Having lived forty-two years in an autistic mind/body complex, it was not the negative attention that I received from my oddities that hurt the most. It was when I actually saw or sensed something that others didn't but would lack the language to express it or be dismissed as nuts. I've often had to watch the organization I was involved in struggle against an illusionary adversity that had a ridiculously obvious solution from my point of view.

#3: Literature that seemed to promote autism as some sort of advantage or superiority. A main point I wish to make in this book is that the different qualities of consciousness or even being in different levels of the Simulation are not strictly better or worse than any other, but clearly different. I know that I see and sense things most humans don't, but there is a laundry list of life situations that I struggle with that most humans seem to glide through.

Spending over forty years autistic without ever being diagnosed makes me an autistic adult who ironically feels a bit like an outsider in the world of autism, simply because I can cite very little of the modern research in the field and am not familiar with much of the vernacular.

However this allowed me to see the non-autistic world through my autistic lens without really realizing that I was doing so. This was a primary genesis of this book. It took over forty-two years, but the world has given me enough experience to finally put my wavy autistic observations into comprehensible language.

A commonality I've generally observed is that most autistic people have small areas of life where they operate at a genius level. This is the result of their connection to the wavy spiritual world. Because of the nature of autism, a piece of them is in the wavy universe, so almost by definition there is a bit less of them in the traditional partically universe that most humans primarily live in. This makes expressing their bit of inherent genius difficult.

Auras:

Angelic Takeaway: An aura is an energy field that projects outside the physical body and is felt by empathic people. Even non-empathic people will find it hard not to notice that certain people have an effect on their environment that goes way beyond their physical actions alone.

Empathic people who feel energy will notice that the power and size of people's auras increases exponentially at every level of the Simulation. The following chart shows how far a person's aura extends out from their physical body. The numbers of this chart were determined by my calibration process, but it correlates very well to what my autistic empathic senses have picked up over the years.

Level of Simulation	Size of Aura
Root	Almost non-existent
Sacral	A few inches from body
Solar Plexus	Half a meter from body
Heart	About one meter from body
Throat	About two meters from body
Third Eye	About four meters from body
Crown	Affects the entire Simulation

Each level of Simulation adds a layer to one's aura, which allows them to affect creation on another level. A being's aura can extend in size and power for short periods of time but this will deplete the being's spiritual energy over time. For example, strong public speakers can fill a large area with their energy for a short period of time. However, this process is not under individual control but happens at the discretion of the universe (tested true).

The Root chakra does not really project an aura. The Root's masculine energy is almost completely contained within the bounds of the physical body. This level is almost exclusively concerned with the physical body's instinctual pain and pleasure impulses. A strong Root will tend to yield strong physiological functioning and a weak Root tends to lead to poor health and survivability.

When a being evolves into the Sacral chakra, a feminine aura extends a few inches from the body. This is mostly noticed with direct physical contact. With this feminine layer of aura, one will like to be touched by people one considers part of their tribe or pack and will be repulsed by the touch of someone they consider outside their tribe or pack. A negative version of this aura will cause the person to be attracted to negative groups.

When a being evolves into the Solar Plexus chakra, another layer of the aura extends out about a half a meter from the body. This masculine layer of the aura seems particularly helpful in handling physical objects, and especially physical combat. Particularly if trained in a valid combat methodology, a person with a strong version of this layer of the aura will almost always best a person with a weak layer of this aura in a hand-to-hand fair fight. A negative version of this aura tends to result in clumsiness and a lack of confidence. Great fighters and skilled craftsmen tend to have a developed layer of this aura.

When a being evolves into the Heart chakra, another layer of the aura extends out about a meter from the body. This feminine layer of the aura feels very positive and tends to give enthusiastic energy to people inside of it. Teachers with a strong layer of this aura tend to move around the classroom a lot in an attempt to keep all the students under the influence of their positive energy. A negative version of this aura will drain energy from others. Great leaders tend to have a strong version of this layer of aura.

When a being evolves into the Throat chakra, another layer of the aura extends about two meters from the body. This masculine layer of aura seems to counter any falsity and reinforce true knowledge within it. If inside the influence of this layer of an aura, it is difficult to not consider what the person in the center of the aura has to say. A person with a negative version of this aura will have a tendency to lie a lot, have trouble comprehending information, and will have trouble being heard. Great scholars and orators have a strong version of this aura.

When a being evolves into the Third Eye chakra, another layer of the aura extends about four meters from the body. This feminine layer of the aura will basically fill most rooms with a pleasant, loving energy. People with this layer of the aura tend to appear more attractive than their physical appearance alone would suggest, and can swing the energy of an entire room in a positive direction. A negative version of this aura will cause a person to be attracted to negativity and false information, and reality will seem reversed to anyone inside their aura. Great saints had a strong version of this layer of aura.

As one evolves into the Crown chakra, the size and power of the aura expands rapidly. One can eventually tap directly into the source code of the Simulation in order to optimize the Simulation for the highest good. This layer of the aura seems to feed more energy to other positive auras within it and tends to be increasingly uncomfortable to the lower energies and often downright painful to demonic energies. A negative version of this aura tends to be uncomfortable to positive auras and feed negative auras. Great beings such as Jesus Christ and Buddha had very strong versions of this aura (tested true).

Karma:

Angelic Takeaway: Any energy that a soul puts out eventually ripples back to that soul. Karma is only a bitch if you are, however. The concept of karma goes to the absolute substratum of the code that runs this Simulation and physics of the universe itself.

Traditional physics probably shows the existence of karma most elegantly with Newton's Third Law, which is my absolute favorite principle to teach as a high school physics teacher.

Newton's Third Law states that "For every action force, there is an equal and opposite reaction force." Stated in another way, "If Mike Tyson punches me in the face and his fist puts 2000 Newtons of force onto my face, my face automatically puts 2000 Newtons of force back on Mike Tyson's fist." This is simply the Simulation keeping itself in balance, which it must always do in order to avoid collapse. However in this particular case, I'm guessing my face will break and Mike Tyson's fist will be more or less fine.

This same basic principle applies up through the dimensions and levels of the Simulation (tested true). It shows up quite obviously in the political world in that the harder an agenda is forcefully pushed onto a people, the more resistance automatically shows up to oppose the agenda. Everything eventually happens when it is supposed to and cannot be rushed.

Unusual events that happen to us often have a karmic basis and often have their roots in our past lives.

From the beginning of this life I've had short bouts of truly terrible pain coming from inside my butt (I'm sure that last sentence was exactly what you wanted to read when you got ahold of this book). It always felt as if my rectum were filled with fire, razor blades, and needles. These incidents were the most intense bouts of physical pain encountered in this life. By grace, none of these incidents occurred when I was around others or in the middle of something important. They always occurred when I was home alone, normally between 6 and 11 p.m. Sleep was always a welcome and needed relief when they were finished.

These bouts numbered about fifty total and normally lasted between fifteen minutes to a few hours. Nothing I did ever alleviated the extreme pain at all, and most of them were rid out in the fetal position on my hands and knees with tears in my eyes. The mind could never come up with a logical explanation. I even completely switched diets a few times in a futile attempt to make these bouts of pain end.

Fairly recently I came across this internet meme:

"Modern life sucks so much... I wish I lived in the past."

The past :

I included it here for explanation purposes and I find it funny now.

After seeing this meme, suddenly, as if by magic, I remembered brutally goring an enemy soldier in the butt with a spear during the Crusades in a past-life. I recall recognizing that the wound was fatal, but not immediately so. According to the warrior ethical code I was following in that lifetime, the correct thing to do was to finish him off and stop his suffering. Unfortunately, in the heat of battle, I failed to do this and the poor soul ended up lingering for weeks in extreme pain.

After seeing that meme, the next evening I had the worst bout of this ghastly rectal pain that I'd ever experienced, but by grace it has never returned as the karma is finally resolved (tested true).

These bouts of extreme lower intestinal pain was the subjective repaying of karma for the pain I inflicted on that man (tests true).

There are also subtle types of karma from the higher levels of the Simulation. In two past lives I had been in a position of significant social influence and had been moral in both. However, in both lives I made a subtle mistake of pushing for the social equality of minority groups with a bit too much force onto a population that was not quite ready for it. Therefore, my actions ended up having the reverse of the intended effect.

In a lifetime after these two, now as a member of a minority group, I joined the military and endured a terrible death for a country that by-in-large was hostile to my existence and unappreciative of my sacrifice.

Karma also plays out on collective levels. Large groups come together to experience disasters or war that are the result of unwise actions of the group as a whole in the past. Souls often exchange roles between being a victim and being a perpetrator in successive lifetimes in order to make better decisions in each iteration (tested true).

A core spiritual principle not genuinely understood by the world is that when either an individual or group endeavors heavily to rise up the levels of the Simulation or spiritually evolve, this tends to draw out negative karma in the lower levels so one can escape them. Broadly, one cannot rise to a higher level of the Simulation while heavy karma still exists on a lower one (tested true).

At the time of the writing of this book, the collective human consciousness is in a state of chaos and still reeling from the COVID-19 pandemic. This is simply because the collective consciousness of humanity is rising to a higher level so karma is rapidly clearing from the lower ones (tested true). If one understands this principle, one understands the essence of the saying "It's always darkest before the dawn."

At the start of the COVID-19 pandemic 1.5% of the human population were in the Angelic stages of evolution and that number has now jumped to 1.7% (tested true). In addition during the massive karmic repayment that was the COVID-19 pandemic, 12% of the human population gained access to an additional level of the Simulation (tested true). This may not seem like a lot but as soul growth happens over eons, this much growth in a few years is an astronomically significant event (tested true).

When one begins putting effort into spiritual evolution or moving up the levels of the Simulation, the person's life tends to become more chaotic in the short-term as negative karma is paid off more rapidly. Not understanding this often leads to spiritual frustration as a soul on a fast rise assumes they must be doing something wrong (tested true).

A nice recontextualization for one's temporary suffering is to realize it's often just karma clearing from a lower level of the Simulation. Karma acts a bit like strings that hold us in the lower levels of the Simulation. Once the karma is cleared, these strings disappear and one will feel lighter, vibrate faster on a quantum level, and will have more upward mobility in the Simulation if one wishes to move to the higher levels.

Everything in the universe must eventually balance; even our linear well-known science shows this. This is simply how this Simulation is programmed and it allows all souls to eventually experience the effects of their own energy and actions. This is a major mechanism which leads to our evolution and attainment of wisdom as we earn our way into the Angelic ranks (tested true).

Chakras Energy Levels and Karma:

Angelic Takeaway: The energy level of particular chakra is indicative of one's karma on its associated level of the Simulation. Certain actions will either strengthen or weaken the energy level of the chakras. These energy levels tend to be heavy determinants of the quality of life inside the Simulation.

Each level of the Simulation has its own karma. The energy level of each chakra of a person is based on their past decisions associated with this chakra and is indicative of their karma on that particular level of the Simulation (tested true). Certain decisions will increase the energy level of the associated chakra, and other decisions will lower the energy level of the associated chakra. Learning which decisions do which is part of the evolution process of the soul.

Here are the individual chakras discussed from a karmic perspective:

Root chakra: A low energy level of this chakra will result in a lack of survival instincts, poor health, and decisions that tend to lead to death. A high energy level of this chakra results in the ability to keep the physical body alive in a number of environments and circumstances.

Positive karma at this level results from keeping one's physical body which is a divine gift alive under difficult circumstances or saving another life. Negative karma at this level accumulates from killing or giving up on one's own life either passively or actively.

Higher-level decisions appear to old souls when the continuance of much life must be balanced, which may include the sacrifice of one's own life.

Sacral chakra: A low energy level of this chakra will result in difficulty being accepted and a tendency to associate with unfavorable tribes or packs. A high energy level of this chakra will allow one to be accepted, popularity will come easily and one will tend to associate with favorable groups that are optimal to the soul's evolution.

Positive karma at this level results from supporting one's tribe or pack. Negative karma results from harming one's tribe or pack.

Going to war results in positive karma if one is defending their tribe or country integrously and negative karma if the war is unnecessarily harming another tribe or country. Not going to war results in positive karma if the basis of the war is unjust, and negative karma if it is the result of 'cowardice' and leaving one's tribe or country vulnerable.

Higher level decisions appear at this level when one is forced to go against one's tribe or country which has become unjust (The American Revolution).

Solar Plexus chakra: A low energy level of this chakra will result in low energy and difficulty succeeding in life. A high energy level of this chakra will result in easy and often automatic success and winning in life.

Positive karma at this level results from using the power from one's success in a wise way and negative karma from using the power from one's success in a selfish or unwise way.

Higher level decisions may appear when one is asked to sacrifice one's personal success for a greater good. For example, this could look like a mother giving up a lucrative career to have a child.

Heart chakra: A low energy level of this chakra will result in difficulty attracting love, a tendency to go after improper romantic partners, and a dull, lackluster attitude towards life. A high energy level of this chakra will result in the automatic attraction of love, the manifestation of ideal romantic partners, and a naturally enthusiastic attitude which will be attractive to other positive people.

Positive karma at this level results from supporting loved ones and negative karma results of hurting loved ones.

Higher level decisions may appear when one has to disappoint a loved one to support a greater cause. For example, this could look like temporarily leaving a new marriage and child to defend one's country.

Throat chakra: A low energy level of this chakra will result in a lack of interest in learning, difficulty comprehending information, difficulties being heard and speech impediments. A high energy level of this chakra will result in one's voice carrying a lot of weight, intellectual knowledge being absorbed easily, and the ability to sway large crowds with your speech.

Positive karma results from the integrous accumulation of knowledge through study and telling the truth even under difficult circumstances. Negative karma results from lying and spreading false knowledge.

Higher level decisions may appear when one has to be subtly dishonest for a greater good. For example, this could look like not telling a suffering person a truth that would only increase their suffering.

Third Eye chakra: A low energy level of this chakra will result in attraction to false information and a dull intuition, and can often cause a person to misread people and situations leading to bad decisions. A high energy level of this chakra will result in the synchronistic attraction of the perfect knowledge one needs for evolution, a sharp accurate intuition, and even psychic abilities at high levels.

Positive karma results from using the intuition's power wisely for the greater good and negative karma results from using the power for unwise purposes such as gambling or scamming.

Higher level decisions may appear when a person must hold back information from their intuition or psychic ability for a greater good. For example, letting someone else live out an important soul lesson without spoiling its ending.

Crown chakra: A low energy level results in a lack of spiritual energy, depression, and a tendency to draw negative life experiences. A high energy level results in being supported by the divine, happiness, and seeming luck as one's life tends to take rapid fortuitous turns and avoid negative ones.

Positive karma results from having faith in the divine even under difficult life circumstances. Negative karma accumulates from militant atheism or taking one's divinity for granted.

Higher level decisions appear when one is forced to keep one's faith under very adverse situations. The Buddha claimed to have been attacked by demons as he approached enlightenment. One may have to keep their faith while experiencing an extremely low hellish state. At certain stages of the journey, souls will be offered worldly power or wealth if they compromise their faith or core ethics. This is a Crown chakra test to see if the soul is ready for a new paradigm of reality (tested true).

Often older souls are given complex moral paradoxes, where a decision must be made that is positive from the point of view of one level of the Simulation while being negative at another level of the Simulation.

An example of this was President Truman's decision to drop atomic bombs on Japan. His decision was positive from the perspective of the higher chakra levels of the Simulation (ended a brutal war and much suffering) but negative from the perspective of the lower chakra levels (ended lives and damaged the environment). However the old-souled President Truman received karmic merit for this tough decision in which many factors had to be taken into account.

I will now go into a personal narrative to provide context to my life and background before making some of the bolder claims of this book. If one is reading this book for strictly academic reasons and can take what I say on complete faith, then the next seven chapters can be skipped, even though certain contexts are provided that makes the other material in the book more understandable.

My Vibrational Swimming Lesson:

Angelic Takeaway: This life unfolded perfectly as if divinely orchestrated by Angels with a practical sense of humor for this book to unfold. In this chaotic life I've experienced all seven levels of the Simulation from my empathic autistic viewpoint. I didn't want to describe my life but Archangel Michael has been very insistent that I explain why I know what I know, and not just say "and so God declared" after every sentence.

My first conscious memory of this reality was at the age of three, where I was thrown into the deep end of a public pool by my grandfather who was an Angel in a human body (tested true). As I went below the water line, I became immediately aware of my existence in this physical dimension and inside of a clumsy animal body. It was not an experience I remember as pleasant.

As my chubby little body which was barely developed to a reptile level hit the water, I called out desperately for help. I believe there was a shared understanding by everyone at the scene that this was simply what had to happen.

As I sunk deeper and deeper into the water, fear began to mount that I'd never see the surface again. It was at the bottom of the pool, where there was no direction left to go but "up," that I regained my orientation, let the instincts of my tiny physical body take over, and swam to the surface.

After this I was very comfortable in the water. I found I could then dive below the surface for limited periods of time, as long as I knew I could eventually return to the surface and get air again.

This early lesson by my grandfather which took place in less than a minute was a perfect microcosm for what the first forty years of this life would become. The shocking realization of life, the gradual sinking to the bottom of the pool as mouthfuls of chlorine and urine-saturated water got swallowed and the gradual rise back to the glorious surface.

I saw that the different energetic viewpoints inside the Simulation experience reality in very different ways. I saw that the rules for one level don't strictly apply to another. The world struggles with this because generally people from every level assume others experience the Simulation like they do (tested true).

In this section I will describe my subjective vibrational experience during this life, but from a more logical perspective than is typical in spiritual narratives. I did not do this to congratulate my own ego, but simply to give an explanation as to why I'm able to write this book.

The narrative format also provides a convenient medium in which to explain some of the core points of this book. As a teacher I've found that information is better absorbed when it comes in the form of a narrative or story. Information is worthless unless attached to something the mind already understands. Context is king!

Previously I described the basic properties of the levels of this Simulation we find ourselves in. The lower vibrations/levels are more associated with the partically/physical domain and the higher levels are more associated with the wavy/spiritual domain.

Quantum Mechanics describes reality as waves or particles in a mathematical black and white fashion. but there seems to be a gradient between these realities that I describe as levels of a Simulation in this book.

These vibrational bands or levels of the Simulation can be sensed by empathic people. My autism which makes me appear odd and socially awkward to the external world allows me to feel these bands of energy quite viscerally. My ability to sense these bands was aided in this life by an Angelically-planned experience that allowed me to personally experience all of them at various stages of this life.

This narrative also focuses on the Crown chakra which we all have. Souls have varying levels of access to this powerful chakra depending on one's stage of evolution. This is actually a divine safety measure to ensure a soul does not do much damage before they can responsibly handle the power of this chakra (tested true).

The health of the Crown chakra is very fundamental to the happiness of all beings. An energized open Crown chakra allows divinity to flow into an entity and will correct the problems in the lower levels of the Simulation over time. A misaligned or closed Crown chakra tends to create compounding problems in the lower levels of the Simulation as energy is choked off.

This graph shows the energy level of my Crown chakra through the first forty years of this life. On the scale I use in this book, 200 could be described as a neutral point.

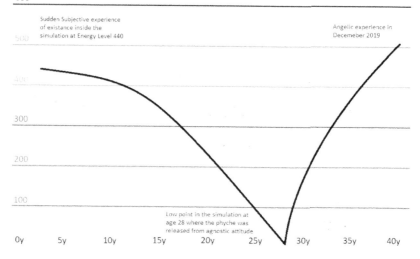

600

Sudden Subjective experience
of existance inside the
simulation at Energy Level 440

Angelic experience in
Decemeber 2019

500

300

200

100

Low point in the simulation at
age 28 where the phyche was
released from agnostic attitude

0y   5y   10y   15y   20y   25y   30y   35y   40y

Note: The reality of these first forty years of this life was much bumpier and chaotic than this simple graph depicts but it captures the overall vibrational trend of this period.

The first twenty-eight years of this life were spent in what could best be described as hypnotic trance. As a certified hypnotist, hypnotic trance is simply the best phrase. I've seen talented hypnotists get a person's mind to not hear a certain word or substitute another word for the one heard. Anytime I heard any mention of God, religion, or spirituality, it was simply not processed.

Despite being basically friendly and well-intentioned, any sort of god-awareness was suspiciously absent in these first twenty-eight years. I was never an atheist or opposed to God, I simply never processed anything from this world. I was radically agnostic, with no opinion on religion or spirituality whatsoever. I actually needed to search my memory hard to find any feeling (positive or negative) on the subject.

This allowed my focus to be primarily on intellectual development, scientifically investigating the world, playing video games and attempting to woo women (with little success) without any interference from that 'spiritual stuff.'

During these somewhat confused twenty-eight years, I managed to always be near the top of whatever academic pursuit I found myself in. I gained a relatively sophisticated scientific view of the universe, got extremely good at a few video games, and achieved a bachelor's degree in Electrical Engineering and a Master's degree in Nuclear Engineering. I even managed to be an officer in the United States Navy. In spite of all this, women were generally unimpressed.

Through this period, despite generally appearing okay from the outside, life did tend to get steadily darker and the amount of suffering that I endured steadily increased. Without a visceral connection to God, I was like a battery slowly using itself up without a way to recharge.

At birth, my Crown chakra's energy level was at 440. This gave me a significant divine reserve to draw from while I explored the physical world exclusively with a non-militant agnostic attitude. However this led to a slow and steady decline in happiness as the energy in my Crown chakra slowly drained. The decline tended to get steeper; as I fell as I was operating with less and less power, and moral compromises became more common as I became more desperate and frustrated with reality.

On occasion I'd run into God or religion but I'd always find a way out of it, not out of hostility or anger, but I'd just find a way to not deal with it.

Some examples:

My loving parents, neither being particularly religious or spiritual, sent me to Catholic Sunday school as a good-hearted attempt to expose me to spirituality and religion. I remember being bored, and irking the good-natured Sunday school teacher with some deep questions that weren't answerable on a logical level.

After a few classes, I realized that there was a playground across the street and I'd hang out there until my parents came to get me. One week, realizing the lie was causing more damage than it was preventing, I confessed to my parents that I'd been skipping Sunday school and they accepted my decision without any anger. The issue was dropped with no drama and I went back to spending my Sunday mornings playing video games and watching cartoons.

Much later . . .

One of my closest friends in college (who would later become a Lutheran pastor) invited me to a weekend Christian retreat with a group of wonderful people I'd become friendly with. Despite being in the midst of prayer, spiritual conversations, and generally loving people all weekend, my main focus was trying to impress a girl (she wasn't impressed) while generally enjoying the loving energy and having fun.

I had a wonderful weekend and got along with everyone at the retreat. I even participated appropriately (at least on a physical level) with all the religious observations of the weekend. Despite this, the main point of the retreat escaped me, and the next week I went back to being a basically good-hearted agnostic student studying electrical engineering.

Things often seemed to be going smooth, but something that could never be verbalized was always missing and elusive. This "missing" thing (mistakenly thought by the ego to be found in worldly success or things 'out there') began a slowly mounting psychic distress. This culminated at the age of twenty-eight when I was in a pit of black despair from which none of the previous coping methods—worldly success, substances, video games, or romantic entanglements—provided any relief to.

After returning from a brutal deployment to the Middle East with the US Navy, I found myself attempting to operate in the world with barely any power or happiness of any kind.

On paper, most people would judge these first twenty-eight years as successful. Not perfect by any means, but a fair start to a typical, successful American Life. The groundwork for this successful life was laid by two outstanding parents, a wonderful extended family including an Angelic grandfather, and great friends.

It was in the pits of despair and psychic distress at age of twenty-eight that a tiny opening just big enough for the power of divinity to creep in through the back door presented itself. Once this opening occurred, I believe the process was irreversible.

During this journey, certain events, people, jobs, and experiences seemed to come into my experience at just the right time as if divinely orchestrated (because it was). I experienced life as the energy level of my Crown chakra slowly drained through the my first twenty-eight years but later re-energized over the next fourteen with God awareness in my life.

It seems one of the lessons the universe wanted me to learn in this lifetime was: "Is reality survivable without God?" The short, unnuanced answer that was revealed to me was "No."

This life has played out in seven year increments. Every seven years, my life has taken an extremely sharp turn in which I was asked to function in a different role in the world, develop a different chakra, and play in a different level of the Simulation. The parameters of the contract my soul had with this Simulation even changed, as I needed to learn drastically different things and experience the Simulation in a different way. At the conclusion of every seven-year segment was a period of darkness and confusion as my role in the world rapidly changed. My Guardian Angel even changed to fit the different need/role of each seven-year soul contracts (tested true).

A close spiritual friend has also observed that her life has played out in seven-year increments, and it seems to be a somewhat common experience.

A better learning experience I could not have planned if I tried. The Angels who seem to have guided me and helped in this journey simply knew what they were doing. Following is my journey described in the seven-year increments or soul contracts.

Soul Contract #1: Ages Zero to Seven, The Root Chakra:

Angelic Takeaway: The first seven years of this life were spent in a simple autistic existence rebuilding the Root chakra primarily. I spent most of the time in my own little autistic world heavily preferring it to grounding into the physical Simulation.

I was a weird kid. I wish there was a more elegant way to state this, but my language ability isn't capable of that. I constantly wore mismatched clothing, and was only really capable of communicating with those who understood my odd sense of humor.

I have less memories from the early parts of my childhood than most. Earlier, I describe the swimming lesson that seemed to startle my soul into its partically existence on this planet. My soul had endured a bad ending to the previous life, dying in the American Vietnam war. As a result, my lower five chakras were in very low energetic states. My first seven years were spent in a reptile-like Root chakra existence, but with strange insight and luck coming from strong Third Eye and Crown chakras respectively. This first seven year period was devoted to rebuilding my Root chakra.

My low physical functionality, counterbalanced by a high IQ and relatively developed Third Eye and Crown chakras, resulted in an Autistic condition described previously. I struggled physically despite having strong wavy/spiritual insight into the world. In my early years, I had an eerily accurate intuition and tended to be led away from bad situations, even though the animal body I was in had no clue why this was happening.

Very few things could get me into a single time and space and focus on partically physical reality. I enjoyed napping, eating, talking to myself, and as my loving mother put it, "marching to the beat of my own drummer." If born into the ancient world, this body would likely not have survived, but now, a strong family structure allowed it to pull through.

If I'd had the ability to verbalize my thoughts during that period, it would have been something like, "If we all just sit real quiet in silence we can just enjoy this wonderful orgasmic vibration." Unfortunately that was not the experience of most of the world around me at the time. The other kids seemed insistent on other activities. They preferred stealing my LEGOs, despite my preference that they take up a meditation habit.

I intuited that Santa was not real before I even started school and was befuddled on why all the other children believed the nonsense. The active Third Eye and high IQ quickly discredited the tale of Santa. I also couldn't understand why all the adults were insistent that I believe in this jolly overweight man who came down through our tiny chimney. Though a wonderful magical thing we tell kids, it can hardly stand up to critical thinking or an energized Third Eye.

When I was extremely young I found out that it was simply less effort to go along with the Santa story. As an older child I kept the Santa thing going because I enjoyed getting Nintendo games for Christmas.

I enjoyed being alone. I could be seen playing multiplayer games by myself and living in my own little nerdy autistic world. I was almost always dirty, as the whole world of hygiene made no sense to me. Bathing and cleaning also requires effort in the partically world, which took me out of my wavy autistic world that I tended to enjoy much more. The poor souls who were tasked to teach me in my younger years tended to have their hands full, as I didn't really behave or respond to anything like a normal kid.

I also had a bad stutter. Although this got better over the years, the core of this was because the vibrational wavy ideas that appeared in my head did not translate cleanly into partically human language, and my Throat chakra which helps facilitate speech was woefully weak.

I've never really spoken any physical language other than English in this life, but talking to my more linguistically gifted friends, I've learned that translation between different languages is often not 100% efficient. It's frustrating being unable to express your thoughts as well as you could in your native language.

The same concept definitely applies to translating wavy vibrational ideas into partically logical thoughts. The stutter is me getting stuck in language when unable to express myself correctly. This book took a lot of effort, as it's an attempt to express very spiritual ideas in logical, physical language. My grandfather, who gave me the extreme swimming lesson, had the same stutter.

When I started school, my overall assessment of the other children was that they were loud, violent, and often quite stupid. Bear in mind this opinion was coming from a kid who couldn't fully read until second grade, and to whom the entire concept of an alphabet was baffling.

I spent two years in kindergarten and developed very slowly. This was because I was floating deep in the wavy universe, so I was slower than the other kids to adapt to the physical/partically Simulation.

I remember in my second year of kindergarten finally having the grand realization about the alphabet. "If I just write these twenty-six arbitrary symbols down on this piece of paper in a certain order, I'll be left alone to play with LEGOs, do math, and play with my imaginary friends." (These imaginary friends I now know were Angels.)

The only subject that made any sense was math. I recall a kindergarten level math book being handed out and being instructed to do the first page. While the class was doing this I completed the first ten. I was yelled at for working ahead and not following instructions.

Honest to form, my rebellious ego having been blocked by an external authority rebelled in the most nerdy way possible, I snuck the math book home under my shirt (easy for a fat kid) and completed the whole thing that very night.

After seeing the completed math book, my kindergarten teacher visited the fourth grade wing of my elementary school and got a fourth grade math book for me, which occupied me better. In my wavy reality, math with its strict black and white rules and tangible results was the only thing that seemed to make sense enough to draw me down into this partically simulated reality.

I recall being at a daycare center with a particularly rowdy pack of boys. This pack was made up of boys, operating primarily from the Root and Sacral levels of the Simulation with one physically dominating leader. This is typical in packs of bullies I find. The feminine version of this kind of pack was captured beautifully in the cinematic masterpiece *Mean Girls*

At one point, the pack leader pulled out a knife and began cutting into a tree, proclaiming he had found an unlimited supply of free chicken. He was cutting away parts of the inner tree (which did vaguely resemble a pieces of cooked chicken) and feeding it to other boys. I remember reading the vibration of this situation and thinking nothing about this seemed right, and especially that none of these boys seemed particularly bright. The wavy senses that come from my Third Eye have always alerted me to when something was wrong, even though I often didn't know how to express it.

We were away from the safety of adults with a mentally unstable older boy armed with a weapon, as he fed us all pieces of wood that were likely wreaking havoc on our young digestive systems. I wanted to proclaim to the other boys that this was a situation we should immediately remove ourselves from, but I did not have the language to express this nor the social clout to do such a thing. I eventually snuck away, retreated into the house, and worked through my fourth grade math book as the girls played *My Little Pony* around me. I would later join them.

I didn't like to talk, and had absolutely no idea how to socialize. Socialization is often aligned with the development of the Sacral chakra and mine was also under-developed, and wouldn't become a priority until the next soul contract.

I would pick up complex concepts very quickly, particularly if I was interested, but would often be baffled by simple concepts.

In first grade, we were playing a game which involved counting dried beans. I quickly realized that I was the best in the class at this particular game. I remember bragging to all the other children how I was clearly the best at counting beans. Imagine being the most popular kid in a first grade class and having to listen to a fat, dirty kid in mismatched clothing tell you in a stuttering voice about how much better he is than you. I'm obviously not in favor of bullying but in certain cases . . . I get it.

As I realized that my skill with numbers was not appreciated by those around me, I decided sports was a better way to fit in. My loving father was a sports fan. During these early years, I imagine his frustration because the world of sports was completely lost on me. The whole concept of sports made no sense in my private wavy universe.

During a tee-ball baseball game, I was in right field. For those of you who know nothing of youth baseball, this is where you generally put the worst player (apologies to Roberto Clemente and Dwight Evans). I was sitting down making a house of flowers, which all great baseball players do when they are playing the field.

At one point, I watched as a ball was hit in my direction, rolling past me only feet to my left. I remember not giving two shits about that little white ball and not understanding why everyone else was so concerned about the silly thing. My team lost that game, but I won because I had created the prettiest house of flowers that evening at the urging of my Crown chakra.

Here is the thing with playing and talking by yourself in a conservative town. When you are two or three years old, it is cute. When you turn four, it's still cute but starts looking a bit odd, and when you go to kindergarten (for two years) it starts getting very concerning. In first grade, folks begin to worry.

Second grade was a particularly tough year. I had a teacher demanding conformity to a vibration I could not resonate with. Reality had gotten too complex and the other kids did not make any sense to me. My teacher banned me from advanced math and recess until my reading, speech, and social skills improved. In a desperate time, the universe sent help in the only form that could possibly help a burgeoning little nerd.

NINTENDO to the rescue.

Soul Contract #2: Ages Eight to Fourteen: The Sacral Chakra

Angelic Takeaway: The ages eight to fourteen were spent rebuilding the Sacral chakra primarily living out of the second level of the Simulation. I learned basic socialization within a tight knit community filled with supportive family and friends.

For this next soul contract I was tasked in re-energizing the more social Sacral chakra while still being responsible for the Root chakra level of existence. This meant a more complicated existence and a need to socialize. My Angels found the perfect way to initialize this socialization. For Christmas in second grade I got an 8-bit Nintendo. Upon opening the box I remember thinking, "Well this is a good gift I guess. It's what the other kids seem to be into, but this looks too complicated for me. Where are my imaginary friends at?"

Still it was a Nintendo, and it was the cool thing to do. My dad and I (neither of us being that technically proficient) managed to hook it up. I took to the Nintendo like Forrest Gump took to the shrimp boat business. It was love at first sight.

Throughout my childhood I was better behaved than average. At worst, anything I did before high school would at worst be described as mischief. My parents rarely had to impose punishment. I never drank or did drugs, and was never grounded or formally punished to any significant degree. However, there was one carrot they used. In short, the ongoing deal I had with my parents was, "Get straight A's and you get a video game." This was enough to get me to put forth enough effort to basically get straight A's throughout school.

At one point I wanted nothing more than a Game Boy. After being given difficult news by my parents that I was not likely to receive a Game Boy for Christmas due to financial concerns, I won one off a coke bottle cap a few days later.

Aside: Manifestation/Law of Attraction.

The Manifestation concept and Law of Attraction are new agey truisms, and often get over-simplified by commercial interests. When presented as, "Picture something you want in your head and it will come to you," it frustrates aspiring spiritual aspirants because their partically ego pictures something in their head. Then they are disappointed when it is not immediately attracted or manifested.

The common misunderstanding with this law is that the power of one's manifestation ability varies drastically with the level of the Simulation one is operating from. From the lower chakra levels, one's psyche has almost no direct effect on the state of the Simulation.

Although beginning in the Solar Plexus level of Simulation, one's psyche begins directly affecting the Simulation space. One's effect on the Simulation space or manifestation ability rises exponentially each chakra level higher than that (tested true).

Someone in the higher wavy levels of the Simulation do not consider themselves separate from the rest of the universe, so what the universe wants and what the personal will wants tend to be almost the same thing. This results in a soul having a very powerful effect on the state of the Simulation, but very rarely making greedy personal demands of it. At this point, thoughts that appear in the head are not because an individual put it there, but the head is simply in tune with the Simulation or God.

As a young autistic child a small part of my consciousness was aligned with higher level Third Eye and Crown levels of the Simulation. While I was not impressing many people on a partically physical level, I had a strange tendency to always eventually get what I wanted, which coincidentally tended to be what the Simulation wanted for me.

In the higher levels of the Simulation one tends to automatically attract what one needs to continue evolution, but in the lower levels of the Simulation one tends to rely on effort and force to grab what one needs or wants. In general the beings operating from the high levels of the Simulation seem to create reality, and beings operating from the lower levels of the Simulation manipulate and fine-tune it.

From the relatively high level of the Simulation, one often tends to get what one needs by seemingly magical means. This includes winning a Game Boy off a bottle cap days after realizing one would not get one by conventional means.

End Aside.

For the first time, video games gave me something tangible to talk to the other kids about. I wasn't exactly a social butterfly yet, but it was progress. I did manage to make a friend. Together we started the video game club. I was the president, he was the vice president, and his little brother was the treasurer. There were no other members.

The icing on the cake was that I somehow managed to convince my mom to get me a subscription to the magazine *Nintendo Power*. With this magazine, reading suddenly made sense. *Oh so that's what letters are for, writing reviews and tips for video games.* This gave me an impetus to learn to read which happened dramatically fast. I went from basically not knowing how to read to reading above grade level in a few months.

After seeing my reading skills dramatically improve virtually overnight, my second grade teacher made an odd implication that I had cheated. This was despite the fact that I barely knew what the word cheating meant.

Just in case someone gets the impression that I think video games are the answer to all the qualms in elementary education, please read my chapter on video games later in this book for a more nuanced discussion.

Concentrating more on the external world my general happiness level began to fall as I now expended more energy in the physical world instead of relaxing in my private autistic world. The energy reserves of my Crown chakra now began to be used up at a higher rate without being replenished. However, both my social and academic abilities improved drastically. Video games gave me a way to relate to this simulated reality and ultimately get karmically tangled up in it.

With games at my disposal, I now spent hours intellectually analyzing games and drawing maps. The old style RPGs (role playing games) and strategy games on both Nintendo and computer were my favorite. The more complex and number intensive the game, the better I tended to like it. This provided hours of figuring out how the computer code calculated numbers so I could optimize strategies. When involved heavily in a video game which I enjoyed, nothing in the universe would distract me, which seems fairly typical of autistic youth.

Sports and physical activity continued to be a challenge for me. I was blessed with below-average athletic ability and still had under-energized physical chakras. I generally enjoyed activities that involved the wavy higher chakras and not the lower physical ones, but the universe seemed to be slowly guiding me into a more partically experience. My father coached youth sports teams and always found that his son was the worst player on the team.

During my first trip into Boston in this life, my father took me to a Boston Red Sox baseball game at Fenway Park against the Toronto Blue Jays on June 4th, 1989. During this unusual game, the Red Sox got an early ten-run lead, and then blew it and ended up losing in the twelfth inning. This early emotional experience along with classic spiritual movie Field of Dreams ignited an interest in baseball.

The day after the Red Sox game, to my father's surprise, I could suddenly catch and make contact with a baseball. Both skills had been completely elusive to that point. Though I would never be mistaken for a big-league ball player, I had another thing to talk to people about and was upgraded to the second worst player on the team.

Baseball statistics became a hobby of mine. I'd look at the paper every day and analyze stats. I enjoyed watching how batting averages and earned run averages changed over time while a player was hot or in a slump. At a slightly different time, I would've been right at home working for Billy Bean (an Oakland Athletics Baseball general manager known for optimizing his teams using complex statistical analysis and documented in the book and movie *Moneyball*).

I'd design fictional baseball teams from characters in my video games and have them compete with each other using dice (this was even more nerdy and pathetic than it sounds).

My baseball career came to a close in a magnificent fashion. I was never a good baseball player and I played three years on a little league team called the Braves, who were not much better. Despite being a wonderful eclectic group of kids, we didn't win often.

Aside: The miracles of the Braves (which no one ever talked about).

A fair assessment of the talent level of my little league baseball team was: terrible! I'd apologize to my former teammates for this blunt assessment, but any of them who thought we were good are probably in mental institutions by now.

In my three years on this team we barely won any games. The games we did win were always due to fluky circumstances, like the other team not having a pitcher or the opposing coach using the game to play all the players who would not play otherwise.

Many of our games were "called" since once down by over twenty runs on a school night with the sun going down, there seemed little reason for even the most ardent adult to keep an unnecessary slaughter going.

At the end of my last season, the Braves were predictably at the bottom of the league standings. In accordance with league rules, we played the undefeated Twins at the top of the league standings in the first round of the playoffs.

This undefeated team had a pitcher who threw so fast that my central nervous system could not even follow the ball. During our regular season matchups with this pitcher, I never even swung the bat, as all my physical energy was focused on not getting hit.

On this particular day, everything went right for the Braves and everything went wrong for the Twins. I was walked twice by the above mentioned pitcher, despite having zero inventions of actually swinging the bat. We won this game, ruining the season for the team that by all logical standards should've been the league champions. In the next round of the playoffs we returned to form and were predictably slaughtered.

Over the years my mathematical nerdy mind has attempted to arrive at the "odds" of the Braves beating the Twins if all the initial conditions were the same. The best my mind can do is come up with the percentage: 0%. Maybe .0000000000000000000000014% if my calculator watch was being particularly generous. Only later in life has it become obvious that Angelic activity was involved (tested true).

I remember thinking a miracle had happened. This game had broken all rules of linear causality that my nerdy fifth grade mind had learned at the time.

However the most unusual thing about this incident was not the results of the game, but how quickly everyone else seemed to let the memory fade. I remember being extremely excited to talk about the miraculous game the next Monday at school but the other kids were not interested at all, which I found very unusual at the time.

I think most kids and adults involved filed the incident in the "do not look too closely at this" part of their minds, as it would've clearly broken many of their worldly perceptions. Every level of the Simulation seems to operate in a bit of a hypnotic trance, and not notice things falling too far outside its perception of reality. I've noticed this at every level of the

Simulation. This is the basis of the Faulkner Uncertainty discussed elsewhere.

Since this incident I've always enjoyed the sports movies and documentaries where a scrappy underdog team wins a championship (Miracle, Mighty Ducks, Bad News Bears). Sadly the Braves will never be made into a movie, mostly because it would be too far outside the realm of believability for most people.

End Aside.

I slowly became more "normal." I had a relatively high IQ so I could do well in school without expending too much effort, and I slowly became good enough at conventional things such as conversations and sports to blend into my environment. I made some very loving friendships and basically became a good citizen, despite true happiness eluding me. I was very protective of family and friends while distrustful of those I considered outsiders, which is a common trait of the Sacral level of the Simulation.

As my happiness level fell (in correlation with the energy of my Crown chakra), I gained an increased capacity to operate in the partically world. However, the sense of almost absolute security which seemed natural to me when I was extremely young slowly disappeared. Now negative emotion crept into my experience more often. I developed a temper, particularly where video games were involved and stress became a reality.

Worst of all, even in a nice small town, kids will be kids. We tend to attract into our lives what we are. As I got older, I noticed kids gradually became meaner toward me. My peer group was getting older and more competitive, and I was concentrating more on the lower physical chakras and less on my higher ones, meaning less power was at my disposal. These two factors contributed to me being bullied at an increasing rate.

By middle school, bullying started to become a real issue. As an oddball, autistic chubby kid with a speech impediment, this should not be shocking. Once again, when things began to get bad, the universe sent help in the form of an alliance of brains and brawns.

Soulmates come in different forms. I've encountered many over the years but what always seemed to be the theme is we both had some characteristic that the other needed that facilitated a relationship and ultimately evolution.

I was academically strong but one of the wimpiest kids in the fifth grade. Patrick was not academically strong, but one of the physical alpha males of the sixth grade. However both of us were primarily aligned with the second level Sacral chakra level of the Simulation. A characteristic of this chakra is viewing the world in terms of tribes or packs. In academic circles I tended to be a pack leader, but in physical and social circles felt like a perpetual outsider. Patrick was in the opposite position. Despite very different physical and mental characteristics, a strong Sacral chakra friendship developed.

My first two meetings with Patrick went like this:

- Trying to give him a hug on the playground and getting knocked in the mud.

- Letting him see my precious Garbage Pail Kid collection on the bus and then when his stop came, he simply kept them and got off the bus. The next day he denied all knowledge of this lol. This denial continued after we became close friends.

I remember my elementary school playground well. There were three distinct vibrational zones. Near the entrance to the school was a wavy zone, where the high values of the upper three levels of the Simulation ruled. All the socially awkward kids hung here. I found that I could avoid negative playground attention if I stayed close to the other socially awkward kids, followed the rules, and didn't purposely draw negative attention to myself. Besides, we were always within earshot of the teachers if trouble occurred.

Then as you moved further out from the building and into the playground, the vibration changed. On the playground, the values of the Heart and Solar Plexus levels of Simulation dominated and enthusiasm and fun ruled. This is where the majority of students played and socialized.

Many small American towns have a strong Solar Plexus and Heart vibration, with many of the residents heavily aligned primarily with these two chakras. Suburban areas where all the yards are well-tended and all the neighbors are friendly tend to have a large percentage of the population operating from these two levels of the Simulation (tested true). The small Maine town I grew up in was a classic example of this energy. Most people in these towns are positive people who care about their neighbors, work steady jobs, contribute to society in some way, and often observe a religion.

However, at the very end of the playground where the woods began, the values of the lower two animal levels of the Simulation ruled. Physical dominance, fear, and tribalism ruled the woods. I recall one time wandering my autistic vibration into the woods with a precious Nintendo power magazine. It was stolen and I was pushed down. This is pretty much what the wavy levels of the Simulation should expect impinging onto the turf of the partically levels of the Simulation unprepared. I don't make the rules, but I've learned to play by them.

Patrick hung out in the woods, where his physical vibration thrived far away from any adult influence. In the woods, it went something like, "the biggest, strongest kid makes the rules." Since Patrick was the biggest, strongest kid, he hence made the rules. As opposed to the reality I enjoyed next to the teachers, Patrick enjoyed the other end of the playground away from the teachers.

Upon entering fifth grade and a new school, the playground suddenly became a more complicated place. The playground was smaller and more homogeneous (evenly mixed). All the different social groups mixed. For a socially awkward nerd, this was very bad news. Luckily the universe sent help just in time. His name was Patrick.

Based on our surface characteristics, Patrick and I should not have been friends. However, we shared a chakra alignment which is a very powerful attractor force. Patrick liked knocking people in the mud and dominating in sports. I liked video games where I didn't have to use my physical body too often. The genius 8-bit Nintendo football Simulation Tecmo Bowl was a perfect meeting point, directly in the middle of our vibrational experiences at the time.

During our Tecmo Bowl matchups, I learned about the finer nuances of winning and losing. Mostly that winning felt good, but what felt better was letting someone else win anonymously. Patrick hated losing, and often I'd let Patrick win a close game as the energy was generally more comfortable that way.

Patrick and I were both rebellious in our own way against our town's culture. Patrick would rather run his pack and physically dominate his environment than conform to the goody two shoes Heart chakra alignment of the town. My autistic wavy vibration at the time would rather read, play video games, or retreat inside my own head than conform to the culture of the town.

Patrick helped me energize my lower chakras, which is what the Simulation wanted me to do anyway, and I helped Patrick develop more into the higher chakras.

I grew up on a little pristine lake in Maine. Most of the kids in my neighborhood were skaters and hockey players. To this day I cannot skate. God chose a number of skills I would learn in this lifetime and skating is not one of them.

Since I was becoming more social, I found a way to become more involved. I became the statistician for Patrick's self-created hockey league. While the other kids skated, shot, passed, and checked, I sat on the side of the ice with my moon boots, notebook and Gameboy. I kept score and produced complex statistics that the league players only found tentatively interesting.

This went on till I beat Patrick in the Nintendo hockey simulations "Blades of Steel" and "Ice Hockey" in back-to-back games. Losing two games of simulated hockey to his little stuttering unathletic friend, who couldn't even skate, was too much for Patrick's poor little ego to take and I was immediately fired from my job as league statistician.

This would've come as a terrible blow, had the role-playing game Dragon Warrior 3 for Nintendo not just fallen into my nerdy little hands. When one door closes, another tends to open.

Soul Contract #3: Ages Fifteen to Twenty-One: Solar Plexus Chakra:

Angelic Takeaway: At the initiation of this soul contract, I moved to a much larger more complex social environment away from my sheltered Sacral level existence. This forced the development of the Solar Plexus chakra and operation in the third level of the Simulation where ambition and expression of individual power arose.

It was in this soul contract where I acted the most 'normal' and lived the life of a fairly typical teenager and college student. A large percentage of Americans operate from the Solar Plexus level of the Simulation, so acting from the Solar Plexus does indeed appear normal.

During this soul contract an accelerating decline in happiness occurred as the increasing complexity of life and continued agnosticism drained the Crown chakra at an increasing rate. Immoral decisions became more common as my connection with divinity continued to sever. However, during this soul contract, I re-energized the Solar Plexus chakra and learned to exert my individual will and power.

In middle school, I moved with the family to Massachusetts where I suddenly found myself in a much larger school, with a much more competitive social situation and complex environment. My intuition and odd sense of humor alone was no longer enough to survive. As with all things, the Simulation encourages us to eventually evolve.

As a socially awkward autistic tween who enjoyed a nice comfortable reality, moving to a new bigger school was my worst nightmare. A recurring fear prior to moving was what to do on the first day of lunch. As a generally introverted youth, I was at best mediocre at starting conversations and making friends. My plan for my first day at lunch was to find a corner to hide in and hope I was left alone.

Walking to lunch on my first day I remember doing something resembling praying, with no real spiritual basis. It was basically a begging of the universe to get me through lunch. Then as if on cue, I was approached by a dorky looking kid (who would later be a best friend throughout high school) and he asked me to come eat with him.

I was led to a lunch table filled with the most eclectic group of tweens imaginable. Each person at the table had a good heart but didn't really fit in anywhere else for whatever reason. The table vibe reminded me of a bargain bin at a store where you find wonderful things, but it's obvious why everything is in there. We were a group of great movies on VHS. Each movie was wonderful and informative, but unfortunately not many people had VHS players so it was obvious why we were all in that particular bargain bin.

This odd but lovely group would end up being my core group of friends in high school and though not appreciated at the time, it was an early sign that the universe and Angels had my back. Miraculously, a socially awkward tween had stumbled into a group of lifelong friends at a new school before the first day was halfway done without any personal effort.

However, moving to this larger school still brought immense challenges. Despite stumbling into a small group of wonderful friends, I was no longer in my safe small town in Maine. I also don't think I appreciated how much Patrick had indirectly helped keep bullies away. For the first time in my life, I faced serious bullying. I was an unathletic, overweight, stuttering, socially awkward kid with a last name that sounded like a swear. A bully's wet dream. Not wanting to dwell on the negative or victim level of things, I'll leave painful details out.

A turning point in getting bullied happened in late middle school.

At the start of a class, I was sitting in the front row trying to mind my own business without the teacher in the room. I was being verbally and occasionally physically assaulted which was fairly common at the time. One particularly aggressive bully was in my face yelling "Fucker, Fucker, Fucker" (a nickname based on my last name) and pushing me to try to get a response. Being a peaceful, friendly nerd, I had no defense against this at the time.

What happened next is not fully explainable in logical terms. Without conscious effort, I found myself in a new vibration; my hand made itself into a fist and I punched the unsuspecting bully in the nose. I don't remember making hard contact, but there was an extremely loud crack and the bully's nose began to bleed quite profusely. I suspect he took the hit worse because the action was very unexpected by all at the scene. My guardian Angel also helped a bit (tested true).

I've heard the term "a punchable face" used throughout the years. I believe this term to be true on some level. Every soul on the planet has karma and all energy must eventually balance. Some people just have a punch coming to their face.

A friend of mine was recently in a legal situation and she described the unethical opposing lawyer as having "a punchable face." By chance I saw a picture of him and I realized that she was correct. Upon seeing his face I felt a visceral reaction arising from deep within my physical chakras to punch the guy. It was like some energy in the Simulation cried out for karma to be balanced.

The bully, mentioned above, simply had a punchable face (said with unconditional love as we are all evolving souls). I was generally nonviolent, but some power in the universe found it necessary to balance this karma out.

As if on cue, the teacher walked in. I remember the bully using notebook pages to sop up the blood. As this was the last period of the day, when the bell rang, I ran to the bus and went home to a night of stress. I didn't sleep as my mind created hypothetical scenarios about being retaliated against along with school and parental punishment.

The strangest part of the incident was that the next day came and nothing really happened. Quite miraculously the bully and I got along after that. Though never becoming friends, we seemed to have established a truce. Bullying also dramatically declined after this as word spread that the little nerd had some teeth.

Please don't take this as a license to use physical violence. It is rarely an optimal solution to problems but in this specific context it seemed the appropriate thing to do. This incident seemed the beginning of teaching me the spiritual lesson that people in different levels of the Simulation do not play by the same rules.

A main point of this book is that people of the world function on different levels of the Simulation and that rules of one level don't strictly apply to another level. Tackling a person is okay during a football game but not okay at church.

I've observed people operating at all levels of the Simulation be surprised when they accidentally wandered into another level's culture, and are shocked by how drastically reality changes. This is much like my surprise when I was pushed down and my Nintendo Power was stolen in the woods of my elementary school. Oftentimes more help is available to people in the lower chakra levels of the Simulation than they suspect, as their level of perception does not notice the existence of the higher, generally more benign levels of the Simulation.

It was clear that to function my current environment I needed to adapt to a new level of the Simulation. This seemed the point where I switched primarily to a Solar Plexus chakra alignment which was the chakra which needed to be rebuilt during this soul contract. I immediately noticed I became more ambitious, competitive, and driven.

One particular downside of moving into the Solar Plexus level came during a track practice during high school. In my early youth, I had considered winning and losing in sports to be almost irrelevant. Sports were interesting, but winning and losing (more losing in my case) came with a grain of salt and no major effort was ever exerted to win.

In the Solar Plexus level, there appeared for the first time a burning desire to be successful and win. Much more effort and force was now exerted in sports and competitive endeavors in general. This Solar Plexus drive may have resulted in a great athlete had this physical body been designed to be one. However, playing for the New England Patriots or Boston Celtics may have to wait until the next life.

One track practice, I was pitted in a sprint against a friend who was a superior runner across the gym. Despite having a burning drive to win, I predictably fell behind early in the race. As I tracked my opponent in my peripheral vision, I watched myself slowly catch him and pass him.

As this happened, the mind created the illusion that I was speeding up as I passed him. However, the reality was that my friend, who was not only faster than me but at least temporarily smarter, was slowing down as we approached a wall at the far side of the gym.

The good news was that I won the race but the bad news was I hit the gym wall at full speed. In desperation, I put my right wrist out and it was forced to absorb nearly all the momentum of my fast moving overweight body as it hit the wall. The result was this:

I got a seven-point break/fracture that never healed completely correctly.

I look back at this incident with humor, as my opponent was quite a bit faster than me. The idea that I had gained some magically burst of velocity to beat him was quite ridiculous. This incident was mostly the result of having recently switched alignments to the Solar Plexus chakra in the third level of the Simulation where one's drive and will to succeed is much stronger in competitive endeavors.

I spent the majority of my high school experience vibrating in the Solar Plexus level of the Simulation. I wanted to succeed so I could serve my country optimally. I balanced many different activities including membership in a state title winning marching band. Along with a strong academic record and high standardized test scores, I put together a portfolio that would look very attractive to colleges in the late 90's, which was my primary goal during those years.

However, at one point it was made clear by my financially responsible father that I'd played enough Final Fantasy and Mario Kart, and it was time to find a job and begin earning one's keep in the world. Even though being forced out of my comfort zone, earning one's own money was an idea compatible with my Solar Plexus view of the world at the time. I wanted to earn my own way and not force anyone else to financially support me.

After a fairly lengthy job search, applying to many jobs unsuccessfully, and looking into a few professional internships, nothing panned out. Finally, somewhat in desperation, McDonald's became the top option since, as was pointed out to me by multiple people, McDonald's is many people's first job. When I went to my local McDonald's restaurant for an application, I was interviewed and hired on the spot. When one is on the path the Simulation desires for us, reality tends to flow very smoothly. I've experienced this over and over.

I'd be lying to say my time as a McDonald's employee was a 100% positive experience (most jobs aren't) but I absolutely loved the interesting cast of characters I met. It is now apparent that the Simulation had dropped me exactly where I needed to be for my continued evolution.

Early in this job, I minded my own business, performed my duties to the best of my ability, and slowly became accustomed to a different vibration and culture. I showed up on time, worked hard, and tried to get along with the other employees, even if we were clearly on different levels of the Simulation so didn't fully understand each other.

Working this job required me to adapt to a faster work environment than was natural for me at the time. My wavy sheltered childhood had allowed me to float by in a relaxed state, but to be a good McDonalds employee, one needed to focus on the partically/physical universe. I needed to multitask, respond quickly to physical stimuli, and perform tasks at a high rate of speed.

Elsewhere in this book I mention brainwave states and their relationship to the level of the Simulation. The work environment and culture of McDonald's simultaneously forced me to function in the faster beta frequencies instead of the more relaxed alpha and theta frequencies which I was far more accustomed to.

In the Simulation, higher is not strictly better. One tends to be happier and vibrationally closer to God in the higher levels of the Simulation, but sometimes operating from a lower level of the Simulation is simply better suited for certain roles. I was now spending more time in bottom three physical animal chakras and less time in my higher wavy autistic chakras. This shift made me focus much more on the physical world and relate to a different demographic, thus helping me function as a McDonald's employee.

After a bit of adaptation and showing the strong work ethic which is quite natural in the Solar Plexus level of the Simulation, I was made a manager. I struggled early in this role as the boss, as I wanted to be nice to everyone and lacked the confidence to put my foot down.

It seems a common experience for socially awkward, nerdy teenagers to get off to a slow start with the opposite sex. I was no different. During high school, I was entranced with a very kind-hearted girl who became one of my best friends, and whom I would have gladly walked through fire for. Sadly this never manifested in the romantic relationship I would've liked, though we always loved each other deep down.

Late in my senior year of high school, the universe finally threw me a bone. Somehow, an absolutely beautiful fellow McDonald's employee, widely regarded to be the hottest woman in the store, took a strange liking to me. This went against every construct of reality that I understood at the time.

It was one night while cleaning the shake machine together that she finally said with a tone of frustration, "If you ask me out, I will say yes." This led to my first date. I picked her up for that date unshowered after a workout, wearing gym shorts and a sleeveless shirt. I saw nothing wrong with this at the time.

Despite my social awkwardness and odd quirks she did not dump me immediately, and it turned out, dating the hottest girl at work gave me a bit of clout. Suddenly the other employees showed me quite a bit more respect, which made managing easier. Now in heavy alignment with Solar Plexus chakra, I walked around with physical confidence and a head held high for the first time in this life.

One night while managing the McDonald's with my new attractive lady-friend, I was visited by a group of high school friends, and my kind-hearted high school crush was among them. Being naturally empathic, I immediately sensed her jealousy, suddenly seeing me flirting with my new attractive romantic interest.

This course of events seemed to immediately present me with a decision. I could've held onto the basic morality I'd developed in my childhood and empathized with my kind-hearted high school crush, and stopped blatantly flirting to minimize the emotional pain of the situation. Instead I chose what most would consider the lower path and chose to purposely inflict jealousy.

I realized for one of the first times in my life, I was in a socially dominant position. I proudly showed off the immense power I wielded as a McDonald's manager and dating the hottest girl in the store. Rather than considering the feelings of my high school crush, I let my ego take over and exert its temporary dominance. I did everything in my power to invoke my kind-hearted friend's jealousy.

This resulted in temporary ego satisfaction but resulted in a loss of innocence, as this was the first time I recall doing something to intentionally emotionally harm another. As a result, happiness became significantly more elusive. The Crown chakra which had been slowly dripping energy was now rapidly leaking. Not only was I less happy after this incident, the apparent 'luck' which seemed to have kept me out of trouble in my youth was now much less present. Trouble now occurred with increasing frequency.

This also seemed to bring me into visceral contact with my animal ego, which is the primitive animal part of us found in every human which I will discuss later. My spirit animal according to Native American tradition is the wolf. I then prioritized fighting for position within the human pack over the happy wavy experiences of my autistic childhood.

An effect of the increasing Solar Plexus alignment and decreasing Crown chakra alignment was that my interest in sports and physical fitness dramatically increased. My actual performance as a McDonald's manager improved greatly, as I now knew how to be a boss. I could exert dominance by simply raising my voice a bit or implying displeasure. For the first time in this life, I could enforce discipline and rules when necessary.

However, this vibrational shift came with a huge downside. Anxiety increased as I now saw my existence as dependent on my physical and financial well-being. Interest in intellectual and academic matters rapidly declined. I was still able to maintain a strong academic record but it was now largely the result of effort, self-interest, and a high IQ rather than any personal interest in learning. Immoral decisions also became more common and negative karma began to accumulate at a faster rate.

As my interest in intellectual activity declined, my interest in physical activity seemed to almost automatically replace it. I began working out with a passion and took a heavy interest in nutrition. Having not been born in an athletically gifted body, I maxed out the athletic potential of my physical body, which was clearly more built for reading than sports.

During the summer between high school and college, I took an interest in basketball and actually got relatively good. I got to a point where I could dominate basketball games played with my nerdy high school friends and relatives, none of whom had ever played any organized basketball. My primitive wolfy ego/id whom I'd recently come in contact with entertained wild fantasies of walking onto the Northeastern University basketball team and leading the team to NCAA glory.

Unfortunately, upon arriving at Northeastern and beginning to play with real basketball players in Boston, I was quickly knocked off my pedestal and was forced to confront the reality of my athletic ability.

The choice to attend Northeastern University seemed to be more of a pull than a conscious choice. As a student near the top of his high school class with strong SATs and a wide range of extracurricular activities, I could've attended almost any university and was offered scholarships and great financial aid packages to a few other prestigious schools. After a visit to Northeastern in Boston (despite being generally adverse to cities and crowds), the decision seemed to have been made from a source way higher than my individual mind could comprehend at the time.

Looking back, it is clear to the intuition that Northeastern was simply the place where I would have the experiences, both good and bad, that would be optimal for my soul to continue its evolution. The application process went smooth and fast.

The choice to be an Electrical Engineering major also seemed to be made for me. As a student with a strong math and science background who desired to make a lot of money, the choice of major seemed ridiculously obvious, despite having no particularly strong interest in the subject. However, like a lot of directions this life took, the Simulation knew what it was doing and was funneling me in a certain direction.

An early potential title for this book was going to be *Angelic Electrical Engineering,* as I wanted to express the idea that all energy flows down from divinity, with the different levels of the Simulation acting a bit like electrical transformers stepping down the voltage so it can be utilized by the lower levels of the Simulation. This is now a chapter title in this book.

My early college experience was wonderful. Being in an academic environment in honors engineering classes had me surrounded by nice energy, and I thrived. However, by the end of second quarter with the energy of my Crown chakra continuing to deplete, I was accumulating more and more negative karma and struggling to find scraps of happiness.

During a summer quarter, I was housed in a suite with three other electrical/computer engineering majors. The summer was quite pleasant, as we all got along very well. Although it was clear, two of us were aligned with Solar Plexus chakra and the other two roommates were aligned with the intellectual Throat chakra. Throat chakra alignment is less common in the world as a whole but is more common in academically elite environments.

We were all in a programming class together. One might suspect the two suitemates aligned with the Throat chakra to perform better academically but the opposite was actually the case. The Throat level aligned suitemates ended up with Bs in the class and the Solar Plexus level suitemates (myself included) got As.

The two other suitemates took a genuine interest in the class material. They took the programming to heart, spending the summer programming a game and fooling around with computer code. The grade they received in the class was secondary. Hence they did well, learned a lot, but did not feel a need to ace the class.

Meanwhile, my other Solar Plexus level roommate and I were taking the class for the grade. We did what we needed to do in order to get a high grade in class, as that was the primary reason that we were taking it. While the other two suitemates applied what they were learning in class to their lives and enjoyed intellectually enriching themselves, we gamed the class to ensure we got our A. We both spent a lot of time at the gym (an extremely enticing activity for those operating in the Solar Plexus level of the Simulation) and played a lot of competitive Starcraft (a popular computer strategy game at the time).

This highlights a difference between the Solar Plexus and Throat levels of the Simulation which both tend to be broadly masculine. Both levels can produce good students, however the Throat level students will be genuinely interested in learning, where the Solar Plexus level students will be more interested in what learning will get them, which is a big difference! I will talk about the characteristics of students at the different levels later in this book.

Growing up as what could be broadly classified as a nerd, a potential career in the military barely ever registered as a viable option, but the Simulation tends to send us to the experiences we need for our soul's growth, and the military was clearly where my soul now needed to go.

When signing a military contract I've always recommended to my students that they carefully consider their options and take their time. Telling my students this is very hypocritical of me, as this was not at all what I did.

On September 11th of 2001, I was getting ready for another year of college. I had gone to college with the goal of being an electrical/computer engineer, but this was seeming like a more distant goal as interest in academics was continuing to dwindle. I was nearing the end of the Solar Plexus soul contract and entering a new soul contract aligned with the Heart chakra. I was awakening to this new level of the Simulation quite abruptly after a series of heartbreaks, and was now seeking some higher purpose to serve.

On September 11th, 2001 I was stacking and chopping wood at my parents' house when a quick trip into the house for water resulted in me seeing a plane fly into the Twin Towers of New York City. Even though it was the news, my mind did not register the event as real, as the idea of my country getting attacked on its own soil was too out-of-coherence with my very safe childhood.

Over the next thirty minutes, I became curious about what I had been briefly seen on TV, so I went back inside to find out the United States had indeed been attacked. At this point, now aligning with the Heart chakra, I formed a reaction which seemed a combination of the Heart and the three chakras I'd been aligned with early in life. My country (Sacral) which I loved (Heart) had been attacked. I wanted revenge (Root) and wondered what I could do (Solar Plexus).

When the Twin Towers came down, my goals were no longer aligned with the goals of being an electrical engineer.

As the Angels would have it, a few days earlier I'd received a letter from a Navy recruiter about the Navy's nuclear engineering program. The contents of the letter had been dismissed, but for some reason not thrown away. Stumbling upon the letter a few days later, the idea of defending my country I loved now seemed appealing. I had the academic record and intelligence to get into the prestigious Navy Nuclear engineering program, so the decision to enter the military seemingly made itself.

The process of getting into the Navy's Nuclear Power program was extremely fast and smooth, which is generally a sign from the universe that you are going in the right direction. A timely viewing of the patriotic film *Top Gun* (which critics complained was Navy recruitment film, despite being clearly the most awesome movie ever created) made what should have been a hard decision with a long touring, vetting, and interview process feel more like a greased pig being pulled through a pipe. Coincidently I would end up serving on-board the USS Enterprise, which is where the first scene in the movie *Top Gun* takes place.

After graduating college and before reporting for formal military training, I went on a vacation with my family to Las Vegas. It was a hot week and I remember not feeling well. Happiness had become even more elusive than ever, as my Crown chakra's energy continue to deplete and my connection to divinity weakened.

At one point I found myself in a shop staring at a wolf T-shirt. An old lady grabbed me by the arm roughly and looked deep into my eyes. She said with alarming intensity, "There is a wolf inside you" and walked away without further comment. This was my first true indicator that my spirit animal was a wolf.

This experience was so unusual at the time as I had absolutely no context to understand it. I immediately dismissed it from my memory as weird, as I was still viewing everything from the spiritual universe as nonsense at the time. However, this incident occurred with proper timing. No longer having the energy of the Crown chakra at my disposal which I'd taken for granted early in this life, I was now existing almost completely in the animal world. The characteristics of a wolf became my primary characteristics. I saw the world in terms of packs and was protective of those in my pack but hostile to those I considered outside of it in a wolfy fashion.

Luckily this was all part of the plan as I was about to enter one of the strongest packs in the world: The United States Military.

Soul Contract #4: Ages Twenty-Two to Twenty-Eight: Heart Chakra

Angelic Takeaway: The ages twenty-two through twenty-eight were spent primarily in the US Navy. The Crown chakra, which is indicative of one's visceral connection to divinity, was now extremely weak, so darkness and unhappiness was the general experience of this period. The Heart chakra searched for love and enthusiasm outside itself but would never truly find it. It took hitting an extraordinarily low spiritual point for the psyche to crack open just enough to let divinity in. The Crown chakra then began to slowly recharge and recovery began.

One would think that a soul contract aligned with Heart chakra would be a happy one. However, rather than the experience of love, I was scheduled to explore a reality where I experienced almost the complete absence of it.

For a large part of this soul contact I was what could be characterized roughly as a hopeless romantic. The heart was constantly reaching out, but being in a very low spiritual place through most of these years, potential partners intuitively stayed away. Even when a romantic spark was found I'd find a way to sabotage it, which is common in a low spiritual state.

This led to the experience of the depths of human suffering, often referred to as hell. However this incredible low, which is worse than most can imagine, led to a slow realignment with divinity and the Crown chakra.

This soul contract was my most unhappy by a long shot, as I operated with a Crown chakra now negativity aligned. In my youth with an energized Crown chakra, the Simulation had been seemingly working for me, but now the Simulation seemed to be working against me. I made many moral mistakes saw the world in very simple negative terms and was very politically opinionated.

To say I was unprepared physically, emotionally, mentally, and spiritually for the military would be understatement. When I signed up for the military my perception of what military life was like and what it actually was like were miles apart. A broad choice people going into the Naval Nuclear Power program face is whether to go onto Submarines or Aircraft Carriers.

I was very insistent on Aircraft Carriers for two reasons. Firstly, I thought that the movie *Top Gun* was representative of day-to-day life aboard a carrier, even though I never got to play even a single game of homoerotic beach volleyball during my entire time aboard the USS Enterprise. Secondly, I actually thought that I could see a bit more sun because I could take my lunch up to the flight deck daily and picnic and casually watch the jets get launched. The idea that I ever thought this is humorous now.

Navy OCS is essentially a boot camp for Navy officers, run by intense Marine Corps Gunnery Sergeants. I showed up unshaven, overweight, with essentially no military bearing and a moderate speech impediment, made worse by nervousness which the gunnery Sergeants quickly realized. I knew immediately from the attitude of the trainers that I had jumped in way over my head.

My first night at OCS, after being brutally yelled at the entire day, I didn't sleep and seemed to slip down further into fear than I'd ever been in my life. Lacking the security of the Crown chakra and any real power, my only hope to survive

OCS was to rely on my inner wolf (my ego) and my new pack (my classmates at OCS).

Given this unpreparedness, Navy OCS went close to how one would expect. I held back as my progress was not satisfactory, which made me feel a bit like I was in kindergarten again where I had also held back. Lots of the would-be officers I was going through this training with had come from a strong military background and were generally much more attuned to this lifestyle. I was having to adjust to this military lifestyle on the fly in a state of great stress, while simultaneously learning to operate from a new level of the Simulation.

As someone who seems to have jumped around between different levels of the Simulation in this life a little more than most, I will say it's not easy, and each jump between levels is like having to adjust to a drastically different pair of glasses.

Aside: *Officer and a Gentleman.*

This iconic but dark 1982 film is about the trials and tribulations of Richard Gere, or "Mayo," going through Navy OCS. I recommend this film for a number of reasons. Its energy level is higher than it appears on the surface, and broadly tells the tale of a young man transitioning from the Solar Plexus of the Simulation to the Heart level of the Simulation.

I'll try to give as few spoilers as possible. A large part of the plot revolves around the romantic entanglements of Navy OCS students as local women try to seduce and date them during their free time.

I'm not sure what happened, but this was not my reality whatsoever. I suspect this is mostly due to the fact that I in no way resemble the handsome Richard Gere. I never left base and spent any extra time resting, studying, or working out. The beautiful Debra Winger never even attempted to seduce me, and my nights were generally spent in a combination of terror and exhaustion, not mingling with beautiful ladies.

End Aside.

The stress of OCS forced a regression from the Heart level of the Simulation to the tribal Sacral chakra level of the Simulation. A downside of the tribal Sacral level of the Simulation is beings operating from here lack much personal power, tend to get brainwashed easily, and pick up lots of fallacious information. What one is told by one's pack and pack-leaders is considered ultimate truth. I bought the information from my military indoctrination completely and without question. When people use 'sheep' as a derogatory term, it is normally referring to someone operating out of the Sacral level of the Simulation.

Luckily, most of the information I received at Navy OCS was true and integrous. Falling temporarily back into a lower level of the Simulation was of Angelic design to facilitate my evolution and get me through OCS (tested true).

One of my better performing days at OCS was the day we fired guns. I earned the highest score in the class, despite having never touched a gun to that point in this life. This earned me a few valuable respect points in the Gunnery Sergeant's eyes, which I sorely needed at the time. What was unknown at the time was that I actually had touched many guns in previous lives (tested true).

By grace, I ended up ranked twenty-three of forty-five in my OCS class. My academic scores were at the top of the class (thank God for a high IQ), my physical scores were near the top of the class (due to sheer willpower and staying on base to improve while Richard Gere was off getting laid), but my military bearing score was dead last in the class. This was a bit of a sneak preview of how much of a fish out of water I was, but it is clear this was the experience the Simulation wanted me to have.

My first ship, the USS Gunston Hall, was a major culture shock. My very unsophisticated view of Navy Ships and Officer Ward Rooms was challenged when I encountered the reality of political posturing, extremely hard work, and uncomfortable conditions. Neither of the ships I was stationed on in the Navy seemed to have an air conditioning system built in the 20th or 21st century.

The phrase "Swear like a sailor" holds a bit of reality. When in a low spiritual state and experiencing fear, you tend to act like the rest of the pack for security purposes and help demarcate the lines between friend and foe. The F-word was used a lot on both the US Navy ships I was stationed on, and this quickly became my absolute favorite and most used word. To this day it still comes out a lot. My apologies to the well-mannered, cultured crowd.

As I was operating with very little power or morality, I was hardly an ideal Naval Officer. Generally I struggled to literally keep my head above water during most of my military time. Off the ship, I felt the immense pain of operating from the Heart chakra without the energy available to express the enthusiasm and love this level of the Simulation lives for.

One thing that saved me was my autistic ability to sense people's vibes, which had remained mostly intact over the years. When operating in a pack, it's nice to know who the high vibe people are and brownnose them as well as you can. An observation of this book is that the people operating from the higher levels of the Simulation tend to have most of the actual power, even if that is not the appearance of things. This paradox is created because the more actual power one has, the less one tends to seek it externally or create an appearance of it (tested true). As I was operating with almost no power during this period, I expended great effort to seek illusionary sources of it.

Another thing my autism and Third Eye has helped me with over the years and probably saved me from washing out of the Navy was my ability to tell what was energetically going on behind the scenes and not just the appearance of things.

At Navy OCS I was taught the Navy rank system. At Navy OCS this rank system was followed to the letter. High ranked officers were treated like gods, and lower ranked people had to struggle just to survive. However, as I got to my first ship, I observed a very different reality. I quickly noticed that despite the fact that everyone wore their ranks visibly on their uniform, the higher-ranking person was often not the person actually in charge.

It was apparent that the William Wallace quote from the wonderful movie *Braveheart*, "Men don't follow titles, they follow courage" was a reality. I observed that often high-ranking officers were given the customary military courtesies of their rank, but wielded no actual power or respect.

The opposite was also often the case. In one division that I managed, a Petty officer third class or E-4, which is relatively low rank in the Navy, actually ran the entire division and had no need to listen to anyone's orders (with the possible exception of the actual captain of the ship). This high vibrating E-4 operated in the high end of the Throat level of the Simulation where significant spiritual power resides.

He understood the division's equipment better than anyone and was smart enough to give higher-ranking people proper military respect. His inherent power was obvious to most, and therefore he answered to no one. Because I could sense vibes really well, I knew immediately that he was actually my boss, even though I was his boss on paper.

I recall one particularly unwise junior officer giving this powerful E-4 an unnecessarily hard time about a minor technicality, thinking he was protected by his rank. The entire division jumped to the E-4's defense and the unwise junior officer ended up in the captain's cabin explaining himself. True Power is somewhat immune to earthly position (tested true).

Another interesting power dynamic exists between the young Junior officers and the Senior enlisted ranks. Legally, a young kid just out of college, having just reported to a ship as an officer, can order a thirty-year salty enlisted Chief who has been around the world six times.

The reality tends to be far different. With my God-given ability to read energy, I immediately understood this interesting dynamic between junior officers and senior enlisted. I was able to sense who was actually in charge and never made the error of using my officer status to order a person around who I shouldn't. I saw many Junior officers make this error and it never seemed to turn out well for them.

Another interesting power dynamic that I noticed when reading the vibes of the wardroom was that on both my ships, the auxiliary officers (the guys who controlled air conditioning units) were significantly more powerful than their rank alone would indicate. Though they were relatively low ranked junior officers they tended to wield power similar to that of the executive officer (the second-in-command of a Navy ship).

Both my ships ended up in the very hot Persian Gulf, and had air conditioning systems not nearly powerful enough to keep the entire ship even close to a comfortable human temperature in the pressure cooker of the world.

If the Captain of a ship had a choice between disappointing an executive officer who often had the unfortunate task of delivering bad news and problems to be dealt with and an auxiliary officer who controlled the flow of cool air to his cabin inside a frying ship, he would face a truly difficult decision.

Despite this small advantage of autistically-sensing vibes, the Navy was an extremely dark time for me. This was mostly due to an almost completely drained Crown chakra which I was still unable to recharge, primarily due to my agnostic beliefs. I would also later learn that I was subjectively dealing with a large amount of negative karma I'd accumulated as a pirate in a past-life, to be discussed later. My first ship was even conducting anti-pirate operations on my first deployment.

To this point in my life, I'd avoided alcohol. Though at the age twenty-four, I had my first drink at a Navy officer party. Even though I only partook due to peer pressure, with one drink in me, it blocked out enough of my nervousness to strike up a conversation with a woman and actually get her number (a minor miracle for me at the time).

To avoid accidentally glorifying alcohol, I'll tell you about my second time drinking. I was alone in my apartment on a Friday night. My roommate (another Navy officer) was on duty and had a very large liquor collection. Mostly out of boredom and general unhappiness with life, I decided to try drinking. However, being alone and being unaccustomed to drinking this probably wasn't a great idea.

I remember pouring myself a large glass of something very high proof and chugging it in a single gulp. Having only drank conventional beverages to that point in my life, this seemed reasonable.

My memories from the night are hazy, but I remember crawling around the apartment on all fours. Trying to turn on the TV but being completely befuddled by the remote control and absolutely ruining a saved game file on a video game since selling my best piece of equipment "seemed like a great idea at the time." I woke up in a pile of poop and puke with just enough time to clean up before my roommate arrived home.

In regards to addictive substances, to make a long story short: THEY HAVE NO ACTUAL POWER. All any chemical can do is temporarily block or rev up certain chakras so different levels of the Simulation can be felt temporarily.

Unfortunately the law of karma dictates that every high needs a corresponding low. After the temporary high has passed one must experience an equal or opposite low corresponding to the stolen high. During the high, one feels like they have access to the power of a higher level of the Simulation when they actually don't. This can lead to some bad decisions, and it did in my case. Real power can only be earned through evolution and learning. This is discussed further in a future chapter.

My third time drinking was at a party. The consumption was more moderate this time, so the transition to the temporary feeling of a higher level of the Simulation was managed. My ego was fascinated by the fact that I loved everyone and could suddenly dance (this was verified by a third party, and was not 100% drunken fantasy).

I loved everyone at the party. This was my first time really feeling a glimpse of the potential of the Heart level of

Simulation. One loves everyone and tends to be loved back. This is the everyday experience in the Heart chakra level of the Simulation when properly aligned and energized.

Alcohol was allowing me to feel a pale shadow of the Heart level of the Simulation. At the time I was operating in a very low spiritual state and was falling back into the bottom three animal level chakras in order to survive, where it's a struggle to get a positive reaction from anyone due to the energy you exude.

What was not understood at the time was that this experience was temporary. However due to this temporary experience, I became a heavy drinker virtually overnight. In my particular case alcohol tended to block out the unhappy lower levels of the Simulation where I was under-energized, and I experienced a pale shadow of the juice remaining in my higher chakras. This felt better than anything I could experience naturally at the time, so addiction to this high state came on fast. This resulted in my natural vibration beginning to fall further due to terrible drunken decisions. The little juice left in my Crown chakra was now being squeezed out like water from a sponge.

As my vibration continued to fall, the relative high felt even better by comparison, but over time I needed more and more alcohol for less and less time in the elevated state. The toxic side effects of alcohol began to accumulate. The relative state of good health I'd earned at the gym in college and OCS quickly faded.

A series of bad personal decisions, mostly due to alcohol and the low spiritual state I was operating in, eventually culminated in me experiencing homelessness for a period of about six months.

Before one feels too bad for me, please consider the following:

#1: This period was largely the result of poor personal decisions.

#2: My life now seems guided by an unseen hand the entire time. Certain negative experiences were part of the plan.

#3: If any soul wishes to experience homelessness, the six warmer months in Virginia Beach USA is about the best place to do it. I now jokingly refer to these six months as homelessness lite.

#4: At least on a physical level, my back was never really against the wall. There were always many options available to me. As stated earlier, each level of the Simulation tends to see the world through its own lens. At the low level of the Simulation that I was operating from, I saw reality as darker than it actually was and that no help was available, even though in reality I was absolutely surrounded by it. Although I did indeed have a lot of options, some as simple as just sleeping on my ship for example, strangely they never presented as an option.

Aside: Subconscious Sabotage.

This is a phrase that gets thrown around a lot in self-help circles. It is fairly common for someone on the brink of success to do something outlandish at the last minute to ensure their success does not arrive.

My homeless period seemed to be a case of this. When one's innermost view of themselves and one's external reality do not match, the mind attempts to re-sync them.

Even when help is physically available to someone in a low level of the Simulation, they tend not to notice it. I've observed this very often as a teacher in an urban school.

An employee desperate for a promotion seems to blow it every time the opportunity presents itself due to unexamined feelings of inner inadequacy. These feelings of inadequacy often hide behind an outward display of over-confidence.

In the lowest levels of this Simulation, my psyche seemed to automatically create the conditions to experience homelessness so that my external reality matched my subjective inner vibrational state.

This is one of the reasons sending purely financial assistance to poor areas without addressing the root issue is notoriously ineffective in dealing with poverty crises.

End Aside.

On a positive note: Turns out, if you know where all the cheap all-you-can-eat buffets are in Virginia Beach and one has a stomach like mine, one could eat fairly decently for about $10 every other day in the early 2000s.

It was a hard six months, but I learned one positive lesson from this period that has stuck with me since. It was that material possessions are not related to happiness as I had once suspected. One can get by pretty well with almost nothing, and one's life actually tends to be simpler and more enjoyable when not weighed down by too much stuff.

My experience and spiritual research has been clear that happiness is related to the energy level of one's chakras, karma, and vibrational vicinity to God. It is very poorly correlated to material possessions.

Having very little to one's name actually turned out to be a stress relief. Since that period I've basically started over a number of times, dumping most of my material possessions. Each starting over felt like the shedding of an old skin and the increased freedom more than counterbalanced the minor feeling of loss that comes with losing partically/physical possessions.

I can't help but noting that increased worldly possessions comes with an added subtle stress. It is more stuff to track and try to be a responsible custodian of it. Most wise spiritual teachers recommend non-attachment to material possessions. If worldly possessions come, enjoy them and be as responsible of a custodian as you can, but if you lose them, it frees you up for rapid change and a more carefree existence. As with most things, worldly possessions come with an upside and downside.

Thankfully, my homelessness came to an end. My ship left for a deployment to the Middle East. Unfortunately, deployment life was even harder. I was never a perfect fit for Navy deployments. Not seeing the sun and working a stressful job that required my attention for nearly twenty-four hours a day, I barely survived. We were engaged in anti-pirate operations as I subjectively paid back karma for my mishaps as a pirate in the early 1700s. After a very tough deployment in which I caught glimpses of the lowest expressions of the human experience known as 'hell,' I reported to the Naval Nuclear Power School.

Upon arriving at Naval Nuclear Power School, I was in bad shape physically, emotionally, mentally, and spiritually. I was so taxed that upon arriving at my duty station, I simply checked into a local hotel for the night, thinking I'd find a more permanent residence in the morning. That one night turned out to be my entire time at the school. Living in a hotel where all my messes got magically cleaned up however was a nice way to spend time after a period of homelessness and a very hard deployment. Unfortunately, I'm messy and unorganized on my best days, and having someone paid to clean up for me did not help that situation.

This year-long academic environment was a much-needed respite. I was back in an environment more natural to my predilections. I met some of the highest quality and loving people I've ever encountered in this year, and my vibration made a partial recovery as I experienced the Heart level of the Simulation without chemical assistance for the first time in this life. I loved the people around me and by the laws of the universe, was generally loved back. At one point while stationed in beautiful upstate New York, I had my first inkling of a past-life memory fighting in the French-Indian war.

At the time all spirituality and past lives were still filed under good-natured nonsense, but the data obtained would be very useful when past-life memories began flooding into consciousness later in life.

By the grace of a fortuitous three-month gap between when my nuclear training ending and my next ship (The USS Enterprise) returning from deployment, I got some more much needed recovery. By the end of this time, I was engaged to a wonderful woman whom I'm friendly with to this day, eating a very healthy diet, mostly done with a master's degree in nuclear engineering and running almost ten miles a day. However, this period was clearly calm before the storm.

The depths of Human Consciousness:

When I reported to my second ship, the Nuclear-powered USS Enterprise, it had just returned from an extremely hard deployment in the Middle East. I recall experiencing a visceral pain in my aura as the vibration on the steel nuclear-powered carrier impinged on mine. The crew, whose morale was extremely low, drained on my personal vibration as their poor energy bodies searched for any life energy available.

Most of the crew were temporarily operating in the lowest levels of the Simulation and had severe addiction issues. This is despite the fact that this was probably collectively one of the best groups of people I'd encountered in this life. Life aboard an extremely old aircraft carrier under the war conditions of the Middle East was just that difficult.

Shortly after reporting, the crew received extremely bad news that the ship would be returning to the Middle East for another deployment, a mere six months after getting home. This was bad news for me, but terrible news for the poor exhausted souls who had just returned from what I heard was dreadful seven months.

During these first six months in port, my main duty was to get qualified and learn about the nuclear plant. At the beginning, through a bit of cleverness and deceit recently learned in the lower levels of the Simulation, I was able to minimize my time on the ship and spend a lot of time with my wonderful fiancée while keeping my vibration at its relatively high level. However, as deployment approached and my responsibility as an officer on the ship steadily increased, my vibration fell, and my relationship with my fiancé collapsed along with most of the hard-won progress in my personal life.

A few days before leaving for deployment while visiting my parents on pre-deployment leave, I was blessed with a few days in the amazing Third Eye level of the Simulation without the aid of any external substances. To this day I'm not sure why this temporary state occurred. It felt orgasmic, but truly was the calm before the storm, and would ultimately set up the quickest energy crash of this lifetime.

For reasons of protecting classified information and avoiding embarrassing details, I'll just say this deployment to the Middle East was extremely dark. The first month of the deployment went somewhat smoothly. I was a new watch officer so I was given an extremely strong enlisted watch team, and we got a reputation as the best watch team on the ship. However, the brass then mistook my watch team's talents for my talents, and I was given a much less talented watch team; problems began to rapidly mount.

At one point there was an accident in the plant, which was partially my fault but fully blamed on me. I was disciplined. After this, I became extremely bitter and fell down into the lower end of the Root level of the Simulation, and I would stay there for a long period. All my chakras were now negatively aligned.

Upon getting home, I was greeted by my loving family. But after a small burst of love and happiness at being back home, I fell very deep in alcohol addiction. On my first bout with alcohol, I'd kept my drinking somewhat under control, mostly due to fear of consequences from my pack if I got completely reckless. However, with all chakras misaligned and in unimaginable suffering, I was desperate and without much meaning to life anymore, I threw all caution to the wind.

For over a year, I only occasionally felt something not hellish when alcohol and heavy caffeine were used. After the high of the alcohol wore off (which it always does), I'd slide down into a new low point that was lower than the previous low point. I felt completely abandoned by all of life, and nothing in the physical world seemed to relieve the constant suffering which seemed never-ending.

For a year my Guardian Angel was working overtime. A steady stream of self-inflicted bad events happened over this year, but by the grace of God, nothing serious occurred.

Although it is often in the depths where a turnaround finally happened. After all the physical, non-spiritual coping mechanisms that had been learned in this life failed, my internal self which had been suspiciously cut off from spirituality finally opened up. This tiny opening was enough for God to creep in the back door and begin the recovery of my desperate psyche.

The turnaround began reading a book *The Biology of Transcendence* while drunk on a hammock in my backyard. This caused a 'crack in my cosmic egg,' which is the name of another book by the same author, the late Joseph Chilton Pierce. The book, which mixed ideas of spirituality and God with science that I was familiar with, was just enough for the Crown chakra to begin slowly absorbing energy from the divine again. I'd spend the next fourteen years in an unsteady climb rebuilding my depleted Crown chakra and re-establishing my relationship with God.

With my military time ending, I voluntarily entered an alcohol rehab treatment program. The group I went through rehab with were kindred spirits and I immediately felt like part of a tribe/pack again. This allowed me to be a somewhat functional human being again in the Sacral level of the Simulation.

The rehab program I went through was nothing short of divine. It gave me a taste for the twelve-step process which would never be my main path but laid out the viable map to happiness which I'd not had in years. Despite the wonderful hearts and intention of the counselors, I absorbed the spiritual intention of the rehab program on a surface level only. However the door to divinity was cracking open that could not be re-shut.

After leaving rehab I began to consume anything wavy and spiritual that I could get my hands on, and a new way of being seemed to slowly emerge. A new world opened up which was unavailable to the former, skeptical, and agnostic self.

The negative karma I'd racked up during my drunken military years was quite thick and many of my old attitudes held firm. Some people have a grand spiritual awakening and seem to immediately jump out of the depths in a single leap. However, my core lesson plan for this life required a relatively slow fall and then a relatively slow rise back up in order to experience contrast fully (tested true). Although with the Crown chakra opening back up again and divinity flowing back into me at an increasing rate, the ending was inevitable at this point.

The rise however was lightning fast in cosmic terms. My life would be chaotic for the next fourteen years as I rapidly cleared karma; I often felt like I was undoing the mistakes from earlier in life during the slow decline. Much later, I'd feel like I was clearing karma from past lives.

Soul Contract #5: Ages Twenty-Nine to Thirty-Five: The Throat Chakra

Angelic Takeaway: In this soul contract I primarily inhabited the Throat chakra or the fifth level of the Simulation. I read and studied profusely during this period. This period was characterized by a steady increase in my spiritual knowledge and energy in my Crown chakra. Life got gradually happier despite the challenges of karma rapidly coming to the surface as I repaid karma for the mistakes earlier in this life.

This soul contract seemed to begin a long process, often referred to in Christianity as Atonement, in which karma accumulated earlier began to gradually be paid back. This process did entail suffering, however, from this point in life I'd experience a steady lightening. As I reconciled past karma, the restrictions and anchors which had tied me to the lower levels of the Simulation gradually lifted.

When I got out of the military, the psyche was still in bad condition, so I did what was natural for any wounded animal and returned to the safety of my pack. I returned home to my childhood home and the security of my parents. I also took up with a group of old high school acquaintances who were facing similar struggles. A vibrational property of the Simulation is 'like attracts like.'

With a temporary period of minimal earthly responsibility, I began exploring the world of the Throat chakra level of the Simulation which entailed reading and study while rapidly paying back karma.

A characteristic of the Throat chakra level of the Simulation is reading. With the recently arisen spiritual interest, I began consuming spiritual books of various quality at a voracious rate. At the Throat level of the Simulation, reading is the most efficient way to assimilate information (tested true).

I floundered a bit, continuing to struggle with alcohol and tending to socialize with other struggling people but a solid nuclear and extended family provided a solid base to recover. As my Crown chakra slowly began to rebuild itself and gain energy, I felt happier and more stable. I gradually found myself drawing more and more from a mysterious loving power source as opposed to the personal self which I'd relied on almost exclusively through the first twenty-eight years of this life.

After a few months at home and watching the wonderful movie *Patch Adams* I decided to attempt to re-emerge into the world by starting medical school and applying to a few jobs in widely varying fields. To do this, it became clear I needed references. My military career had ended in a less than stellar fashion, so on Christmas Eve I gathered the courage to call my former boss in the military and ask him what he'd say about me as a reference.

I felt a lot of guilt and shame before making the call. My wildest dreams involved my former boss giving me a neutral report for medical school applications and job references. However the reaction of my former boss exceeded these wildest dreams by a wide margin.

This conversation involved the re-telling of a few humorous sea stories and genuine heartfelt concern on both sides, and ended with unconditional forgiveness as we both acknowledged the challenges we'd faced on the USS Enterprise. The former boss agreed to give me a good reference. Though not a complete resolution to the trauma, it relieved the soul of a lot of guilt.

This unconditional forgiveness brought tears to my eyes after the phone call had ended, and put my recent hardships into perspective as the educational experience that it actually was. I am forever thankful to this boss for a boost during a time when I desperately needed one.

I've always remembered this conversation and the unconditional forgiveness and have tried to return this favor when I found a soul that was lost like me. Oftentimes a struggling soul will not feel like they deserve forgiveness but they are often the ones who need it the most. Since we are all actually one unified wave, forgiving something outside of yourself is actually forgiving yourself on a metaphysical level and quickest way to relieve your karma (tested true).

Almost immediately after processing this forgiving conversation, I felt a bit of actual usable energy in the Crown chakra for the first time in many years. This yielded enough productive energy to begin the medical school and job application process. I began enrolling in medical pre-req classes at a local university, applied to a few jobs, intensified my spiritual study, and started the process of getting my life reorganized.

I also got back into the gym and began eating well again. With life energy returning after only a few months, my physical body was back to reasonable condition after a year of living primarily off red wine and cheap liquor.

I filled out formal medical school applications and began doing job interviews. I also took up with a few integrous spiritual book clubs that were accelerating the development of the Throat chakra.

I even dated a couple of wonderful women. Each of these relationships seemed to revolve around a life lesson that we were both meant to learn together. The most painful lesson of each relationship was that each one had to ultimately be let go of, as my life was in rapid transition and none of them were meant to be.

Many great spiritual books came into my life during this period, most prominently among them the contemporary spiritual tome, *A Course in Miracles,* that lays out a 365-day study program which I was regaining the discipline to follow. My life was taking a good direction for the first time in years.

Unfortunately I still had a lot of negative karma, bad habits, and addiction issues. The next year went erratically with a few falls and major errors. My Crown chakra was gaining energy steadily, but was still quite weak. Its recovery went in spits and bursts as I worked through difficult issues of faith.

Nothing about trying to go to medical school from the application process to the pre-reqs went very smoothly. It never felt like the direction the universe wanted me to go. I was also still in a relatively low spiritual place, which simply wasn't too compatible with medical school in general. As it became increasingly obvious that I simply wasn't going to Patch Adams and I continued to strike out with potential jobs, things grew desperate.

I eventually found myself in my last week of unemployment with no real clear signal on where to go next. I was living with my loving parents, and though the relationship was good, having an unemployed son with no money coming in and no real prospects living with them at home was not a reality they'd accept.

Teaching mostly had popped up on my radar because I'd heard from a friend that substitute teaching was a nice way to earn some extra money (which I knew I'd soon be desperate for).

On a Wednesday I went to the education department of a local college to discuss options. I really had no idea what the licensing process or procedures were. The lady in the department seemed generally unimpressed by my general lack of knowledge about teaching, but the important thing was that I was added to their email list.

On Thursday I got an email from this list saying that an urban school was in "desperate need" of a chemistry teacher. I called the woman from the email whom would later be my boss and my opening line was something along the lines of "Umm . . . I have no teaching experience, no education in the field, and basically have no idea why I'm calling. I do, however, have a Master's degree in Nuclear Engineering and am a former Lieutenant in the US Navy. Interested in meeting?" To which I got a surprisingly enthusiastic "Yes" and an interview was scheduled for the next day.

On a Friday afternoon I drove to the interview and gave what I perceived as a terrible interview. I honestly didn't know what I was talking about and stutter badly when not confident.

After the interview I was told to wait in the office. I remember being a bit peeved, because I thought the interview had gone so poorly that I wished they'd just let me go home and enjoy my last night of collecting unemployment (and probably a good deal of alcohol).

When called back into the office I was asked to come in and start teaching the next Monday and was told to wear my military uniform. I would later learn that the school's situation was indeed desperate. It was early in November and I was teacher number six of the year for this position.

The thinking of my to-be boss who had already been through five chemistry teachers early in the school year was that if she put a former military officer in the room then at least some skulls would get cracked and perhaps the students would get scared into behaving.

A running joke we had over the years was that although she hired a former military officer what she ended up with as a teacher was about as far from that as she could get. On the Myers-Briggs personality test I'm an INFP (Introverted Intuitive Feeling Perceiver), which is the least likely of the sixteen personality types to end up in the military. Ironically, I first learned of my INFP personality type at military leadership class and I learned that I was in a room full of ESTJs (Extroverted Sensing Thinking Judgers), the most compatible military personality type and my opposite.

I absolutely loved my students that first year but make no mistake, this was not the same nerdy crowd I had taken AP classes with in high school. I was teacher number six of the year for a reason. Being completely inexperienced as a teacher, I came into my new school with a distinct plan for teaching, which involved strict discipline and adherence to the virtues of Law and Order. As the universe has a sense of humor, this isn't at all what ended up happening.

At the start of my first day of teaching, dressed in an official Naval officer's uniform, I set out to lay down a strict unwavering law. However in my first minutes of attempting this, a student made a particularly dark remark meant to intimidate me, to which I replied back automatically with a humorous and even darker remark. This drew a laugh from the class and the rest of the day was spent introducing myself to my classes with the rough and dark humor I'd learned in the military in a relatively informal manner.

This actually became an integral part of my teaching style which has gotten me a bit of trouble over the years. The rough and dark sense of humor that I picked up in vibrational hell during my military years actually allowed me to relate to my urban students better, who often came from horrid circumstances.

Over the years, I've often tried to lean into a more traditional style of teaching, however, I've always been a bit disappointed to find that the rough, chaotic, and humorous style that came intuitively on my first day of teaching simply worked better with my students. When I tried proper mannered lectures in the queen's perfect English, generally at the urging of other adults, I tended to find myself talking to myself.

The first year was a struggle as I learned to be a teacher on the fly in a tough situation while rapidly working through karma. If one wishes to work through negative karma rapidly, teaching at an urban high school is probably one of the best places to do it.

I showed up for work every day and did my best to be of service, despite dealing with major personal issues. This commitment to service was what finally pushed my Crown chakra back into the positive range. Showing up to an integrous job every day, even if one is doing it imperfectly, will tend to pull negatively aligned chakras back into the positive range (tested true).

At one point during that first difficult year of teaching, I was quite sure I was being fired. As a result, I went and interviewed at another school. I received a call from the other school one morning, and a meeting was established for later that day in order to formally accept another job offer. Less than an hour later, I was mysteriously called down to the front office. Out of the blue, I was made a formal offer to continue teaching at the current school, which would end up being my home for over a decade.

During my first year of teaching, I found myself at a party where I was far out of place vibrationally. At one point I made an out of context video game joke, to which I got many strange looks but one snorting laugh.

The laugh was from a young lady wearing all black who had just returned from a family funeral, and was also far out-of-place vibrationally and not in the mood for dating or men. Despite this, we were seemingly magnetically pulled towards one another and were de-facto life-partners an hour later.

This was a relatively short, extremely loving, but extremely tumultuous relationship where past-life karma between us was resolved. We were both operating from the Throat level of the Simulation with some fairly serious substance abuse issues. We both hid the extent of our addiction issues from the other in a slightly dysfunctional, try-to-appear-strong-for-the-other type of love. It was in no way a coincidence our Guardian Angels had arranged for us to meet up to resolve our karma at this time.

After a tough first year of teaching and relationship issues, the aforementioned girlfriend finally came to her senses and kicked me out. I bought a condo in a quiet area where I could spend the summer in solitude and concentrate on a steadily growing interest in spirituality. Being away from worldly and social drama for a while sped up my spiritual evolution. I began very serious work with *A Course in Miracles*.

By the time I returned to school in the fall, I was operating with all Seven chakras positively aligned for the first time in this life. I found functioning primarily from the Heart level of the Simulation in many ways was the optimal level to teach from in the Urban high school environment that I was in.

Teaching from the Heart level of the Simulation made the job go immediately smoother. Over the next few years I'd gain a positive reputation at school as I operated from the Heart at school while teaching. At home, I'd transition to the Throat level of the Simulation as I studied *The Course in Miracles* extensively along other assorted spiritual and scientific texts. These two lives existed in a strange juxtaposition.

During this time I also continued to manage the health of my other chakras while my connection to divinity grew with my Crown chakra. Addiction and karmic issues did still surface regularly as tends to happen during periods of rapid growth. A series of short-lived Romantic relationships presented with each seeming to present a specific lesson.

In the middle of one school day, I longed for people to discuss *The Course in Miracles* with. In the middle of administering a test, I searched "*Course in Miracles* Groups" on my school computer and less than fifteen seconds later I'd been guided to an active group just down the street from me. Synchronicity at its best.

I showed up to this group a few days later. Among the core members I'd be the only male and the youngest by twenty years. This group was me and a bunch of older ladies discussing a spiritual text beyond the life's scope of most humans. Over the years I called this weekly meeting a 'book club,' as this did not require further explanation.

The Course in Miracles teaches us that our external world is a projection of inner attitudes. As this lesson sank in, I saw this and other lessons from the course play out in my external reality at school, home, and in the people I attracted into my life.

After a few years of teaching and spiritual study, my Crown chakra became steadily more energized, which caused the rest of the chakras to generally follow suit in fits and starts. I lived alone and read a lot, as a main purpose of this soul contract was to rebuild the intellectual Throat chakra.

As my Throat chakra strengthened, my stutter improved and I found people (my students in particular) became more inherently interested in what I had to say. When I'd make a spiritual error, the Throat chakra would temporarily de-energize, the stutter would come back, and I'd find it harder to hold my student's attention.

However on a whole, things seemed to be going smoother and smoother. Though life was not perfect, I was generally happy and successful.

One weekend I listened to a spiritual podcast on my daily run. On this podcast I heard an old man who seemed to find everything funny. Everything the old man said resonated with me. He even spoke positively about an HBO miniseries called *The Pacific* that I'd just finished watching. Upon getting home I downloaded his first book *Power vs. Force* and then forgot about it for a few weeks. The man was Dr. David Hawkins.

On a late spring Sunday morning I'd signed up to participate in a charity 5k race. I should note that charity races are a very common activity for people operating from the Heart level of the Simulation. You get to remain healthy while helping the world, and still allow the personal self to get a bit of public credit. That's as Heart level as Heart level gets.

While waiting for the race to start I began listening to Dr. David Hawkins' book, *Power vs. Force*. Once the book started, that took priority over any of the heart-based positive energy swirling around me. I ended up walking in the back of the pack with the pregnant women with strollers.

When I got home, I ordered most of his works immediately and went to work studying. In the coming weeks I'd read his entire library that he had available at the time. My Crown, Third Eye and Throat chakras now exploded with energy, as the inherent truth and importance of these teachings were recognized.

That summer I returned to a state of serenity that I'd not experienced since I was a child. I spent the summer reading, eating a healthy diet, communing with nature, and stayed away from addictive substances for the first time in a long time.

With a more bird's eye view of reality, I felt far less need for external stimulation and I now meditated naturally; it no longer felt forced. I now felt as if I was co-creating the Simulation rather than just manipulating it.

However, the downside of moving up the levels of the Simulation and resonating with a higher level of the Simulation is that karma from the lower levels tends to be drawn out, and I still had a lot. The next two years at school would be chaotic, and it would take that long before I was able to stabilize permanently again in this new higher state.

In these next two years I found myself operating with real power at school and could influence others. I did not always use this power wisely and a few major mistakes occurred. One particularly bad mistake led to me falling back to the near the bottom of the Simulation and the fight back up was painful.

By my mid-thirties, I'd stabilized again with all my chakras positively aligned and had a reasonable handle on most aspects of my life. I was spending a lot of my free time reading, with more and more time in contemplative meditative states. As I drew closer to an infinitely loving power that defied all attempts at verbalization, the Crown chakra continued to energize and life got steadily less hectic and happier.

After a few violent changes in my personal life and series of struggles at school, my classroom was moved to a quieter section of the building. I was placed next to a teacher who was another cusp autistic, versed in Quantum Mechanics, and operating primarily from the Throat level of the Simulation like me. Many ideas of this book were flushed out with her. As this life has played out in seven year soul contracts, at the age of thirty-five, a new one was starting.

Soul Contract #6: Ages Thirty-Five to Forty-Two: Third Eye Chakra

Angelic Takeaway: During this soul contract I'd begun resonating primarily in the Third Eye level of the Simulation. Shortly before my fortieth birthday in December of 2019 I experienced an Angelic experience of such epic proportions that verbal description only provides a pale shadow. This experience provided a significant energy boost, but also rapid surfacing of karma which coincided with the COVID-19 pandemic. This period of cleansing led to growth in my personal consciousness along with the collective consciousness.

The spiritual growth of the previous contract had felt like a recovery and a gaining back of ground lost during the first twenty-eight years of this life. It involved a lot of study and reading, which is typical in the Throat level of the Simulation. Now my life was as quiet as it ever had been and spiritual practice, faith, and prayer had become prioritized over study. I now seemed to be exploring brand new territory with Dr. David Hawkins as my primary guide.

I maintained a boisterous personality at school which I'd found to be effective at teaching, but at home I now occupied the Third Eye level of the Simulation and began sensing truth very viscerally. To a bit of dismay, I realized how incorrect many of my early life attitudes and the attitudes common to the world actually were. This realization was in juxtaposition to the realization that everything was actually playing out exactly as it should.

At the initiation of this soul contract, I was relatively stabilized in the Third Eye level of the Simulation. This was after a few chaotic years of karma rapidly coming up to be healed and forgiven. It was now clear to me that a rapid rise through the levels of the pulled negative karma from the lower levels of Simulation rapidly in order for it to be resolved. Any period of swift growth in this life has been followed by a period of chaos and cleansing.

Life events now seemed to bring in new teachings and concepts in a divinely orchestrated way. A few major distractions presented themselves during this period, though afterward it was always clear that the distraction was a lesson in itself.

At one point while living in a quiet condo complex which I'd become quite comfortable in, a truly horrid energy moved in directly below me that would blast loud Satanic music all night long. My Third Eye felt on fire whenever this energy was home. This seemed to force a move and I ended up buying a house across the street from a church and large cemetery, rich with Angelic activity. None of this was random (tested true).

When I moved from the condo I donated over 200 books, and was proud that my book collection could again fit onto a single bookshelf.

This all occurred while holding onto a job as a high school physics/chemistry teacher as life settled down and I experienced a period of relative peace.

During my late thirties, I kept to myself the overwhelming amount of time. I spent a lot of time in nature and meditation as I went deeper into understanding and merging with the universe. An old habit that remained in addition to other addiction issues was playing video games. I still played them often. This was entertaining and it didn't force me to leave my own little personal autistic energy bubble. However, I often found myself during this period expecting to enjoy them more than I actually did, and then finding myself desiring a deeper experience while playing them.

Over these years I also attended a number of wonderful bi-annual weekend retreats at a local monastery which centered around the spiritual text *A Course in Miracles.* The ladies in my book club were the organizers so this was one of the few regular social events that I attended. The grounds were beautiful and a truly wonderful eclectic group of people attended.

Through my late thirties, life got quieter and more serene as I settled into the Third Eye level of the Simulation. An advantage of the perception at this level which I'd enjoyed to some extent throughout life is the ability to sense and sidestep trouble. This tends to make you a bit of an outsider, as the trouble you sidestep tends to be exactly what some people around you need for their evolution. I got a reputation as a party pooper during this period.

The nature of this Angel-evolving Simulation is that it loves evolution. Shortly before my fortieth birthday and onset of COVID-19, I had an experience that would change everything.

This is an only slightly altered version of the write-up written only a few weeks after the experience. The language and style is a bit different from the rest of the book, but I've been guided to minimize changes to this to preserve the visceralness of the experience.

Heavenly foxhole the meeting of two Angels:

In the summer and fall of 2019 I had settled into the Third Eye level of the Simulation. I was active in a number of spiritual groups both local and online, taking care of myself physically in a very scientifically minded way, spending a lot of time in nature and contemplation, reading the great spiritual texts of the world, and teaching physics and chemistry as a job while enjoying strategy-type video games.

Late in the fall of 2019, in a discussion with friends, the topic of video games came up. In this nerdy yet sophisticated discussion, the final conclusion seemed to be that they don't need to be labeled as bad. However they do occupy the linear mind and have a tendency to draw one down into the physical/partically universe and away from the spiritual/wavy universe, which was the opposite direction that I wanted to go at that time.

Largely due to this conversation, I decided to quit all video games cold turkey which turned out to be way easier than I thought it would be. Without the daily dose of intellectual stimulation and escapism that the video games were providing, it seemed to initiate a rather rapid transformation of this consciousness.

My leisure activities automatically moved from stimulating activities to more purely spiritual activities like meditation and prayer. At school, creating a loving, fun and supportive environment for the students was prioritized above intellectual work.

The last week before Christmas break in 2019, I watched the movie *Interstellar* with my physics classes. Normally the discussions resulting from this movie tended to be in the scientific Throat vibrational range, but this week I found the conversations naturally gravitated towards the Heart and Third Eye vibrational range and the philosophical themes of the movie such as the "the power of love." During the nights I enjoyed a state of absolute security and serenity which I had only enjoyed sporadically to this point in life.

Once I got home from school at the start of the 2019 Christmas vacation and knew that I was away from most earthly responsibilities for two weeks, I was able to float up into a new vibration that the conceptual mind could not classify at the time.

The next day, a Saturday, a friend had gotten me tickets to the New England Patriots vs. Buffalo Bills game. The process of driving to the game, meeting my friend at a bar, getting into the stadium, and finding our seats was of very different quality than I'd ever experienced. I typically would have used the logical mind to look at maps and signs to navigate around the stadium, but instead something resembling intuition navigated the body around the stadium very efficiently.

I had been a Patriots fan most of my life, but watching the game from this state of consciousness was of a different quality. This was an important late-season game with major playoff implications, but I only seemed to prefer if the Patriots won. A higher knowing assured me that whatever team won would be for the highest good of the universe.

Watching the game from this state, a new layer of causality emerged. Football before had been viewed on an almost completely partically/physical level. From this new 'wavier' vibration, I saw an energetic/psychic level of the game emerge. Bill Belichick's powerful Throat vibration naturally helped the Patriots players stay aligned with team strategy.

Tom Brady's aura seemed to contain a bit of the vibrational energy I was now experiencing. It provided the team a strange "luck" (which was simply the subtle influence of the higher dimensions on physical reality). A group of Buffalo Bills players who had prayed in the end-zone before the game had unusually high vibrational energy levels and were having a larger effect on the game than most would've thought based on their physical role alone.

Aside: Athletes and Vibrational Energy Levels.

Many athletes who are attracted to playing contact team sports seem to operate largely from the Sacral and Solar Plexus levels of the Simulation. On a personal level, I was most interested in both watching and playing team contact sports while in these vibrational ranges.

At this vibration, one naturally tends to reach for individual ego goals that can be detrimental to team success. Coaches operating in the Heart and Throat levels of the Simulation are good at aligning the individual egoic goals with higher team goals. Bill Belichick brilliantly summarizes the fallacy of chasing individual ego goals with the quote: "Stats are for losers."

Great athletes sometimes seem to have a bit of wavy energy in their aura. These athletes appear to have luck going for them, which seems to be the subtle effect of wavy spiritual energy on the partically physical reality. These rare athletes seem to also have the ability to go into higher states of consciousness for short periods of time. This results in them getting a reputation of being particularly great at the end of big games when it's all on the line. Tom Brady and Michael Jordan are two athletes who seem to fall into this category. Even a brief look at their careers makes a good logical case for it.

End Aside.

Most of the fans around me were drunk. The man on one side of me provided a running commentary of the game, which involved a high number of euphemisms for penises and homosexuals. The man's low vibrating partically energy was subtly uncomfortable in my current extremely empathic state, especially when the game took a negative turn from the Patriot's perspective.

Despite all this brutish behavior, the obviousness of love was present. Every soul was acting out their own level of evolution in a perfect process. All the players, fans, and coaches were at the game for their own reasons, and fate had brought us together to co-evolve and share this experience.

Two rows ahead of me was a couple obviously in love. This was actually more interesting to watch than the game. At one point, the couple was trying to take a selfie. I eagerly volunteered to help them take a picture and I was handed a phone. Unfortunately, I wasn't in my familiar state of consciousness so the ability to use my logical mind to manipulate the phone's unfamiliar camera technology wasn't online. As a result, I took multiple pictures of my thumb. The guy finally took the phone away, not with negative energy, but he just realized that this friendly stranger was basically worthless in regards to the task he'd volunteered to perform.

The Patriots won, I was glad in part for the obvious reason why any fan was happy that their team won. However, the bigger reason for my happiness was because the energy in the stadium immediately increased in vibration and I realized that the walk to my car and wait in the parking lot was going to be much more pleasant in this higher energy. I'd always been sensitive to energy/vibration, but today this sensitivity seemed to have been turned up even higher.

Walking back to my car, I felt the wavy field that keeps a flock of birds or a school of fish in formation without conscious attention. I was walking back to my car in a huge pack of football fans. I was in a contemplative state, and very little conscious effort was being applied to tracking where I was. Despite this, the body somehow navigated to my car through very unfamiliar territory. The same phenomena was occurring for other fans. Some were in a state of severe drunkenness;

they made turns and walked in their desired direction with little or no conscious thought to navigation.

Aside: Morphogenic Fields.

"Morphogenic fields" is a term generally used to describe what keeps a flock of birds all flying together, and the reason why the same species of an animal tend to have common characteristics. This also applies to humans. A large number of people can be under the influence of the same field, and this manifests in them all thinking and acting alike.

This phenomenon is particularly common in entities in the tribal Sacral level of the Simulation and helps pack animals communicate with each other, as the individual entities aren't fully individualized but are being controlled by the same field (tests true).

For more reading on this interesting and paradigm-breaking phenomenon check out Rupert Sheldrake's *Morphic Resonance* or Charles MacCay's *Extraordinary Popular Delusions and the Madness of Crowds.*

End Aside.

I got home very late and attempted some normal activity. I put on an old episode of *The Office* but couldn't concentrate on the general plot, and was moved to tears by a romantic moment between Jim and Pam. Sleep finally came.

The next morning, I woke with relief as I now realized that I had a few weeks with very little earthly or social responsibility. As I enjoyed my morning coffee, I decided to lay down and meditate/pray on my couch to slow relaxing music.

My vibration steadily began to rise. Eventually there was simply too much energy available to lay down and the body began dancing to the music presented. I intuitively switched from meditative music to higher energy music that was a better vibrational match to what the body was doing. I (my ego) was not a part of this process.

The concept of "Angels" had never been a major part of my spiritual repertoire. As a person exploring the world of spirituality for the previous twelve years, they had come up but had never been a major area of interest or focus.

Now dancing around my living room and kitchen, listening to Lindsey Stirling's "Roundtable Rival," the idea entered that I was now vibrating at an Angelic frequency. Angels were around me. I had no logical proof of this, but I knew the sky was blue, grass was green, and that I was experiencing an Angelic frequency. I was surer of this than anything my logical mind had ever perceived. This was unusual, because my mind had rarely even thought of the word 'Angel' or 'Angelic,' but those were the words appearing in my mind.

Suddenly and unexpectedly, the body found itself in a higher dimensional construct.

I was never under the impression that I was "teleported" somewhere else. I always knew that the physical body was in my house. Just that there was an Angelic overlay on my reality. This is similar to the experience of having a daydream while walking. Your attention is focused on the daydream, but you always know that the physical body is just walking.

There was no way to describe this extremely wavy experience perfectly with my so-so language skills, so this is my best attempt to reconstruct the experience.

I was in a World War Two style foxhole with two magnificent beings. To put it simply, I was beat up. A bloody miserable mess. On one side of the foxhole was a heavenly realm that was indescribably beautiful. On the other side was fire, brimstone, imps, and demons. There was an intuitive impression that I had just splashed up from the fireside and jumped into the foxhole scared and confused.

There was an impression that these two magnificent beings were doing a sort of higher dimensional first-aid on me. They gave off an energy of unconditional love stronger than anything that I had felt on earth. Angels had never been part of my philosophy, but it was obvious that these magnificent beings were indeed Angels. How'd I know? I did!

The Angels were completely open to be read by me, and there was an intuitive understanding that I was completely open to be read by them. This realization immediately triggered a large amount of fear, as I knew these Angels could see all that I had done in this life. This fear quickly subsided as they both gave me the impression that they did not care about any of that "lower dimensional bullshit" (this was a term from my earthly mind). I got the impression that they viewed my silly antics on earth with a sense of humor that I didn't fully grasp at the time.

This "did not care" attitude from the beings was not apathy at all. It was simply that whatever had happened "down there" (on the fire side of the foxhole) was simply about what had to be done down there to survive and bring me to a certain point in evolution. They gave me the impression that confusion "down there" was rampant, terrible actions were expected, and mistakes were part of the process; their only real concern now was getting me patched up and out.

The Angels exchanged a cryptic joke that I got the impression was mostly beyond my level of comprehension, but the punchline was roughly, "This idiot is feeling guilty for things he didn't even do, the ego had done them." I then sent the Angels the impression that I hoped they could forgive me as I'd done the best that I could "down there." There was an awkwardness at this request as I realized that the concept of forgiveness was basically absent from them. From their point of view, nothing had been done "wrong." From a wavy, vibrational point of view, the universe was perfect and the chaos of the partically/physical universe was expected.

Aside: Guilt.

Though guilt plays a major role in the lower vibrations and is often used to control behavior on earth, as one moves into the higher vibrations, its role rapidly diminishes. Eventually it becomes clear that all souls are doing the best they can under the circumstances they are in. Most souls in this Simulation are dealing with ego programming errors and karma that is way beyond its conscious awareness.

Bill W, the founder of Alcoholics Anonymous, said eventually a "reasonable regret" and a willingness to correct the error is all that is needed. Human life is difficult under nearly optimal conditions, and mistakes are basically unavoidable.

End Aside.

Since the two Angels were open to be read, I saw that even though they loved me unconditionally and nothing could either add or subtract from that, they had read my energy, and though they knew that I still had a long way to go to get back to my true self, they had actually seen others in WAY worse shape.

When I'd first entered this foxhole, the guilt of appearing in front of these beings knowing all the mistakes I'd made was palpable. Their initial assessment of me, which was like a higher vibrational version of a doctor's quick assessment, was that I was a vibrational mess.

Because they were reading my consciousness directly, they immediately imprinted a comforting thought, "You are financially stable and have a good job, you have addiction and karmic issues to still deal with but we've seen people show up here in way worse shape. You could be on the edge of death passed out in an alley. The fact that your soul was allowed to vibrate this high means you are actually in pretty good shape. Relax!"

This impression gave me great comfort, as I knew my current vibrational signature was a mess compared to what belonged in front of these beings. I could tell they were viewing reality from a higher vibrational place than me and saw my current issues as minor and temporary.

The beings seemed to understand the relative situation well. Compared to these heavenly beings, my current state was indeed a vibrational mess. However they saw the need to put my mind at ease and assure me that I was indeed doing okay. Comparing my vibrational state at the time to the vibrations of these beings was like a major league baseball player comparing his batting skills to that of a little leaguer. Unless a jerk, the major league baseball player would still congratulate the little leaguer for his hit into the outfield, even though he could've easily hit it out of the park.

I then went into one of the most relaxed states I'd ever been in, and let whatever first-aid they were doing on me continue. The entire body was in an orgasmic state.

Later research would reveal that sexual orgasm is simply the physical body temporarily experiencing the highest vibrational level available in physical form (tested true). I was now vibrating at the top of the physical spectrum and the bottom of the non-physical heavenly spectrum. This is why the physical body experienced this as an extended full body orgasm and the mind had pictured me in a foxhole directly between heaven and hell (tested true).

It became obvious that I'd never been in the presence of such talented healers. At this point, the earthbound mind began to intrude and list the multitude of minor problems with the physical body. Unconsciously, I realized that I was now directing the Angel's energy towards these physical problems, and it was actually slowing down the process.

I then got a scolding from one of the Angels. It was not scolding in the way we know it on earth, but that is simply the closest word to it. The scolding did not imply disappointment or punishment, but it was just an acknowledgment that certain things that I didn't understand yet needed to happen fast. I was vibrationally told that time was an issue here, I had no way of understanding what they were really doing, and that my ego was not a big concern to them.

One of the Angels then told me in a non-verbal way that even though they could quite easily fix the problems with the physical body, they were much more concerned with problems at the level of the soul and energy body. The Angels then assured me that once the problems were fixed on this level, the problems on the level of the physical body would mostly heal or attenuate greatly. The state of my physical body (particles) was just an effect of my current state of consciousness (waves) which was actually the cause of my physical life situations. It was this implanted non-verbal thought which would plant the seed, which would later become a concept of this book: 'waves create particles.'

This allowed them to get back to their work. They explained that they were rushing because I could not stay in this realm very long. I was not yet in a condition to vibrate at this level permanently, so karma dictated that I needed to go back down into the physical dimension. This was not a judgment, but simply a fact of nature. When I went back down into the midst of the chaos of the physical dimension, they told me to take advantage of this time and call upon this vibration.

Soon I felt this realm fading from my experience. I was given specific instructions; the first two I sensed were standard and the rest were custom to me.

1. *You just received an influx of energy . . . take good advantage of this and use it properly.*

2. *Patience is your ally, we are now actively working to pull you out, let your energy rise normally.*

Additional Context:

"Pull you out" was the phrase that was used. At the time, my sense was being trapped in this reality/Simulation and wanting to escape or become enlightened. Another phrasing might be that my vibration was now being raised so I could resonate with the higher levels of the Simulation. No "pull you out" would be necessary or even desirable until the karma in this dimension was concluded. I believe this phrase was used because it would resonate with my mind well at the time. This experience did seem to trigger a rather rapid process of repaying karma in the lower levels of the Simulation. The next couple years after this experience was a never-ending string of loving but tumultuous relationships, none of which worked out. Past-life research revealed these were past life entanglements that were never fully resolved.

- *Act normal. Don't draw unnecessary attention to yourself because of this experience.*

The Angels seemed to understand I have a tendency to act a bit odd and let my ego get on a soapbox. After this experience, which was probably the most significant spiritual experience of my life, I had to wrestle with the urge to start telling everyone about it. At this point I was completely unprepared to handle or explain this experience properly. Whenever I mentioned this experience to anyone early on, it was obvious that it was a mistake.

- *Avoid artificial substances. A steady rise of vibration will be much more pleasant than the very bumpy ride up that addictive substances will cause.*

The Angels seemed to understand that I had addiction issues that linger on to this day.

- *Gloria Excelsis Deo*

This is a favorite spiritual quote often said by my favorite spiritual author Dr. David Hawkins

Since this experience, the following changes have been steadily occurring:

- Angels became a main focus of my experience. I noticed Angels where I never did before. I entered environments and noticed Angel decorations that had been there all along, but never even noticed them. My parent's house even had a Willow Tree Angel statue display which had been present my entire childhood which I'd mysteriously never noticed. Any reference to Angels now grabbed my attention. I now have a strong impression that I am being guided by Angelic energy. This has increased over time.

- I've re-watched many movies and re-read books, and noticed Angelic themes that I'd completely overlooked when watching or reading them before this experience. This led to the unusual discovery that though I tended to be heavily attracted to things with Angelic themes in my early life, the ego always attributed my liking them to some other reason.

- Spiritual evolution in general sped up drastically. Before this experience, I wished for this. However, now seeing my reality changing at its current rate, the phrase "be careful what you wish for" took on new meaning.

A common new age fallacy is that when vibration increases on either a personal or collective level, life will automatically transition to a happy dance in the celestial gardens. However, the opposite tends to happen in the short term. The higher levels of the Simulation tend to draw out remaining karma both individually and collectively. Life actually becomes temporarily more chaotic as negative karma is rapidly burned off so one can resonate in the new higher frequency. The COVID-19 pandemic was this happening on a collective level (tested true).

As already pointed out, the higher levels of the Simulation are not strictly better. I've had to adjust gradually to these new levels, as they make functioning in the physical world more difficult.

Manipulation of technology and small talk now seem even less natural. The brainwave frequency is now generally slower and more relaxed so responding to events fast is more difficult. I also sense energy even stronger than before. At one point this would've seemed like an awesome thing, but the reality is different. Being in negative and controlling crowds and around certain people is almost unbearable.

- Synchronicity happens at a much greater frequency.

- Far less interest in a lot of former low vibrational interests. Video games, dark movies and sensory stimulation are examples of this.

- A general difficulty concentrating on intellectual issues. Staying in a prayer and meditative state now seemed more natural than being in a "thinking" state. Before the experience, thinking was my natural state, and prayer and meditation took effort to do. Now prayer and meditation is my natural state, and going into a thinking state takes effort.

- Unless with very particular people, I've learned over time that I need to tone down my spiritual language so as to not appear like a nut. Most people aren't actually too interested in discussing things like Angels, karma, Kundalini energy, different dimensions, Simulation theory and auras. People are all actually living in the reality that is optimal for their current level of evolution, and it is not in the highest good for them to be exposed to higher realities prematurely (tested true).

- The spiritual reality I'd been intellectually learning about before this experience has been slowly becoming an obvious experiential reality.

- I now feel an extremely strong connection to Archangel Michael. Calibration of the statement 'I'm a cell in Archangel Michael's body' now gives a true response.

After this experience, I floated in the Crown level of the Simulation. At this point, I was gifted with a little over two months of this new blissful reality where very little karma came up to be healed, and I floated through life with almost no effort.

I loved everyone, and so by the laws of Simulation I was almost universally loved back. I saw that the process of life was flowing perfectly. Everything happened as if orchestrated by the Angelic kingdom, which I would later find out was the literal truth.

However, as mentioned earlier, a downside of the higher levels of the Simulation is that one can be spiritually vulnerable, especially if one is not balanced in the lower chakras. Although one is in a blissful, incredibly loving state, one is still vulnerable to the proclivities of the physical world while in a physical body, and not everything in this Simulation has your best interests at heart.

During this time, my priorities as a teacher shifted more to healing the energy bodies of my students and creating an environment as loving, fun, and happy as possible. Due to my experience, I got through the more mundane aspects of the job on auto-pilot.

My reality had shifted into a mode incomprehensible to most of those around me. Part of my Angelic guidance from the aforementioned experience was to hold off talking about it immediately. There was a reason for this guidance.

As the weeks passed, I settled into this new near-celestial state where seemingly no problems existed. I naively became more comfortable and bold talking about Angels, out-of-body travel, how much I loved everyone, and my new blissful reality. To my external reality I was appearing more and more like a spiritual nut.

My devotion to God was nearly infallible and my Crown chakra was now rapidly charging. However I was enjoying this Crown level of the Simulation so much that the lower six chakras all suffered, and slowly began misaligning due to neglect.

A few weeks after the Angelic experience, my reality was ecstatic and my happiness was nearly impossible to hide. The only thing that required effort was acting anything resembling normal.

My retired parents were spending the winter in sunny Florida, so during my school's February vacation, I made plans to fly south to spend a week with them.

The morning my flight for Florida was to occur I found myself lying in bed in a prayer and meditative state, blissed out beyond comprehension. I received a text from my mother asking if I was safely through airport security and at my gate, to which I told her I was still in bed.

What remained of my earthly mind then did a bit of math, and it became obvious I was going to miss my flight. Snapping back to physical reality, I found a cooler and recklessly threw the bare essentials I'd need for a week in Florida into the cooler.

I arrived at the airport less than an hour before my flight was to take-off with uncombed hair carrying a cooler instead of luggage like most sane travelers. Miraculously crowds seemed to part as I ran towards my gate. I made no wrong turns even though the logical mind had no clue where I was going in the unfamiliar airport.

I went through airport security (which miraculously had no line) with a completely disheveled appearance carrying a cooler as luggage. A very high-vibrating TSA agent seemed to empathically sense that despite appearances and my apparent confusion, I was the furthest thing from a threat and helped me get through security extremely fast within the limits of the law.

I boarded the plane bound for Florida, with minutes, if not seconds to spare.

The weather that week in Florida was blissful. It was sunny every day I was there. I went on long walks where I'd let the physical body get recharged by the sun after enduring the low sun of a New England winter. During these walks, I listened to Angelically themed music and seemed to downloading information from the Angelic kingdom.

I began to remember a past life I'd shared with a fellow teacher and became excited to tell her about it. However I did not have the maturity at the time to realize that this is rarely a good option, as past lives are temporarily held back from memory for a reason.

After a blissful week in Florida, I flew back to New England and landed on one of the coldest nights of the year. I walked my physical body back to my car in a sleeveless shirt and shorts after becoming adapted to a temperature nearly 80 degrees Fahrenheit higher.

This gave a me a feeling similar to stepping back aboard the USS Enterprise for my second deployment after spending a few days in the Third Eye level. It had the feeling that vacation was officially over, and reality was to strike again.

Returning to my house and eventually school, I was forced to confront the reality that I'd let a lot of menial maintenance tasks associated with my physical life fall by the wayside. I'd have to play a bit of catch-up.

However I found myself resisting returning to normal life and dealing with issues in the lower levels of the Simulation. Instead of re-integrating into normal physical life like the Angelic guidance I was receiving suggested I do, I simply became weirder and probably appeared to most as a recluse who had fallen off the deep edge of reality.

The day after my fortieth birthday, I received a distinct message from the universe which was impossible to ignore.

This was the day I was planning on having a conversation with the teacher I'd remembered a past life with. I now know would've been a pretty grievous error for a number of reasons that I did not understand at the time.

I arrived at school a bit early to find a physics class already in my classroom. They had all chipped in and had bought me a Lindsey Stirling cardboard cutout. Lindsey Stirling's song *Roundtable Rival* had been part of what triggered my Angelic experience and as result had become an avid fan of her music.

This particular class had a very high group vibe. They loved when I played her music in class, as their collective vibe matched the vibe of Lindsey Stirling's high energy music well. The thoughtful gift which remains in my classroom at the time of this writing warmed my heart.

As a result, I immediately began blasting *Roundtable Rival* and let the high energy flow, to let the party begin.

At this point in my spiritual evolution, I was going in and out of the physical body quite regularly. This skill was still quite new and I was not harnessing it well; I was still very unskilled in controlling it. In the excitement of the loving, ecstatic energy, I jumped into the air as high as I could to do a kick.

At the apex of the jump with only one leg under me, I went out-of-body and my unathletic physical body was left up to its own devices to make an awkward, almost impossible landing. My students watched in horror as I landed extremely awkwardly on my left leg and my left knee bent completely in the wrong direction. I had torn pretty much everything holding my left knee together.

I sat at my desk the entire rest of the day, ordering my students to do everything for me. At the end of the day I did an awkward one-foot hop to my car through the parking lot. The few times I put even the slightest weight on my left knee I felt excruciating pain.

With a bit of Angelic help I managed to hop and drive my way home. Exhausted, I downed a few Advil and collapsed on my couch for the night. At the time I thought a night off the knee would heal everything, and that a faculty basketball game I was scheduled to play in soon was still a viable reality.

When I awoke the next morning the wounded knee was even worse. I stumbled to school and scrapped my way through the day again, ordering my students to do everything. I fended off rumors that were spreading about what had happened and my apparent mental instability.

I struggled on with one working leg in complete denial of my condition for a bit, but eventually was ordered by my boss to stay home and deal with my knee. Concurrently, "COVID" was quickly becoming an increasingly used word. A week after I was ordered home by my boss, the school was shut down as the world went into COVID-19 quarantine.

Later spiritual research would result that the knee injury happened for broadly three reasons:

- Negative karma that was rapidly coming up as my consciousness evolved. I had even accumulated a bit more negative karma directly after the Angelic experience. I had been shirking earthly responsibilities, telling people information that they were not karmically ready to hear and talking about my spiritual state out-of-context, completely unprepared to talk about it maturely. As previously mentioned, adjusting to a new level of the Simulation takes time as one finds oneself in a drastically different reality. A challenge of adapting to a newly energized chakra is not letting lower ones misalign, which is exactly what I did.

- The day of the injury I had plans to tell a fellow teacher about a past-life, which would have been very karmically inappropriate. I've found past life knowledge is information that is controlled quite tightly by the Angelic kingdom to optimize everyone's evolution. In the Crown level of the Simulation unbalanced by the lower levels, one tends to live in an 'everything is awesome' sort of reality and thinks errors are impossible, which ironically tends to lead to one making them. The Angelic kingdom stepped in to prevent this error from happening.

- This injury got me out of the world a couple weeks before COVID-19 quarantine would have naturally. At the time I needed solitude to adjust to my new state and was largely unprepared at the time to deal with normal human society. This knee injury and COVID-19 quarantine were strangely synchronistic for me, as it gave me solitude when I absolutely needed it.

Over the next few months as most humans focused on the COVID-19 pandemic and its effects on society, I barely registered it. I was in an almost constant meditative and prayer state, stopping only to handle the basic responsibilities I still had as a teacher, dealing with my knee, and briefly hanging out online finding my new soul tribe online as my circle of confidants rapidly changed.

As my vibration continued to rise, some very dark nights of the soul occurred as karma came up to be healed. Certain higher level spiritual paradoxes presented themselves to be resolved. In order to occupy a higher spiritual state, one must experience its hellish opposite and reject it (tested true). One could view these as spiritual tests.

I now understood the Buddha's words when he claimed to have been beset by demons as he approached enlightenment.

Part of karma being activated came from past life relationships. A seeming steady stream of women entered my life whom I'd shared romances with in past lives. As the karma with these feminine souls had not been completely resolved properly, all these feminine souls magically re-entered my life as the universe tried to balance its karmic books.

I've decided to leave the details of these relationships out as they happened in recent history and do not want these loving women exposed unless they choose to be.

Returning to school in the fall of 2020 was a great challenge. Though my Crown chakra was now more energized than at any point in this life, ALL six of the lower chakras were now misaligned.

I had barely noticed COVID-19, but now re-entering the world of conventional endeavor in the fall of 2020, I saw a masked-up world that was severely misaligned spiritually. Adding to the trouble was the fact that my lower chakras were now a mess, so I was barely able to function as a conventional human.

The next two years were spent dealing with high-level spiritual paradoxes, slowly realigning the lower chakras in order to function in the physical again while karma rapidly came up to be resolved during COVID-19.

When an entity endeavors to evolve spiritually, karma rapidly surfaces from the lower levels of the Simulation so that the entity can stabilize at a new higher level. This also happens on collective level. The COVID-19 pandemic was this phenomenon happening on human collective consciousness level, which I was experiencing in my own way (tested true).

By my observation, everyone was affected in some way by COVID-19 and was forced to resolve karma at their appropriate level. I barely registered the virus itself, but was internally dealing with eons old karma during this period.

The human collective is now in a higher spiritual state than prior to the suffering of COVID-19. This is well reflected in the fact that 1.5% of the human population was in the Angelic stages of evolution prior to COVID-19 and now 1.7% of the human population is at this stage of evolution (tested true). 12% of the human population also gained access to a new level of the Simulation during this time (tested true). This may not seem like much but as consciousness evolves over eons, this much growth in only a couple years is an divinely significant event (tested true).

Just prior to my forty-second birthday, a significant relationship ended, and I was guided to make some major life changes. Work on this book in its current form began. I now understand that I'm in a new soul-contract, and await with excitement as to the changes God will bring to all of us as our collective evolution continues. Gloria in Excelsis Deo!

Angels:

Angelic Takeaway: Angels are the very experienced players in the Simulation who work directly for God and have earned the right to make alterations to the Simulation's fundamental code via prayer. If they are in your presence, you'll feel a sense of divine bliss and often see them display their delightful sense of humor.

At the time of the writing of this book in the summer/fall of 2022, 1.7% of the human population are in the Angelic stages of evolution, which is up from 1.5% just prior to the COVID-19 pandemic (tested true). It is clear that COVID-19 was a massive clearing of collective karma and has resulted in our collective evolution.

It is no coincidence that the word 'Angel' is spelled almost the same as the mathematical term 'angle.' When vibrating at the level of an Angel, direct physical interaction in the Simulation is no longer the main role; the main role becomes to 'angle' wavy divine energy to correct major imbalances in the Simulation or promote large waves of evolution, which is most often accomplished via prayer (tested true).

A common job for the lowest choirs of Angels who operate just above the physical constructs of the Simulation is to greet and comfort those who have just died. At death, one does not immediately need to know the secrets of the universe, but needs a loving presence for comfort and reassurance that everything is okay. This makes it a perfect job for a junior Angel. The actor Cuba Gooding Jr. does a wonderful job portraying an Angel in this role in the film *What Dreams May Come.*

Angels tend to be associated with particular Archangel who are the next higher stage of evolution beyond Angels. The Angelic kingdom exists in nine choirs, and in order of ascending power they are Angels, Archangels, Principalities, Virtues, Powers, Dominations, Thrones, Cherubim, and finally Seraphim.

Angel wings are symbolic. Angels generally exist outside the constructs of the physical Simulation but can temporarily appear in physical form and play a character. The wings are symbolic of their ability to move up and down the levels of the Simulation (tested true).

Angels appear in human bodies, but oftentimes their mission on Earth requires that they forget this fact, as telling people you are an angel generally precludes you being taken seriously or being trusted with money.

Oftentimes in this life when I've gotten myself into a pickle, an Angel in a human body has shown up, seemingly out of nowhere, to save the day.

One such incident happened while living in a condo complex. I was working with an older style pressure cooker and for those of you who know nothing of these, leaving one of these unattended on a stove burner basically creates a bomb.

I had the stove burner on full with the pressure cooker on it. Realizing I had trash to take out, I left the cooker unattended in order to bring the trash out to the dumpster, which normally would've taken only a couple minutes.

As I put the trash in the dumpster, I immediately realized I'd forgotten my keys inside. I had locked myself out of my condo complex with an active bomb brewing on the third floor.

Just as panic hit, a very shady-looking stranger whom I'd never seen appeared seemingly out of nowhere. The man seemed to notice my distraught energy and shouted, "Hey buddy, can I help you with anything?"

I quickly explained that I was locked out. The shady-looking man then immediately pulled out a tool which resembled a knife, and magically opened the locked door without effort in only a few seconds.

I quickly thanked the stranger and ran upstairs to stop the impending disaster brewing on my stovetop.

The incident was written off as luck at the time and the stranger was never seen again. As Angels began entering my experience more often, I slowly intuited that this stranger had indeed been an Angel in a human body. Once calibration became available, I was able to verify it.

What was particularly interesting about this event was that the appearance of the Angelic stranger was typical of a homeless person or criminal, and not of any of the stereotypes associated with Angelic appearance. Though very friendly, the Angelic stranger had technically committed a crime during our brief meeting. It seems Angels can exist in a number of guises which may help them serve the highest good more effectively. This incident seems to highlight the importance of the lesson, 'don't judge a book by its cover.'

As previously stated, 1.7% of the human population are Angels in human bodies. Here are a few broad commonalities I've noticed.

- Tend to be successful in whatever field of endeavor they are in, but in an unconventional way.

- Often deal with a constant sense of 'not being home,' which presents as a subtle unhappiness.

- Can have substance abuse problems, particularly early in life as the substance can make them feel temporarily at home.

- Move up and down the levels of the Simulation more often than most. Recall Angel wings are symbolic of their ability to fly up and down the levels of the Simulation.

- They tend to change careers more than most, in order to meet the needs of the Simulation.

- Generally have a mission or something they feel they must accomplish in life. This often presents later in life.

- They are not necessarily serving in the highest levels of the Simulation. Angels have missions in all the levels of the Simulation. They are found providing empathetic support to those in pain primarily out of the Root chakra level, providing ethnocentric leadership primarily out of the Sacral chakra level, and even as great fighters and folk heroes operating out of the Solar Plexus chakra level.

Moving on Up:

Angelic Takeaway: Putting one's faith in the loving true God and forgiveness are the most efficient ways to move up the levels of the Simulation and relieve one's karma. Even if one puts no conscious effort into spiritual growth, one will tend to gravitate up the levels of the Simulation as natural random life events are actually karma coming back to the soul to be resolved in divinely orchestrated lessons.

Before mentioning specific recommendations on moving up the levels of the Simulation, it bears mentioning that if one is simply living out a human life in any level of the Simulation and not actively inflicting suffering or imposing one's will on others, progress is being made.

Even the mundane aspects of life involve critical spiritual lessons. Some of the most important spiritual lessons of this life were assimilated while doing specifically non-spiritual things, like working a McDonald's drive-through or struggling through a video game. Life itself is the perfect school.

Under even the best of circumstances, human existence involves a bit of suffering. This is hardly pleasant, but one can rest in the knowledge that this is your negative karma subtly coming to the surface to be healed.

The nature of the Simulation guarantees that our karma eventually finds us to be balanced, so even if one lives a life without a specific spiritual pursuit, spiritual progress will be made by simply living out a life with basic morality, not imposing one's will on others, and handling one's responsibilities at whatever level of the Simulation one is operating. It's even okay if life is lived imperfectly and errors made. God loves us all infinitely, and His plan takes our temporary shortcomings into account.

The direction one moves in the Simulation depends on what one places their faith in. Faith in a loving God causes one to begin gravitating up the levels of the Simulation. Putting faith in a principal from a higher level of the Simulation tends to gravitate one towards that higher level, even if one does not fully understand it. Putting one's faith in principle from a lower level of the Simulation tends to cause one to fall through the levels of the Simulation toward that lower level principle. In one past lifetime described later, I put faith in piracy as a way of accomplishing my goals. It did not work out too well for me.

The hardest yet most common way to relieve one's karma is simply by living it out. The easier way to relieve one's karma is forgiveness. The nature of the Simulation causes our energy to come back to us via supposed external sources. Complete unconditional forgiveness of something outside oneself heals the karma and one is then free from it.

Karma is like tiny energetic strings that hold one in the lower levels of the Simulation. When these strings are finally broken, one's soul is free to vibrate at a faster rate so it's possible to resonate with the higher levels of the Simulation.

Real forgiveness happens on a spiritual/wavy level. Something unpleasant outside of oneself is symbolic of an unaccepted aspect of the self. Forgiveness of the aspect outside oneself is actually self-forgiveness. Forgiveness can also happen on a physical level, but one can use common sense. One can forgive a negative person in one's life on a spiritual level but still realize it's not in one's best interest to keep them physically in one's life. In general, I find myself praying and forgiving the folks in the bottom levels of the

Simulation, while simultaneously trying to keep my physical distance.

The Buddha claimed to have been beset by demons as he approached enlightenment. This seemed to have been experiential true in my personal case. Each time a higher level presented itself, there was a need to experience an opposite hellish low and reject it.

One such high-level attack came while flying internationally at the height of the COVID-19 madness during a very busy travel time.

Before the trip, my Angels assured me that everything would be fine, and that I was very protected and being looked out for. This turned out to be true, as the trip which included over forty hours in many airports and planes went miraculously smooth. The only apparent hiccups ended up always working out in my favor in the end.

Despite this, I was surrounded by chaotic energy the entire trip. I saw a constant barrage of travelers being delayed by the COVID-19 testing protocols and travel plans needing to be changed due to flight cancellations. Everyone was in masks and immersed in terrible fear-inducing energy.

Although the whole trip went smoothly, the appearance of things constantly seemed to be attempting to draw me into this fear inducing energy despite the fact that my guardian Angel kept me in a small bubble of complete safety and love the entire time. Had I believed the fear-hype, my trip would not have gone as smoothly.

The temptation, or some would call demonic attack, was to fall into fear and believe what I was seeing going on all around me. By grace this never happened, and upon landing back at home, I was overcome by a peaceful feeling. I was intuitively given the impression that a test had been passed.

Other tests occurred on a completely subjective level where I'd experience truly grim realities (often in my bed at night) and have to keep my faith through the experience. Those tests were a protective mechanism of the Simulation to ensure power does not fall into unprepared hands (tested true).

As one moves up the layers of the Simulation, one becomes more and more threatening to the entities playing in the lower levels of the Simulation, who keep others in the lower levels by perpetuating illusions.

When in the presence of a great power like our sun, the lower mass planets automatically take up an organized orbit around it and enjoy the sun's energy. Any other lower force trying to affect these planets will find it impossible to break the Sun's hold.

What a fascist dictator can get away with in an underdeveloped third world country, with most of the residents in the Root bare survival level of the Simulation, is significantly different than in a heavenly realm, with Archangel Michael standing there with his glorious sword of truth.

As one evolves, one gains access to higher and higher levels of the Simulation. The average soul gains access to a new level of the Simulation about every twenty human lifetimes (tested true). The good news is that if you are reading this book, you are probably NOT an average soul and are currently on a fast-track of evolution.

Here is a broad view of what human evolution looks like when moving into a new level of the Simulation.

Note: When evolving into a new level of the Simulation, one still remains in the lower levels of the Simulation while in a physical body. This is shown in evolutionary biology in that nature builds on top of itself. The newer evolutionary structures of the human brain are built on top of a reptile brain at the top the spine. This is well documented in the book *The Biology of Transcendence.*

When moving into a higher level of the Simulation, it is prudent to give the proper attention to the previous levels of the Simulation and not let one's life go completely out of balance. As each level of the Simulation feels exponentially better than the lower ones, this is a common error I've made in this life and in previous lives.

Root to Sacral:

The Root level of the Simulation presents a bare, survival-based reptile existence. Moving into the Sacral level involves joining a tribe or pack and beginning to work with others. To someone at the Root level of the Simulation would be fear-inducing at first, as it means putting faith in another for your survival.

Early in life, I experienced this transition when I began making friends and found that Nintendo games were something I could talk about with the other kids. This was anxiety-provoking at first with my speech impediment and poor social skills, but the rewards were clear as I made loving friends and my existence became exponentially richer.

Near my spiritual low point of this life I was living a life of near full-time intoxication. I had fallen into bare subsistence

Root chakra existence, where I was just barely clinging to life for the temporary relief of alcohol. Nearing the end of my military service, a close friend told me of an alcohol treatment program which had helped him.

One afternoon I sat in my car in a parking lot, considering two options. Drive home and have a night of drinking, which was my only apparent pleasure source left, or return to my ship and volunteer for the rehab program. The latter choice was made, and I walked to my ship with a feeling I imagine is similar to what some criminals face as they walk to the sheriff's office to turn themselves in and face the music. At rehab I immediately fell into a pack of fellow addicts who became my temporary family, and almost immediately allowed me to re-access the Sacral level of the Simulation.

This is a common way people in the modern world re-access the Sacral level of the Simulation. A person in depths of addiction, barely scraping by in a Root level existence, finally surrenders to God and joins a twelve-step group. An immediate benefit of joining such a group is one finds themselves in a loving tribe, which facilitates functioning in the more social Sacral level of the Simulation.

Unwanted pregnancy is a way the Simulation can present a lost soul with an opportunity for an evolutionary leap. Someone barely keeping themselves alive is suddenly presented with the potential for a family. If one is willing to take a leap of faith and pull oneself up by their bootstraps (with God's help), get a job, and care for people other than themselves, the reward is access to a higher level of the Simulation and an exponentially more satisfying way of being.

Sacral to Solar Plexus:

The Sacral level of existence presents a reality where one lives inside a tight family, tribe, or pack. Outsiders are generally viewed with hostility, and any deviations from the pack's ways tends to carry severe punishment. Eventually the soul hungers for a more holistic existence where one's individuality can be expressed.

Some souls are born into closed-off, ethnocentric communities, unsatisfied with their simple existence. They strive to explore the larger world and earn one's way. This archetype fits within to the Sacral to Solar Plexus stage of evolution.

At the age of fourteen, I moved from a town where I enjoyed a tight-knit group of friends and a supportive family. I was living primarily in a nice Sacral level existence. I then moved to a much larger school and complex environment, where I had to deal with bullies and more social complexity. This was my evolutionary call in this life, to move into the Solar Plexus level of the Simulation and express my individual power.

After the military and still in the throes of addiction, I returned home to my parents' house. I was largely operating from the Sacral level of the Simulation at the time, and returning to the safety of one's family is common at this level. After a certain degree of recovery, the opportunity to become a teacher arose. The decision to become a teacher meant a return to daily responsibility and challenge, but re-ignited full access to the Solar Plexus level of the Simulation, where expression of true individual power is available.

Solar Plexus to Heart:

The Solar Plexus level of the Simulation offers an existence where one wields significant individual power and can be a positive success in the world. However the soul will eventually sense a reality above the somewhat lonely hard work and struggle of this level.

A successful businessperson suddenly seeming interested in more holistic social endeavors that seem to compromise his or her personal success is indicative of someone at this stage of evolution.

However success often increases rather than decreases. This is because the person is now operating from a higher level of the Simulation therefore has access to exponentially more power, so success is more automatic and no longer needs to be forced by individual will.

I was raised by parents who instilled in me a drive to succeed, and I attended a high school that encouraged it. It was the perfect recipe to fire up my Solar Plexus chakra and be a success in the world. It led to me choosing electrical engineering as a major, as it was one of the highest-earning fields at the time.

By the end of college, this success-driven life had lost its luster, as I yearned to serve something higher. This ultimately led me to join the US Navy, which allowed me to serve something higher than myself and move into the Heart level.

Heart to Throat:

The Heart level of the Simulation is a happy place to hang out, but it is still not perfect. One is friendly, charismatic, and tends to be loved by many at this level. Significant spiritual power is also wielded from this level, so this level tends to be the movers and shakers of the world.

This Heart level of the Simulation tends to go along with the predominant good causes of one's culture. However, if one reads history, it becomes obvious that a culture's perceived good causes are not always truly good. Remember, the Nazis were briefly perceived as the good guys in Europe.

Eventually one hungers for a more nuanced worldview, which is offered by the Throat chakra.

In my late twenties after spending my life doing what others told me and trying to do what I perceived as the best thing, I found myself in a dark spiritual low-spot, which I'd never wish upon another soul. This initiated a period of voracious reading and studying as I re-energized my Throat chakra. I strived for a more holistic understanding of the world and wanted to make sure that my efforts were better placed.

A thorough reading of the great books of the Western world (excluding Marx) will aid one greatly in evolving into the Throat chakra level of the Simulation (tested true).

Throat to Third Eye:

The Throat level of the Simulation offers serenity and a calm, happy, and wise existence. Great academics, scientists, authors and engineers have operated from this level of the Simulation. However, eventually the soul yearns for an even more holistic communion with the universe. This is when the soul begins gradually gravitating from the cold world of logic and academic learning and sensing what everything is at its core.

Another layer of security is added here as even the greatest intellects are occasionally fooled by a clever presentation of propaganda. As the demonic world has been perfecting pious sounding propaganda for eons, they've become quite good at it. The Third Eye will not be fooled by this propaganda (tested true).

A career academic or high-powered leader who suddenly takes an interest spiritual matters (which often seems irrational to the external world) is an example of someone in the midst of evolving from the Throat to Third Eye level of the Simulation.

Third Eye to Crown:

The Third Eye level of the Simulation gives one a relatively carefree existence away from most trouble and social drama. However, one still notices the suffering of others. Eventually a deep, unexplainable desire arises to commune directly with the highest source of love, truth, and power in the universe.

The desire to ascend to this level is not an easy one, as it involves surrendering almost all remaining aspects of the personal will to God and being a servant of the divine. Abusing the power one gains access to at this level of the Simulation comes with ghastly, long-term karmic consequences.

This level of consciousness is rare, and roughly corresponds with the Eastern concept known as "enlightenment." Here one fully understands the Spider-Man saying, "With great power comes great responsibility."

Oftentimes, a spiritual aspirant will walk away from everything a previous life offered to pursue this level of the Simulation in order to be of service to God. If you are unwilling to sacrifice everything considered normal in this Simulation, then setting one's sight on a humbler spiritual goal might be more optimal.

Just committing to being unconditionally loving to all life will eventually land one in the Third Eye level of the Simulation, which is an existence beyond the wildest imagination of most of Earth's residents at this time (tested true).

Laws of Conservation:

Angelic Takeaway: Mass, Energy and Life cannot be created or destroyed. Everything in the universe must balance or things in the Simulation would go haywire in a hurry.

In common physics and chemistry, there are two commonly taught conservation laws. I'll discuss one additional one which is not yet known officially to science. These three laws are:

The Law of the Conservation of Mass (from low end of Throat level)

The Law of the Conservation of Energy (from high end of Throat level)

The Law of the Conservation of Life (from Third Eye level)

Most people who have taken a high school chemistry class have probably done conservation of mass problems. One of these looks like this:

$\_H_2 + \_O_2 \longrightarrow \_ H_2O$

This is the chemical reaction of Hydrogen gas combining with Oxygen gas to form water. When I taught chemistry this was always Problem #1, because it is easy to get the solution:

$\underline{2} H_2 + \underline{1} O_2 \longrightarrow \underline{2} H_2O$

This shows that the amount of hydrogen and oxygen atoms stays the same before and after the chemical reaction. 4 hydrogen and 2 oxygen atoms go into the reaction, and 4 hydrogen and 2 oxygen atoms come out of the reaction. No mass or matter gets lost in the process.

This Law comes out of the lower end of the Throat level. This means it's a way of understanding the universe optimally if one is vibrating near the bottom of the Throat level of the Simulation.

This Law is not the ultimate truth however, as one the great scientific Angels of all time Albert Einstein came up with a famous equation $E=mc^2$. This equation tells us that mass can actually get converted into energy, so in the ultimate sense of things, mass is not always completely conserved.

I have a master's degree in Nuclear Engineering and briefly helped run the nuclear reactors on the aircraft carrier *USS Enterprise* of *Top Gun* fame (greatest movie of all-time and not up for debate), so an explanation of basic nuclear physics is in order.

Nuclear reactors are useful onboard Navy ships and submarines because they produce a very large amount of energy (ability to do stuff) with a relatively small amount of fuel, and because they convert mass directly into energy. This is a very efficient process and Albert Einstein's equation tells us why:

The 'E' in $E=mc^2$ stands for Energy (measured in Joules).

The 'm' stands for mass (measured in kilograms).

The 'c' stands for the speed of light, which is 300,000,000 meters/second which is really fast. "I feel the need, the need for speed." (Random out-of-context *Top Gun* reference.)

'c' is a very large number, and when you square a very large number, it becomes a very, very, very large number.

So let's say we have 1kg of Uranium onboard the *USS Enterprise*. How much energy could be extracted from this in theory? By simplifying the physics a bit, we can calculate:

$$E = (1kg)(300,000,000 \text{ m/s})^2 = 90,000,000,000,000,000$$

Joules of energy.

We don't actually get nearly this much energy for a number of reasons. I've simplified the physics and engineering to make it more understandable, but it demonstrates the principle. A little mass converts to A LOT of energy.

I've observed in myself and others that when we lose weight or mass, we typically feel better and have more energy. This is largely because the soul now has access to far more free energy inside the Simulation, and it isn't trying to manage as much mass (tested true).

I've had to move a number of times in this life, largely due to the rather crazy Angelic curriculum I've endured. In every move I've had to go through the difficult process of throwing or giving away stuff or mass. Though this letting go process was never easy, when it was finished I always felt lighter, like the soul had access to more energy again by managing less mass. Mass again converts to energy very favorably.

The Law of the Conservation of Energy comes out of the high end of the Throat level of the Simulation. This means it's a way of understanding the universe about as good as the reasonable or logical mind can do, if one is vibrating near the top of the Throat of the Simulation.

This Law states that energy is neither created or destroyed, it just changes forms. A common way of demonstrating this is with a Nerf gun. Energy is stored inside a spring in the form of elastic potential energy. When the trigger is pulled and the Nerf dart flies off, the energy stored in the spring gets converted into kinetic or movement energy. Calculations are commonly done with this law, which I won't go into here as I feel non science-nerds falling asleep.

There is actually a higher order of this law that is not yet known to science and may never be, as it only becomes obvious in the Third Eye level of the Simulation and is not provable using the scientific method of the Throat level. Though not proved, the body of work of the late hypnotherapist Dolores Cannon demonstrates this principle about as well as one can.

The same basic principle that we talked about with $E=mc^2$ applies to a higher order concept.

Before I give this equation, I urge my physics and engineering friends to resist the temptation to see the letter 'L' as meaning angular momentum or liters. I use 'L' for simplicity purposes.

The equation is $L=Ec^2$. Life equals energy times the speed of light squared (tested true). Energy gets converted into a lot of life.

If one reads of near-death experiences or has been blessed enough to be out of body, one finds themselves in an ecstatic state, as the soul does not need to manage the mass or energy of the physical body. One can just be its divine life essence, completely unrestricted by the laws of the Simulation.

Mass and energy gets converted to a lot of life. This is actually our natural state, and it will come as a very pleasant surprise to those of you who have not yet been outside their physical body. Thomas Campbell's book *My Big Toe* gives a very rational view of being out of the body, and like this book, posits that we are inside a Simulation.

Those who've recalled past lives or have had a past-life regression by a hypnotherapist see the truth of The Law of the Conservation of Life. When the physical body dies, the core of the being, its life essence, goes into another form uninterrupted (tested true).

In my case as I've traced out past lives, the level of the Simulation I was operating in and my level of karma went on uninterrupted by the death of a physical body. I was simply born where I left off at the end of the previous life, in a situation divinely perfect for my soul's continued evolution.

Power vs. Force:

Angelic Takeaway: These two principles are what moves everything in the Simulation. To be short, one works in the long-run and one does not. The Angelic utilize true power which flows from an unlimited divine source while the demonic utilize force which is rooted in time and subject to the rule-set of the Simulation and always eventually backfires.

Power vs. Force is Dr. David Hawkin's first book. Its name points to the two motives that keep this Simulation humming along.

Power flows from divinity and has no need to do anything. It simply just sits there and lets less powerful things draw energy from it and move around in its field. This is similar to how the Sun just sits in the middle of our solar system, giving off energy as the planets utilizing that energy dance around it. The Sun does not give orders to the planets, but its inherent power keeps the planets aligned automatically.

Force, on the other hand, does things. A property of force is that it automatically generates a counter-force. This is the principle described by Newton's Third Law in physics, which in my humble opinion is the most important principle of conventional physics to know. This basic principle applies all the way up through the levels of the Simulation (tested true). At one point I was planning to name this book *Newton's Third Law All the Way Up* but *Angelic Physics* was easier to write.

Force tends to be notoriously bad at accomplishing its goals because of the counterforce generated. On the other hand, power accomplishes everything it needs to do effortlessly, by simply by being what it is. God would have it no other way.

As one moves up and down the levels of the Simulation, the tradeoff between an entity utilizing power and force seems to happen almost automatically. High-level entities that have a lot of power will find using force and then dealing with counter-force tiresome and inefficient. Low level entities that lack power must utilize force in order to survive (tested true).

The below graph represents the reciprocal relationship that exists between an entity utilizing power vs. force. The blue line represents the power utilized, and the red line represents the force utilized. As an entity gains access to power, its utilization of force decreases. As an entity utilizes force more, its inherent power declines.

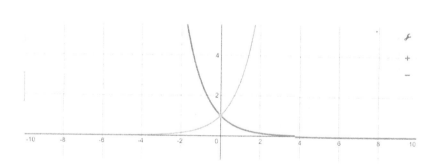

The history of war reveals that it is quite common for the lower vibrational side of a conflict to utilize its increased access to force or physical might in order to take an early advantage. However this advantage is only in appearance and the force and physical might creates a lot of noise, suffering, and counter-force.

Eventually, the true power of the higher vibrational side more aligned with divinity turns the tide and restores balance. One can study the American Revolutionary War, the American Civil War, or World War Two to see clear cases of this power vs. force dynamic in war. I'm sure many other wars provide great examples of this dynamic, but I was too busy playing video games in high school to pay close enough attention to any of the others.

True power creates no counter-force or resistance so will eventually accomplish its goals. The nature of the Simulation guarantees it. Force is always rooted within the strict rules of the Simulation, so it is always inherently limited and automatically draws resistance.

Confusion can arise because true power is more subtle and less easily observable than the short-term immediate effects of force. Force often puts on a big show, because deep down it knows intimidation is one of its only cards. On his path to enlightenment, the Buddha was said to have stood off a giant army of forceful demons, as he realized the power of his true Self could not be defeated by force.

The world often confuses power with access to a lot of force. For example, take a fictional case of two men. One man is the CEO of a large corporation, who rose to his position by political posturing, brown nosing, and backstabbing those above him. The other man is a humble custodian who works for the same corporation, but is friendly and beloved by all.

The first man operates from a low level of the Simulation, works over sixteen hours a day, has abundant enemies, a disastrous personal life, and is always on the brink of having the board of directors remove him from the job. The second man operates from a high level of the Simulation, lives a simple but enjoyable life, comes and goes from his job as he pleases and has more friends than he can count. I'd ask the reader to consider which man they believe has more true power.

I've observed that people operating from a high level of the Simulation often do not even strive for a high position in society. This is based on an evolved comprehension of life. When one is power, one tends to not need or want the external symbols of it.

It's actually easier for a person operating from a high level of the Simulation aligned with true power to affect things from afar and handle things anonymously, rather then get caught up in the details of earthly life. The book *Way of the Peaceful Warrior* by Dan Millman and the movie based on it (*Peaceful Warrior*) are entertaining ways to see this principle in action. A main character Socrates is a humble gas station attendant, who is clearly more than what the world sees him as.

The lowest two levels of the Simulation tend to operate almost completely from the principle of force. Then as one moves into the higher levels of the Simulation, true power rises exponentially and utilizing force becomes less necessary. Life becomes more peaceful and joyous as a result.

Use of political force is common in the current political environment of the world. Political causes which attempt to accomplish its goals using political force, like pressuring others to vote a certain way, silencing the opposition, or even committing blatant corruption always trigger counter-forces. This dynamic tends to set things further apart from the original goal of the political entities utilizing the force.

The rare political entities that had access to true power needed to use surprisingly little force. Examples of these entities are Gandhi, Nelson Mandela, Mikhail Gorbachev, and the most successful US presidents.

The critical error that the world made in combating the COVID-19 pandemic was over-utilization of force. Forcing people to wear masks, forcing people from jobs, forcing vaccinations and forcing quarantines cemented a large faction of humanity against the efforts to combat the pandemic (tested true). A more powerful solution would've been presenting the reality of the situation in a way understandable to each level of the Simulation (tested true).

Both as a student and teacher I saw this Power vs. Force principle broadly operative. Teachers and professors who had something legitimate to offer (true power) had to use very little force with their students. On the other hand, uncharismatic teachers and professors pushing political agendas on their students must use great force. Examples of this force are punishment, threats of bad grades, and screaming.

Surprisingly, most in the world are surprised when counterforce occurs, even though it's extremely predictable. Low-vibrating, forceful entities live an existence of perpetual frustration as their schemes never work out as well as they planned, due to unanticipated counterforce.

Looking at the marketplace, one sees examples of good products that sell themselves with almost no need for advertising. Other terrible products only stay in the marketplace because millions of dollars are spent on marketing and forcing them onto the populace.

This is also why entities wishing for help moving up the levels of the Simulation or needing spiritual assistance must ask or pray for it. The high-level Angelic kingdom operates almost entirely from the principle of power, so by the rules of the Simulation simply cannot force themselves on a stubborn soul struggling but refusing all help (tested true). Any move up the levels of the Simulation is voluntary and cannot be forced.

Generally an entity forcing themselves onto you without your permission does not have your best interests at heart.

In conclusion, the tradeoff between power and force is almost automatic. Entities that make unwise decisions tend to lose their power and become more reliant on force. Entities that utilize what power they have wisely are rewarded with more of it in the Simulation. The statement, "That which has true power has very little need for force . . . That which lacks true power is completely reliant on force" succinctly summarizes many characteristics of this Simulation (tested true).

If one understands this principle, it becomes very obvious why the Angels always win in the end. Tyrants always eventually fall, bullies are always eventually bullied, but the way of love and truth always eventually triumphs, because it's invulnerable and not subject to counter-force. Gandhi often made this observation during his career in slightly different language. The Angelic kingdom has been watching the temporary rise and fall of force in the lower levels of the Simulation for eons, and is basically unaffected by it (tested true).

Evolution vs. Creation:

Angelic Takeaway: Stop arguing over this! Both concepts are true but from an opposite view of reality. Evolution is the study of energy flowing up through the levels of the Simulation and creation is the study of energy flowing down through the levels of the Simulation. For a night of comedic entertainment put your militant atheist scientist friends with your bible-thumping religious friends and watch their arguments contradict each other into logical absurdity.

Evolution and Creation are two sides of the same coin. There is no real conflict between the two philosophies. Evolution is a bottom-up view of reality, as life evolves from the lower levels of the Simulation into more complex forms in the higher levels of the Simulation. Creation is a top-down view of reality, as divine energy flows down from the higher levels of the Simulation to ultimately create everything. Scientists tend to prefer evolution because it can be studied. The religious tend to prefer creation because of its core tenant of faith in God, which is ultimately how we draw spiritual power in the Simulation (tested true).

Another analogy is to think of evolution and creation as two sides of a reflection in a mirror. The lesser-evolved look at the other from their side of the mirror and see a complete reversal or opposite of their reality. However the more evolved notice that they are not just opposite reflections of each other, but actually two ways of describing the same fundamental reality.

The Theory of Evolution was masterfully described by Charles Darwin, who operated primarily from the scientific Throat chakra level of the Simulation and was an Angel in a human body (tested true). He masterfully described the ever-increasing organization and complexity of biological life. Since the beginning of life on Earth, atoms have been arranging into more complex structures or bodies. However unthinking atoms are unable to arrange themselves into complex structures. They needed help form the core of life itself, a spark of God.

Aside: Material Reductionism.

I'm not sure what to say about this philosophy that has gained a strong foothold in the scientific community. To say mindless atoms arranged themselves into structures as complex as human bodies or even trees seems ridiculous to this soul.

I played with a lot of LEGOs as a kid. I'm pretty sure I could've spent my entire forty-two years dumping bins of unassembled LEGOs onto the floor and they never would have arranged themselves into anything too complex or beautiful. Maybe with extreme luck, a cool-looking color pattern would emerge or a couple would stick together and orient themselves just right to create a very simple structure. Nothing approaching the complexity that even a lazy kid such as myself could create would likely emerge.

The scientific concept of entropy also needs to be considered. Entropy is a measure of the amount of disorder in a system. The famous Second Law of Thermodynamics states in simple terms that in a closed system (no energy coming in or out) the amount of entropy always increases. This is an easily observable law. If one puts no energy into cleaning one's house, the house tends to become messier and less orderly over time.

Let's say we try to assemble a complex LEGO structure by the simple processes of randomness. We have a giant bin of LEGOs and dump them on the floor. This would cause a few of them to indeed stick together. Then we pick them up and put them back in the bin, leaving the ones stuck together intact. We could then dump them on the floor again. It is the thought of material reductionist evolutionists that untold iterations of this process would eventually result in complex structures, similar to how it is thought that atoms randomly bumping into each other would eventually result in enormously complex structures such as DNA.

It is clear that every iteration of randomness would result in change. Some LEGOs would indeed stick together in every dump. However, if each iteration were truly random with no higher creative energy coming into the process, whenever a rare complex structure began to form, it is far more likely that the structure would break apart with a dumping than another piece would mysteriously stick to the existing structure in just the right way as to improve it.

If an intellect can look around this world and see this all created from randomness, I honestly don't know what to say, except maybe, "Why didn't you pay attention to your high school statistics and science classes?"

A higher order of energy clearly is needed for physical life for life to exist. How a person can take a walk through nature just to see a randomly created mess of stuff and not the divine spark that created it is borderline humorous to me. As the point of this book is not about arguing for the existence of divinity, I won't waste more time with this. I don't think many true material reductionists or atheists are actually reading this anyway.

End Aside.

The best explanation for Creationism in logical terms is in relating transformation of divine energy to electrical transformers. This is why the Angels guided me sit through four years of electrical engineering classes, despite not being a particularly talented engineer. You can thank the Angelic kingdom for this next metaphor for creationism, since it tends to lack logical explanations.

Angelic Electrical Engineering:

Angelic Takeaway: All the great religions are monotheistic, meaning all the energy of the universe is ultimately derived from a single source. The power level of this source would vaporize us mere mortals. Thank God we have the Angels and higher levels of the Simulation which function a bit like electrical transformers, whose job is step-down this ridiculous power into levels that can be utilized on Earth without fear of anyone getting Angelically fried.

The beginning of this chapter is designed to be a highly simplified explanation of transformers and power grids providing only the **bare** minimum detail to understand this book. My fellow Northeastern Electrical Engineers and pretty much anyone working in an electrical or engineering field can probably skip this. Anyone seeking more detailed information can consult anyone I just mentioned above.

An electrical transformer is a device designed to either increase or decrease the voltage of flowing electricity. A basic diagram of a transformer, the basic schematic symbol for a transformer, and an actual picture of a transformer as you'd see from the street are pictured below:

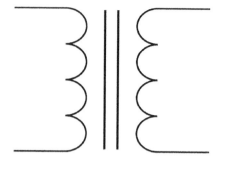

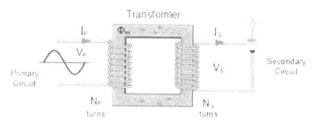

Transformer

I_P Φ_m I_s

V_P

Primary
Circuit

V_s

Secondary
Circuit

N_P
turns

N_s
turns

Electrical power is generated at power plants at extremely high voltages. This is because high voltages travel much more efficiently to their desired source with less loss or waste. We do not keep the electricity at such high voltages flowing into our houses for obvious safety reasons. Computers and home electronics are charged most efficiently by very low voltages. This is why transformers are needed. (Not to be confused with the colorful robots in the movies who are needed to defend Earth.)

A series of "step down" transformers will lower the voltage of electricity as it flows from the power plant towards its ultimate destination. Higher voltages can carry massive amounts of electrical power extremely efficiently, medium voltages can flow safely through populated areas somewhat efficiently but safer, low voltages can be utilized by homes, and even lower voltages can be used to power smaller devices.

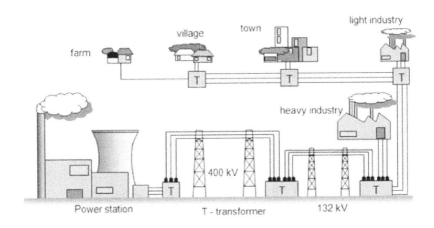

The picture above shows a highly simplified power transmission system. Power produced at a power station at 400kV (400,000 Volts) is able to be transported across the countryside very efficiently. Eventually it stepped down to 132kV by a set of transformers as it gets closer to its destination. These then get stepped down again to lower voltages where it can be utilized by heavy industry. These then get stepped down again where it can be utilized by light industry.

It then continues to be stepped down as the electricity moves into populated areas. Hopefully common sense dictates why we don't want 400,000 voltage electricity running through our living rooms where our kids play. It eventually ends up all the way down at 120V (if you live in America) for your wall sockets.

If you are charging an electronic device, then the charging cord also has a transformer which steps down the voltage even more, as fine electronics don't do well with high voltages. My iPhone charger uses only 5 volts of electricity to avoid frying the electronics inside my phone.

If an electrical engineer designs a grid and tries to step down the voltage too early, then the system becomes horribly inefficient. If the voltage was never stepped down, houses would catch on fire and electronic devices would be fried.

Very broadly speaking, high voltages transport better and lower voltages are more utilizable for actual work.

Now if you have understood the basic idea of how a power distribution system works and you are able to switch your brain from literal mode to metaphorical mode, just change 'voltage' to the 'level of the Simulation' and picture God as the power station producing massive amounts of electricity at ridiculously high voltage levels.

This ridiculously powerful God vibration can probably only be absorbed by beings more powerful and wiser than our wildest human dreams. This is the role of the highest choirs of the Angels that goes WAY beyond the scope of this book (tested true).

At this point, these great beings step down this voltage to the Archangel realm. These vibrations are then passed down from the Archangel realm to the Angelic realm, who directly interact with this Simulation. A common vision I've received is picturing Archangel Michael as a giant Tesla coil sending incredibly powerful bolts of electricity to smaller antennas who represent Angels on Earth.

Information and energy is passed down gradually from the higher levels of the Simulation to the lower levels of the Simulation. The great founders of religions such Jesus, Buddha, and Lord Krishna were transforming energy at the peak of what could be handled safely in the human dimension. This is why their teachings have lasted thousands of years.

In this way, different voltages of electricity and the different levels of the Simulation are similar in that they shouldn't be labeled as better or worse, but serving different purposes.

Individual humans can act as transformers themselves. The great American Football coach Bill Belichick, who operates heavily out of the intelligent Throat level of the Simulation, interacts primarily with football players who often operate from the Solar Plexus level of the Simulation. He provides strategy and motivation to players at this level to win Super Bowls. In this way, Bill Belichick acts as a transformer, transforming divine energy from the fifth level of the Simulation to the third level of the Simulation. Bill Belichick also has a history of signing players who have 'Heart.' Players from the fourth level of the Simulation would help in this transformation process.

When humans face a major crisis in the lower levels of the Simulation such as war, it can originate from a problem in the higher levels of the Simulation. The energy/information gets continuously distorted as it transforms down the levels of the Simulation (tested true).

A professor operating in the Throat level of the Simulation can create multitudes of problems in the lower levels of the Simulation by teaching an incorrect piece of information or incorrect concept. Recall Spider-Man's saying, "With great power comes great responsibility."

One reason why I like Dr. David Hawkin's technique of describing different levels of the Simulation with a number system is that it is easier to relate to a transformer system.

Below is a metaphoric schematic showing the insanely high divine 'voltages/vibrations' being stepped down successively into the various 'voltages/vibrations' utilized by the various levels of the Simulation. It bears reminding that the numbers on Hawkin's scale are exponential so 400 is not twice as powerful as 200 but orders of magnitude more powerful. These numbers are symbolic, not to be taken too literally.

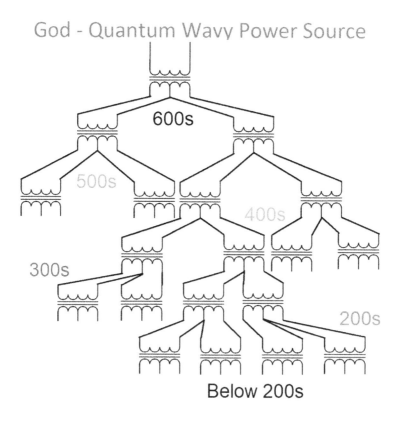

God - Quantum Wavy Power Source

600s

500s

400s

300s

200s

Below 200s

This same diagram can be made using the chakra level names used primarily in this book. The Crown chakra handles the highest voltages coming from the divine and the voltages get transformed down into the lower chakras that function better at lower voltages and handle the more physical aspects of life.

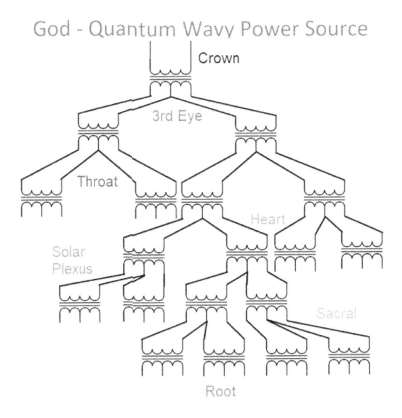

No level is strictly better than another. But if the higher chakras are misaligned, it will mess up the lower chakras over time by passing misaligned energy to the lower chakras.

On the bright side, if the Crown chakra is aligned, which only requires faith in a loving God and prayer, then the lower chakras will tend towards alignment over time as they are being fed aligned divine energy (tested true).

Creating great spiritual teachings, designing modern computers, and fixing plumbing are all important to human life. However, the vibrational energy that accomplishes each of these tasks is very different. Much like how different voltages can accomplish different tasks easier, different levels of the Simulation are better suited for different life activities. This is analogous to how different devices in your house run optimally on different voltages.

The most important thing to take from this Angelic electrical engineering metaphor is all the power of the universe is generated from a single point. The infinitely high voltage of power generated at this single source is transformed down through the levels of the Simulation in a variety of ways for the use of all beings. All the great time-tested world religious and spiritual systems were monotheistic, meaning they agreed there was ultimately one power source despite having many surface differences. This is much like the differences one would find in different transformer systems if one travels between various countries.

As biological life evolved into more advanced forms, eventually souls or waves could have more complex experiences and co-evolved into smarter energetic structures. This Earth School, as it co-evolved as both waves and particles, provided souls with more complex/educative/more fun ways to evolve on earth in a the physical Simulation. With very advanced biological organisms and lots of variance of life in this Simulation, very old souls could be enticed into incarnating here.

Nature of Time, Brainwave States:

Angelic Takeaway: Ever notice that spiritual people tend to be a bit odd and spacey? This is because they are less connected with time and experiencing reality at a lower frame-rate. This does not make them better or worse, just weirder and not good at sports.

This Simulation has a master clock which is used to synchronize everything. This clock ticks away at a very fast rate, with only 10^{-43} seconds between ticks. This time is known in physics as the Planck time. It is the smallest unit of time that we are able to measure. In case any of you slept through math class, 10^{-43} equals .000000000000000000000000000000000000000001 seconds. This is a very, very small unit of time and imperceptible to normal human consciousness.

Also imperceptible to our somewhat crude human senses is something called the Planck length. This is 1.6×10^{-35} meters which is also a ridiculously small number. Any Simulation or video game is pixelated. This is more noticeable in older video games or if one puts their eye right next to the monitor.

Our Simulation is also pixelated, but with pixels that are way too small to be observed with the naked eye, or even the fancy microscope you got for Christmas in sixth grade. Reality isn't smooth, but contains tiny pixels. The Planck length is the length of these pixels.

When one divides the Planck length by the Planck time, one gets the speed of light, which is the ultimate speed limit of the Simulation. This is how fast something travels through the

Simulation space if it moves 1 pixel per tick of the master clock. Most things travel WAY slower than this.

When things begin traveling near the speed of light, you end up with this crazy thing called time dilation, which is simply our poor little Simulation experiencing something like LAG. This is similar to when I tried to play graphic intensive 3-D shooter games on my 1980s era 386 computer as a child.

Time dilation is where time is experienced at different rates in different places. It also occurs when one is near a giant gravitational body, like a black hole. Though I'm unfamiliar with the finer details of the code that runs this wacky Angelic video game, I'm guessing you need a lot of RAM and a pretty fast processor to run a black hole.

The mathematics of time dilation are quite complicated but one can see time dilation physically demonstrated wonderfully in the movie *Interstellar*.

Spoiler Alert:

In the movie *Interstellar*, the astronauts visit a planet orbiting a black hole. They spend only a few hours on this planet orbiting the black hole but while they are on this planet, twenty-three years pass on Earth. The physics of the scene are a bit exaggerated, however it's forgivable as the scene is wonderful to watch, moves the movie's great plot along, and makes an abstract physics concept understandable, which is not easy to do.

Spoiler Safe.

With a master clock ticking away every 10^{-43} seconds, one could say the Simulation updates itself 10^{43} times every second.

A relatable concept is computer monitors run on a frame rate. A typical one is 60 hz, for example. This means that the monitor updates its image 60 times per second (or every .0167 seconds). For those of you familiar with video games, a common concept is fps (frames per second). This is how many times per second your computer updates the game. A high fps results in smooth gameplay, and a low fps results in choppy, less fun gameplay.

If playing a game on a great computer, it may run a graphics intensive game at 60fps. The same game will run at only 15fps on an older/slower computer. I once tried playing the computer game *Doom* on the aforementioned ancient 386 computer, which produced a pathetic framerate of 2fps (which is basically unplayable). This was actually a blessing, as I had *much* better things to do with my childhood than playing a game about hell and demons.

Using this analogy, we could say that the universe is a Simulation with a 10^{43} fps frame-rate. Given the size and complexity of the universe (which the earthly human mind can't begin to comprehend) and this framerate (too fast for the earthly human mind to comprehend) this Simulation is being run by something immensely powerful with a friggin' lot of processing power. Spoiler alert: It's God.

A human nervous system cannot come close to experiencing all 10^{43} stop frames of the Simulation every second. Most of us experience the Simulation at around 8-16 fps under normal circumstances.

The framerate in which we experience the Simulation varies with our state of our consciousness. This has been documented scientifically and is a relatively well-studied phenomenon called brainwave states.

There is plenty of literature available on the topic of varying quality. I'm not particularly well-read, but will give what I've learned from first-person experience and limited personal research.

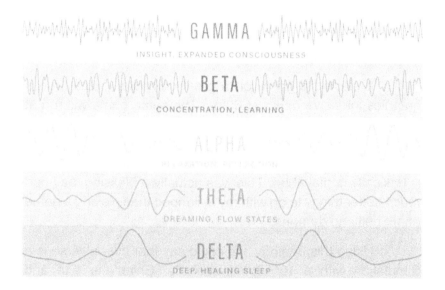

GAMMA
INSIGHT, EXPANDED CONSCIOUSNESS

BETA
CONCENTRATION, LEARNING

ALPHA
RELAXATION, REFLECTION

THETA
DREAMING, FLOW STATES

DELTA
DEEP, HEALING SLEEP

In the lower partically levels of Simulation we experience a higher framerate of physical reality. The state the world considers normal is classically referred to as the beta brainwave state, which operates at approximately 16ish fps.

This is optimal for fast worldly functioning, manipulating the devices of the world, and responding to emergencies. As one moves up the levels of the Simulation, this framerate slows.

A bit higher one finds the Alpha state, traditionally associated with meditation. Here one experiences a lower framerate in the high single digits and low double digits. As one moves to even higher levels of the Simulation, one eventually experiences consciousness from the theta and delta states with very low framerates. Though a slower frame rate makes operating in the physical world more difficult, it allows for a better interface with higher levels of the Simulation and the source code running this entire Simulation. As consciousness experiences physical reality from a lower framerate, it naturally takes a wider view. It's more likely to notice the subtle, more energetic things going on around it.

A person completely focused on a television will miss things going on around him or her in the room. The beta state represents an almost complete focus on the physical world.

Operating in a higher fps consciousness is well suited to manipulate technology or handle itself in a fight, but would not have enough leftover resources to philosophically look at the reasons why it was manipulating technology or in a fight in the first place.

Observation of time-tested enlightened beings clearly shows that they were generally experiencing reality from a very low fps. From this view they gained a very pixelated view of physical reality, but could provide valuable wisdom about the larger happenings of the vibrational universe and God-country. The cost of this cosmic knowledge might mean they did not have a clear understanding of earthly political events or how to use power tools.

This also ties into the Heisenberg uncertainty principle, which states, "The more we know the exact position of an object, the less we know its momentum. The more we know the exact momentum of an object, the less we know its position."

This principle can be applied to other sets of dualities. Turns out, the more one tunes into the higher levels of the spiritual/wavy universe, the less one knows of the physical/partically Simulation. Vice versa, the more one tunes into the physical/partically Simulation, the more one loses sight of the spiritual/wavy universe. We've probably all observed a person so engrossed in a videogame that they are completely oblivious to what is going on in the outside world.

The chart below shows the various brainwave states. The bottom of the chart represents more wavy consciousness states where partically/physical reality is experienced at a very low frame rate, like playing a graphically-intensive computer game on older slower computer. The top states represent experiencing partically reality at a higher frame rate, like playing that same game on a state of the art computer. This is a good example that demonstrates that the higher levels of the Simulation are not strictly better than the lower levels of the Simulation.

Brainwave State	Natural for the Following Levels of the Simulation	Frame Rate for Experiencing Partically Reality	Good For
Beta	Root, Sacral, Solar Plexus	13 - 30 fps or hz	Concentrating on physical reality, dealing with emergencies, panic, animal

			learning, and survival.
Alpha	Solar Plexus, Heart, Throat	8 - 12 fps or hz	Relaxation, laid-back view of life, meditation, academic learning.
Theta	Throat, Third Eye, Crown	2 - 7 fps or hz	Deep relaxation, very laid back view of life, light sleep, energy sensing, hypnosis, creativity.
Delta	Highest levels of the Simulation and deep dreamless sleep	1-2 fps or hz	Deep Sleep, communication with the divine.

Note: This chart lays out the brainwave states discreetly, which is needed to talk about them in language. However, my empathic experience tells me they actually blend together. Maybe a future nerd can classify them as something like Beta, Beta/Alpha, Alpha/Beta, Alpha, Alpha/Theta, etc. I attempted to do this in an early version of the book but did not feel confident enough in my knowledge, and it was too in the weeds. I may try this again in future, but have no problem if some anal-retentive, empathic nerd steals the idea.

Very broadly, the higher the level of the Simulation one operates from, the lower the framerate physical reality is experienced at. However, human consciousness is flexible and functions in various modes, depending on what is required by a person in the moment. A loud noise in a room tends to cause most of its occupants to jump temporarily into beta, no matter what they were doing. A talented hypnotist can put an entire room into a theta state.

Aside: Hypnosis.

I'm a certified hypnotist but to keep this book short I've decided to not talk about my experience with hypnosis. I'll say one point that is missed often by both practitioners and teachers of hypnosis. Hypnosis is actually a person holding a relaxed Theta state of consciousness so the people they hypnotize resonate with Theta too (tested true). In this Theta state people can heal their body, recall past lives, be immune to social anxiety, and even reprogram their consciousness which are some of the main things hypnosis is famous for.

The late hypnotist Dolores Cannon understood this and authored a number of wonderful books. She operated from the Third Eye level of the Simulation and is a good source if one wishes to begin to learn about hypnosis or is interested in past-life regression.

End Aside.

This book was written to an extent in all four states.

I'm simply not smart enough to have come up with the main ideas for the book myself. During my Delta states which occurred during sleep or in extremely deep prayer I downloaded the material for this book in a wavy vibrational form from the Angelic kingdom.

I have short sentences and notes thrown about my house and phone where these vibrational ideas that I downloaded in vibrational form were translated into very basic language and pictures in the Theta state. This occurred in extremely deep relaxation, hypnosis or walking deep in nature.

These notes were expanded on and typed out in a language the reader would understand in the relaxed but alert Alpha state. This is the state I often walk around the world in.

Corrections, organizing, recall of painful moments, and dealing with technology were done in a more stressed beta state. This was my least favorite part of the process.

This process shows how energy works its way down from the high levels of the Simulation to lower levels of the Simulation as described in the 'Angelic Engineering' chapter of this book. The levels of the Simulation tend to act a bit like transformers slowly 'stepping down' the voltage of divine information so it can be understood on Earth. God's direct thoughts would literally fry us so we should be thankful to the higher choirs of Angels that step down the energy of God's thoughts so us mere mortals can absorb them.

People familiar with these states can see most people switching between these states as they adapt to their various life conditions. Empathic people will notice people feel different depending on their brainwave state. Most people walking around will be in a beta or alpha state. In America, cities generally favor beta and rural areas generally favor alpha.

Most humans go into a delta state when sleeping. Research shows that humans are not completely unaware of their physical environment when asleep, but are obviously much less aware than in the waking states. This is shown by the simple fact that most of us wake up if a loud noise is heard. I found I generally slept better in the higher levels of the Simulation than in lower levels of the Simulation. This may be as simple as the fact that the sleeping delta state was not as big of a jump from my normal waking state.

Sleep and the delta state is a way to go deeper into the wavy universe, restore one's energy, and get orientation from one's Angelic guides if you believe they exist. Many famous scientists and artists used dreams as a source of information and inspiration. Some mystics have learned to function on a limited physical basis while awake in this state. Dr. David Hawkins once calibrated on stage during a lecture that his brain was operating at a brainwave state of 2-3 Hz (Homo Spiritus: Devotional Nonduality 02/2003).

There is another state often mentioned in brainwave state literature called gamma. I have not discussed this one as much, as my knowledge of it is limited. Here humans experience a very high frame rate of over 50fps. This one is the least understood, but humans can enter this for short periods of time.

A phenomenon athletes call 'in the zone' corresponds to this state. Though not an athlete per se, I've experienced this briefly a few times playing sports. Things around you will slow down. This is not due to external reality slowing down, but your vibration moving faster so external reality seems slower relative to yours.

One also has an expanded awareness of everything going on around them and is able to anticipate other's actions better. Everything flows smoothly. I believe certain athletes like Tom Brady and Michael Jordan have the ability to go into this state at critical moments. Not being particularly good at sports in my normal brainwave states, I have entered this gamma state and have been in the zone just enough times to occasionally convince myself I was good at sports.

Observer Effect:

Angelic Takeaway: Weird physics has shown us that when you look at something, you affect it. How much you affect it depends on what level of the Simulation you are operating in. The lower levels of the Simulation exist so entities can experience suffering, war, and all kinds of temporary nonsense for evolutionary purposes, without actually damaging the structure of the universe.

This scientifically studied phenomena is the core of how all true spiritual power manifests. A Quantum Mechanics phrase for a consciousness directly affecting partically reality is 'collapsing the wave function.' If used properly, it can make you sound smarter than you actually are even though it simply means transforming wavy/spiritual reality into a partically/physical reality.

An important thing to note and ties into another chapter on Simulation theory is:

The partically/physical level of the Simulation world has no power on its own or of itself (tested true).

However it tends to symbolize something that is real and has power in the wavy/spiritual world. Souls incarnate into this physical Simulation to evolve and learn lessons. They always find themselves projecting or experiencing the perfect physical reality/hologram to learn a particular lesson or pay back a particular piece of karma (tested true).

Let me give a simplified example. A soul sitting in the heavens in an invulnerable, heavenly wave state would have no way of learning the negative effect one's actions can have on others without affecting the infinitely blissful conditions of the higher Angelic realms (tested true). Most of us on earth realize that things are only truly learned when a bit of hardship is involved.

Upon incarnating in the Simulation, the energy put out to the Simulation by an entity begins reflecting back on it through its external surroundings. The entity experiences the effects of its own energy on a time delay, depending on the level of the Simulation it is operating in. The lower the level of the Simulation, the longer the perceived time lag is between putting energy out and then seeing it show up outside oneself (tested true).

Most of us who have suffered in or been the apparent victim of something outside ourselves would never wish this upon another soul. However, sometimes the opposite happens. A soul who has suffered tends to get bitter and wishes suffering on others. This simply means that the lesson has not completely sunk in, the soul still needs time, and unfortunately more suffering for the lesson to sink in. While the lesson is sinking in, the person will continue to project a negative reality.

On my second deployment in the US Navy while in the depth of suffering, an accident in the plant which I perceived as outside of myself led to increased suffering on my part. Instead of the lesson being learned, I became bitter and further separated myself from others. I wished suffering on those who had made the errors leading to the incident and those who had punished me.

This was because I was not quite ready, and my absolute spiritual low point had not been reached. My soul needed a bit more time for the ultimate lesson of this life to take root. I'd spend the next year sinking even lower away from God, until my psyche was left with no option but to confront a dark part of myself. As soon as the core of the lesson was accepted, which in this case was that ultimate answers came from within and not some illusionary idol outside oneself, the lesson was learned and spiritual recovery initiated.

If one remembers that the outward picturing of the Simulation has no power in itself, once a lesson is learned or a dark truth is accepted, the observer effect immediately goes to work on the Simulation and physical reality often adjusts faster than one expected (tested true).

When one begins noticing this phenomenon, it is observed that certain negative people are constantly collapsing the wave function around them into a negative reality. These poor souls are often referred to by the world as 'losers.'

However, other people are constantly collapsing the wave function around them in a favorable way. These people tend to dance through life, and have the appearance of being lucky to most people around them, who are unfamiliar with this tenets of spirituality and Quantum Mechanics.

One eventually realizes that everyone is just radically who they are and experiencing the effects of their own energy, in a perfect learning and evolutionary process (tested true).

People are also affected by others observing them. This is reason why many have fear of performing in public. An increasing source of societal angst unknown to many is the rapidly increasing number of security cameras (tested true). When in the view of a security camera, the person is actually being observed and affected by everyone who has access to that security camera footage. As the the source of the Simulation is outside of time and causality, the time of the footage actually getting observed is irrelevant to the physics of the Simulation (tested true).

If one wants harder evidence of the observer effect, then I recommend researching 'The Double Slit Experiment.' Discussion of this experiment was cut from this book to keep it a shorter, entertaining read and it's well documented elsewhere.

Masculine and Feminine, the Two Halves of God:

Angelic Takeaway: A long time ago God thought it would be fun to experience itself in two halves inside a Simulation. It split itself into the logical masculine and the loving feminine. All sorts of fun high-jinks and wacky nonsense resulted from this. Generally speaking, the more you function from both the masculine and feminine at once and not try to see the world through the lens of a single one, the easier life becomes.

The masculine and feminine are sometimes referred to as the heart and the mind. They represent the original split from the undifferentiated oneness of God. This is described in the Biblical sense in the allegory of Adam and Eve. The loving, feminine Eve thought it would be a great idea to experience this strange Simulation, but she has had to put up with annoying masculine Adam, trying to get them out of the Simulation ever since.

The higher the level of the Simulation one operates from, the more aligned the masculine and feminine aspects of the person are (tested true). In the highest levels of reality, the masculine and feminine are seen as perfect mirrors of each other, both equally important and necessary. High level entities such Angels see themselves as neither masculine or feminine, even if they temporarily need to take on masculine or feminine roles to help correct imbalances in the Simulation.

Any talk of trying to make the masculine or feminine greater or more important than the other always results in nonsense, as they are perfect divine reflections of one another.

The relationship between the masculine and feminine is best visualized by the holy cross: a symbol of Christianity, one of the world's greatest religions.

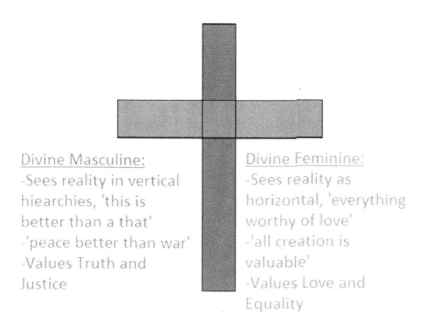

Divine Masculine:
-Sees reality in vertical hiearchies, 'this is better than a that'
-'peace better than war'
-Values Truth and Justice

Divine Feminine:
-Sees reality as horizontal, 'everything worthy of love'
-'all creation is valuable'
-Values Love and Equality

The masculine sees reality in terms of a vertical hierarchy. It sees certain things as better or more desirable than other things. The feminine sees reality in terms of a horizontal hierarchy, where all things are seen as equal: nothing higher than anything else.

A trend well observed in Spiral Dynamics in that the levels of the Simulation alternate broadly in nature between the masculine 'service to self' principle and the feminine 'service to others' principle. This is by divine design, as it makes every level of the Simulation well-equipped to correct the errors arising from the level directly below it.

Both the feminine and masculine levels of the Simulation are important stages in the growth of the soul. As one moves up the levels of the Simulation, the gap between the feminine and masculine extremes closes. The closer aligned the masculine and feminine principles are, the better everything functions.

The bottom Root level of the Simulation is masculine; it organizes life in a vertical hierarchy where pleasurable activities are prioritized over painful activities. This is how the lower stages of life stay alive. Eating is pleasurable, while getting eaten is painful.

The next higher level is the feminine Sacral level. Here, life works together in packs. All members of the pack are protected, assuming they don't start wandering into the ways of another pack. The health of the pack is prioritized well above the accomplishments or development of individual members. Human societies run too heavily by this level of the Simulation have a tenuous existence and often degrade to mob rule, as the less functional members of the pack are given equal say to the stronger more functional members.

Above this is the masculine Solar Plexus level of the Simulation. Here, integrity and doing the right thing is valued. True spiritual power first shows up here, as being integrous aligns with the power of the universe as a whole. This level is still quite physical, however. Mechanical objects that have lost their function and integrity tend to be fixed by this level to restore their function and integrity. Coincidentally, folks who operate heavily from the Solar Plexus level tend to have an amazing talent for fixing things. I've always stood in awe of this talent, as my energy in this life has had a relatively small alignment with the Solar Plexus. This causes my trouble with mechanical inclination and tendency to not follow rules well. No one is perfect.

Next we come to another feminine level, the Heart level of the Simulation. Here what is considered good and loving by the prevailing society becomes the priority. This often takes the form of helping the less fortunate. Some of the most successful teachers and police officers operate from this level, as both professions are geared towards helping society with an emphasis on helping the less fortunate. A problem of this level is the tendency to not use one's energy as efficiently as possible and be a bit too self-sacrificing.

The masculine Throat level tends to solve this self-sacrificing problem by both rewarding and encouraging individual accomplishments. This is the level of traditional science and academic achievement. The grand output from this level of the Simulation is largely motivated by the individual, but tends to wind up providing great service to the whole.

A brilliant quote attributed to the US president John F. Kennedy is a 'rising tide lifts all boats.' This simple statement tends to rectify the Heart and Throat levels well. For society to function optimally, we should try to lift the tide so as to help all of the boats (feminine), not just the ones that are sinking (masculine).

Societies dominated by the achievement-driven Throat still leave some souls behind. The feminine Third Eye sees all reality as connected and lovable. Folks who operate from this level tend to be positive and loving influences wherever they go. However, the rose-colored glasses one views the world from and the ease at which one functions at this level tend to leave one a bit spiritually unaware of the way things actually function in this purgatorial Simulation. The lessons of this level seem to revolve around learning to be loving to all of life, while realizing not everything in this Simulation has your highest good in mind. One learns they can help the drug addict while not taking on the drug habit and surrendering one's individual power.

As we move up into the wavy levels of the Simulation we find the vibrational Crown chakra beginning to channel divine assistance into the Simulation for the benefit of all.

Above this are levels largely beyond earthly comprehension that continue to alternate between the masculine and feminine, but over 99% of the human experience takes place in the levels already mentioned.

In political America, the Republicans traditionally argue for the masculine side of reality and the Democrats argue for the feminine side of reality. Optimal resolutions happen when both sides empathize, see the other perspective, and eventually compromise. Unfortunately, much of American politics is now split over tribal lines. National politics are now dominated by the Sacral level of the Simulation, instead of the Heart and Throat levels that predominate when a government is functioning well.

The split between the masculine and feminine in the physical world shows up quite distinctly when discussing economic systems. The masculine tend to trend towards systems that reward individual entities for achievement, with capitalism coming out of the masculine Throat level of the Simulation and being the flagship of masculine economics. The feminine tends to trend towards systems that equally distributes wealth so that no one is left behind, with socialism being the flagship of feminine economics.

In traditional America, our economic system functioned very well as it helped produce one of the wealthiest and most powerful nations to ever exist. Its economy functioned broadly masculine, with the Capitalism principle being dominant. However it still allowed feminine systems such as free public education, churches, and charities to operate strongly to help fill in the wealth gaps created by the masculine system. Systems that allow both the masculine and feminine to function strongly tend to be the most successful.

In economic systems, as with reality, the closer the masculine and feminine are allowed to work together the more power becomes available; everything tends to operate more efficiently. The bottom two levels of the Simulation tend to have the masculine and feminine working in opposition to each other.

It should be noted that economic systems such as Marxism that come out of the Sacral level of the Simulation tend to actually penalize the high achievers of society in an attempt to force equality. Marxist systems are disastrous in the long-run. History clearly shows this.

However, as one rises through the levels of the Simulation, the gaps between the masculine and feminine principle close and they tend to work in concert with one another with both respecting the other's role. In the highest levels of the Simulation, the two principles are seen as reflections of one another and entities tend to contain nearly equal qualities of both.

Another way of visualizing the masculine and feminine is with the following graphic:

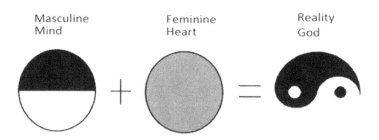

The mind or masculine looks at reality as black and white. It classifies certain things as better than others. The heart or feminine sees all creation as equally gray and worthy. It is when these two fundamental aspects of consciousness are integrated that we see reality clearest and God shows up. Functional masculine energy contains a bit of feminine and functional feminine energy contains a bit of masculine. This is symbolized by the yin-yang symbol.

Most scales of consciousness/development including Spiral Dynamics, Dr. David Hawkin's numbered scale, and the chakra system presented in this book are traditionally laid out vertically, with the lower vibrations on the bottom and the higher vibrations at the top. This is the best way to lay it out as to make sense to a logical masculine mind. This book, which draws heavily from all these masculine scales, came through a male body so it is broadly masculine in energy. However, I hope I defend the feminine principle enough and emphasize that both the feminine and masculine are equally important in creation.

The masculine scales of consciousness and the way I laid out the levels of Simulation creates a subtle illusion that the higher levels are better because it's a vertical hierarchy. This is partially true. I do prefer charity workers over child molesters. Happiness is much greater in the higher levels of the Simulation, with suffering beyond comprehension in the lower levels of the Simulation.

However, particularly where society is concerned, higher is not strictly better. I personally functioned best on the worldly level when able to operate from multiple levels of the Simulation. All levels of the Simulation contribute to the panorama of life in their own perfect way. The Root and Solar Plexus are likely most useful in a fight, the Sacral and Heart are most useful with one's family, and the Third Eye and Crown are most useful for spiritual comprehension. It can seem silly to say that material on Channel 7 is better than the material on Channel 3 simply because the number is higher.

Evolutionarily speaking, it's clear life evolves from the lower levels of the Simulation to the higher levels of the Simulation where life gradually gets calmer, more loving, and more enjoyable. However, all the levels are necessary. A basic understanding of ecology shows that life on this planet would not exist without single-celled organisms, but only the most ardent Marxist would argue that those single-celled organisms are ready for a university education. Each level of life clearly plays an important role in the overall thrust of life in this dimension.

With this in mind, one could just easily lay out any integrous scale of consciousness and development horizontally in a feminine way, as it is clear no level of life is strictly better. No one looks at a rainbow and says that the green light is better than the purple light. All the feminine levels of the Simulation attempt to do this in their own way. The downside of this view is the post-modern trap of living a life of 'anything goes.' The soul left completely directionless can end up in ghastly places.

One can even demonstrate the advantage of aligning the feminine and masculine using basic vector multiplication and geometry.

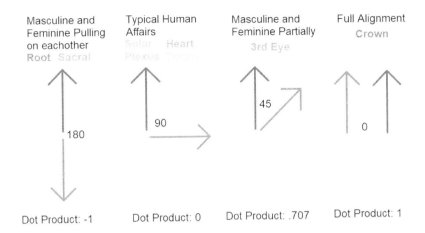

In the first picture we find the broad situation that we find in the bottom two levels of the Simulation. The two fundamental energies of the Simulation are pulling on one another.

The Dot Product is simply a way of multiplying vectors and is beyond the scope of the book but just ask a nerd friend or google it, you can probably get it. The Dot Product of vectors 180 degrees out-of-alignment is −1, meaning the result is negative and will eventually lead to war, violence, and all manner of bad things.

In the next picture we see the state of affairs Jesus observed in normal human activity, which seems to be broadly typical of the Solar Plexus, Heart, and Throat levels of the Simulation. The masculine is trying to advance society and achieve. It views reality vertically. The feminine is constantly trying to even things out. It views reality horizontally. Together, they form a cross. In this situation the dot product is zero. This is just how humans operate at this level, and no power advantage is gained.

As we move into the higher levels, the actions of the masculine and feminine become increasingly aligned. When they are only 45 degrees out of phase we find the Dot Product jumps to .707 which gives us some serious power to work with for the betterment of all things.

In the highest divine levels of the Simulation, the masculine and feminine work together harmoniously and no longer oppose each other. A matter of fact any difference between them is seen to be illusionary. Completely in-phase, the dot product is at its maximum value so power and efficiency are maximized.

The Heisenberg Uncertainty Principle applies also to the masculine and feminine (tested true).

The Heisenberg Uncertainty Principle, stated in very basic terms, is, "The more we know the exact position of an object, the less we know its momentum. The more we know the exact momentum of an object, the less we know its position."

This can be restated as, "The more you try to understand the universe completely in terms of the masculine the less you understand the feminine, the more you try to understand the universe completely in terms of the feminine, the less you understand the masculine.

Here, a subtle illusion presents itself that creates problems in the world. As one gains a better understanding of reality through a feminine or heart lens (the position of the object), the more one fails to see the masculine or mind lens (the momentum of the object). Therefore, one operates with a distorted view of reality.

The reverse is also true. As one gains a better understanding of reality through a masculine or mind lens (the momentum of the object), the more one fails to see the feminine (the position of the object). Therefore, one operates with a distorted view of reality.

This Heisenberg principle can actually be applied to any duality or pair of opposites (tested true).

A healthy view of the universe corresponds to the Buddha's 'Middle Way' which means seeing the universe equally in terms of both the masculine and feminine at once. One's view shouldn't skew toward the masculine or feminine extreme; one sees the clearest with a moderate view.

A common saying is "What does not bend is likely to break." I've observed this in every social system I've been involved in, from companies, schools, families, and the military. The masculine likes to set up linear structures, with strict black and white rules. The feminine, with its all-gray view of reality, tends to know where the rules can bend safely to relieve pressure.

In both the masculine and feminine extremes, structure tends to break down completely. A structure that cannot bend will eventually break when it meets a larger force, and there always is a larger force.

A masculine structure that integrates the wisdom of the feminine will actually be stronger. This is visually shown when a powerful storm hits a forest. It's not the unbendable hardwood trees that tend to survive the worst storms, but the trees that bend a little in the wind.

The world tends to swing from masculine extreme to a feminine extreme over great periods of time. The masculine extreme tends to result in war, and the feminine extreme tends to lead to anarchy and lawlessness. The peaceful good times tend to happen between these extremes. The Buddha gave us his advice 2600 years ago to follow the middle path, which seems to be what humans do during the good times.

Addictive Chemicals:

Angelic Takeaway: "Don't do Drugs." Even though this is my advice, I know reality is far more complex than this simple advice can comprehend. Addictive chemicals don't have any true power but can only temporarily rev up or block certain chakras, often leading to a temporary higher state. Karma still applies, so any high will eventually be met with a corresponding equal and opposite low.

First and foremost, I must make a statement that my personal calibration research has revealed over and over again:

Addictive substances or drugs have NO power in and of themselves (tested true).

They only have the power we give them and can only temporarily manipulate the chemistry of the body, which alters the levels of the Simulation we temporarily experience.

An even more important understanding is that use of addictive chemicals still falls under the purview of karma. Whatever temporarily high is experienced will eventually be matched by an equal and opposite low (tested true).

In the long-run, no real gain tends to come from them other than a temporary boost, which must be paid back; or a bit of higher insight, which comes at a steep cost.

In this chapter I'll discuss the three addictive chemicals I've used in this life and the effects they had on my chakra system. The three chemicals are caffeine, alcohol, and THC (the most psycho-active compound in Marijuana). All three have had a broadly negative effect on my life, but as nothing happens by accident, they all played a role in my personal evolution that my earthly mind will never fully comprehend (tested true).

Caffeine: This chemical fires up the nervous system, which gives the Root chakra a temporary boost that must be paid back at some point (tested true).

I began using caffeine regularly in college. In college, the energy reserves that my Crown chakra had come into this world with at birth were running dry. Energy was becoming harder and harder to come by. I was in an academically demanding program with all the normal stresses of college. This was compounded by the fact that I was acting primarily from the Solar Plexus chakra, so I was very interested in physical fitness and expending enormous energy at the gym.

I began using caffeine pre-workout so the physical body would have more energy to burn. This did give me a temporary boost in the fitness world, but took a toll everywhere else. What I did not realize at the time was that the caffeine was not giving me energy, but allowing my Root chakra to draw from my depleting energy reserves at a faster rate.

Eventually, I was needing caffeine to get started in the morning. I was using my Root chakra's energy faster than it could be replenished, which caused its energy to gradually drop.

Out of sheer exhaustion, I began using caffeine before classes and studying to rev myself up. This was counterproductive as I was studying electrical engineering, which required higher thought.

Caffeine revs up the survival Root chakra which gives the reptilian nervous system more energy but not the higher chakras where it was actually needed for study of complex phenomena. On caffeine I became better at rote memorization and habitualized math but broadly worse in all other academic categories.

Towards the end of college I realized caffeine was doing more harm than good, so I spent a trimester quitting it. I was extremely tired and miserable during this trimester and it was my worst academically-performing trimester in college.

Over the next decades I'd tend to begin using again when the stresses of life and spiritual development put energy at a premium. A temporary boost was always provided, but it always took a long-term toll.

However, caffeine need not be demonized. Many people use it in moderation, and research on a single cup of coffee in the morning is broadly positive. This may give a Root chakra of some people a pleasurable startle to come out of sleep faster. Then the cost of this startle is gradually repaid throughout the day so is hardly noticeable.

Alcohol: Alcohol blocks out the input from the Root and Sacral chakras temporarily (tested true). In extreme use, it will eventually block out the input from all the chakras. The result is a blackout.

A blackout is a temporary experience of the void or absence of any experience. This is a state that many Buddhists strive for, which is achievable (tested true). However this is far from the ultimate state—even though it is often confused as the ultimate state—as nothing feels way better than suffering.

An alcohol-induced blackout will feel temporarily good to a suffering soul. But with all addictive chemicals, the karma of an artificial high must eventually be repaid, so when the person wakes up, their suffering will be even worse. This is often referred to as a hangover.

I began drinking alcohol in the military at first due to peer-pressure, then later as a desperate attempt to relieve suffering.

By the time I was in the military, my Crown chakra's energy was below 200 (negativity aligned) so my existence was experienced as primarily suffering.

In early drinking, I found I could block the input from my Root chakra (which had been weakened due to caffeine use) and the tribal Sacral chakra, which caused me to not see enemies across perceived tribal lines. This allowed me to primarily experience my empowering Solar Plexus chakra and my developing Heart chakra. The result was that I was fun at parties, loved everyone temporarily, and had my first success with the opposite sex.

However this was relatively short-lived. As this temporary high felt so much better than my primary state, addiction came on fast and furious. As I drank more, my core spiritual state fell so I felt worse without alcohol in my system. Over time, I needed more alcohol to spend less time in the temporarily elevated state.

Drinking eventually transitioned from a party and meet-girls-activity to a blackout-alone-activity to escape suffering.

During my military time I quit a few times, which always seemed to have a positive effect. However, drinking would always re-ignite when a trying event such as a breakup or deployment would occur.

At the end of my military service, I attended a wonderful alcohol rehab program. Though the alcohol abstinence would not stick, it was a great help beginning my spiritual journey. This began the re-energizing of my Crown chakra and faith in God, which was the ultimate solution to my drinking problem.

Similar to caffeine, research on a single drink in the evening can be positive. If one has a stressful job, this may allow one to temporarily forget the tiredness and stress of the day from the Root chakra, as well as grudges and interpersonal issues from the Sacral chakra. The karma is likely repaid the next day at work when one must deal with these inconvenient karmic issues anyway.

THC: This chemical has recently become legal in many parts of the United States. It blocks out the input from the Root, Sacral, Solar Plexus, and Throat chakras, leaving only the Heart, Third Eye, and Crown relatively unimpaired (tested true).

The impairment from this chemical gives us a person who is generally loving and spiritual, but far less functional in the physical Simulation. Unfortunately many pothead stereotypes tend to be true.

I only used this substance once before it became legal in my home state. This came when I visited a fringe acquaintance for an outdoor party.

Upon arriving, I recall thinking that I was the only true adult at the party. As the night wore on, many drugs were being used and bedlam predictably broke out. Now feeling a bit like a lame babysitter, I accepted an offer of marijuana. Having never used it, my tolerance was low and I probably took a bit too much.

At the time my Heart, Third Eye, and Crown chakras were all operating at a relatively low level, so when I began to lose input from the remaining four, panic struck as I comprehended that I was in an unsafe place, and quickly losing the faculties that would allow me to respond to an emergency.

I ended up locking myself in my car and praying that no police showed up. I spent the night writing pages and pages of notes about spirituality and Angels, which was COMPLETELY out of context at the time.

I left the party very early in the morning as soon as I'd regained my physical faculties. I decided then that marijuana had been a mistake. This decision would hold until it became legal in my home state, which re-ignited my curiosity.

When it became legal in my local area, THC oil became an occasional pleasurable activity which was only done in moderation. I found meditation and prayer more effective and spiritual music enjoyed on a deeper level.

An obvious result of my Angelic experience in December of 2019 was a massive upgrade of my Third Eye and Crown chakras. This is when addiction to the chemical began to rear its ugly head.

Now the blocking out of the lower chakras gave me a temporary ecstatic Angelic experience. On THC I'd temporarily enter Angelic realms beyond the comprehension of my early life and the vast majority of humans.

However, I'd not escaped karma, so these highs were matched with truly hellish lows.

When under the influence of the THC, I'd temporarily escape the limitations of the physical body but after the effect had worn off, I'd sink deeper into the limitations of the physical body. I gained a lot of weight during this period. When the effect wore off, I would be unable to resist my body's urge to virtually eat itself to death.

Higher spiritual insight did come during this period, but I was so physically impaired that it was integrated extremely slowly. At one point, I was so out of balance that my Crown chakra was strong but all six of my lower chakras were negatively aligned. The result was a human being who was only interested in lying in bed praying, and had lost all interest in any other aspects of life.

Over a long period of time, I was able to taper off THC and re-balance my life. However this was tough process as it became intuitively obvious that I was repaying the stolen THC highs with a constant dull spiritual low and some ghastly dark nights.

Moderate use of THC is minimally harmful, and when used as a pain-killer has advantages over many of the commonly used pharmaceutical drugs.

Past Lives:

Angelic Takeaway: You don't generally win video games your first time playing. The players in this Angel-evolving Simulation game don't master it in a single lifetime either. We evolve in this Simulation by seeing life from many perspectives in many different bodies. Karma and lessons carry between these different lives.

As one learns the nature of past lives, all the apparent injustice of the world melts away. One realizes everyone is experiencing the effects of their own energy.

Sidenote: Be extremely careful and nuanced if you choose to talk to others about this. I pray that this is a truth that everyone who finds this book is ready for. For example, it would simply be extremely out-of-context and quite cruel to tell an abused child that they are experiencing the effects of their own karma.

I have many people in my current life with whom I've shared past lives with. A few of them know, but generally when I ask my calibration process if it's in the highest good for me to share the past life memory with them, I get 'no.'

Past lives are temporarily forgotten for a reason, and they reveal themselves in perfect timing when a soul is ready. Often the first remnants of past-life memories are noticed by a person in a joking, non-serious fashion. A recurring pattern is noticed in one's current life, and the person will eventually say jokingly, "Wow, I must have been so and so in a past life." Strangely, these light-hearted jokes often turn out to be the truth.

When a body dies, the non-physical part of the individual (the soul) follows a buoyancy-like principle, finding itself in a new body. It will be in a perfect situation for the resolution of its karma and lessons appropriate to its current level of evolution.

Traditional Christianity tells us that a soul that committed good actions during a life goes to heaven, and the soul that commits bad actions during a life goes to hell. In essence this is correct, but the reality is less binary than that. There are not only two places to go after death, but infinite variations of places to go between the two extreme states of heaven and hell.

Traditional Christianity was founded during a time when the average human soul on earth was far less evolved than they are now, so this simplified model of reality was appropriate for its time and place, still holding value for many souls.

In my personal past life research, my soul always incarnated into a body and situation at the Simulation level that it found itself in at the conclusion of the previous lifetime. The situation I was born into was not always celestial, but always perfect for the evolution of my soul at the time.

There was generally a period of between three and fifteen years between incarnations, which provides a period of rest, free of a physical body. This rest/review period is needed because the purgatorial nature of this Simulation makes it challenging, even under the best of circumstances. This purgatorial nature is by divine design, so all possible energies exist together in order to provide nearly infinite options for the soul to have maximum evolutionary potential.

About every twenty human Earth lifetimes, a soul gains access to a higher level of the Simulation (tested true). If you are reading this book, you are probably on a very fast-track of evolution (tested true).

Sam Bellamy:

Angelic Takeaway: In the early 1700s, I met a beautiful lady on Cape Cod, Massachusetts who was way out of my league. I decided to become a pirate to impress her, which was probably a bad idea. After causing all sorts of mischief on the seas, karma caught up with me and I got myself killed before I could get back to my beautiful Cape Cod lady-friend. I've been paying the giant karmic bill, since events from our current life tend to be a reflection of our past lives.

My personal past lives are not the focus of this book, but I've been guided to share this one in particular. This was one of the first ones that I have recalled in detail, and provides many good opportunities to illustrate the concepts in this book. I'll share a particular instance where I was a pirate during the Golden Age of piracy, named Sam Bellamy, also known as Black Sam or the Prince of Pirates.

73% of the historical record on Sam Bellamy is correct (tested true). I have no interest in trying to correct the historical record or 'prove' that I was Sam Bellamy. Calibration also shows that this would not be in the highest good. Most of the historical errors are minor factual details that do not interfere with an understanding of the general thrust of the man's life. In this section I will be very light on the partically details of the life and concentrating on how this life relates to the subject material of this book.

In April of 2021, I was drawn to a Netflix documentary called *The Lost Pirate Kingdom*. I binged the entire six-part series and was particularly drawn to the character Sam Bellamy. This also began a fascination with pirate culture, which had actually repulsed me up to that point in this life (not a coincidence).

Through synchronicity, the Angels slowly began revealing bits of truth to me. In August of 2021, in a hypnotic state, I recalled the lifetime in significant detail. The initial reaction was positive and the individual self swelled up with pride at the idea of having played the role of a famous pirate. However over the next months the painful, darker details of this life and the karmic disasters came into focus.

During this lifetime I was born in the late 1600s in the British Isles. I came into that lifetime operating from the Third Eye level of the Simulation. I had a very strong faith in God and wanted what was best and most loving for those around me. I eventually left my native home due to disagreements with the religious authorities, which is quite common when operating from the Third Eye level of the Simulation.

When operating from the Third Eye level of the Simulation, one has significant power and influence. In addition, I was relatively balanced in the lower chakras so was still functioning quite strongly on a worldly level. A danger of operating from the higher chakras is one can begin ignoring the lower chakras (as they don't feel as good) and lose interest in the mundane details of everyday life, which can lead to withdrawal from the world. This very thing happened briefly during this life after my Angelic experience in December of 2019.

In that life, I became involved in a number of business ventures and eventually sailed to present-day America. Early life was characterized by a great success, especially when considering my low-social stature at the time and difficult life conditions of the times and professions I was in.

At one point, I found myself on a merchant ship with a very cruel captain. As conditions on seafaring ships at the time were quite horrific under even the absolute best of circumstances, I was left with a very bad taste in my mouth about merchant captains. This would be a contributor to the decision of becoming a pirate.

Eventually my journey led me to Cape Cod, Massachusetts, where I met the absolutely beautiful Maria Hallett and a very intense romance began. Both Sam and Maria were operating heavily from the higher levels of the Simulation. A characteristic of these levels is one tends to be very attractive to others and falls in love easily, so a romance between the two was destined.

This short but intense romance was complicated by the fact that Maria occupied a higher social and financial station than Sam did, and her father did not approve.

At this point, with the help of good friend Paulsgrave Williams, I saw my best option was to take to the seas to make a fortune in order to be with my Beloved. Unknown to me at the time was that Maria was pregnant with my child, which would eventually add to the karmic complications of this life.

The details of Sam Bellamy's short but very successful pirating career are documented elsewhere, but success came quickly as I was operating at a high level of the Simulation, so I had significant power at my disposal. As the original intention of taking to the seas was noble, early endeavors were generally successful, especially when my inexperience were considered.

During an early salvage operation, I hired Black and Indian divers and was confused as to why the others I was working with were extremely hostile to the idea. This was a significant challenge of this lifetime as when operating from a high level of the Simulation, certain concepts like greed, racism, and cruelty are not prominent in one's consciousness. However, difficulties occur when it is encountered in others and one does not understand why others have these undesirable characteristics and don't see their obvious fallacy. In general, pirates are not a very evolved lot and tend to display these characteristics regularly.

When the actual pirating career began, success came fast and furious. As I was literally operating from a higher level of the Simulation than the merchant captains I was raiding, it was easy to anticipate their actions and ultimately outwit them.

Unfortunately, pirating is at best a morally ambiguous profession. As my fame, crew, and influence grew, I began making more and more immoral decisions out of alignment with my core beliefs from the Third Eye level and strong faith in God.

As a result, as my worldly power grew, my personal power waned, and I remember feeling less happy. This is known as a Luciferic Fall in which one gives up their spiritual power and integrity in exchange for empty worldly power. During my pirating career, I lost my wings (tested true).

I remember my motivation early on in the pirating career from the Third Eye was the love for Maria Hallet.

It was later felt to be the most reasonable and logical thing to do in order to be with my beloved while doing good in the world when I'd dropped into the logical Throat level.

It then dropped into being a fun, heroic adventure in which the nickname Prince of Pirates was taken to heart as I dropped into the Heart level.

Even later it became a mission to rid the sea of cruel, corrupt merchant captains abusing their crews when I'd dropped to the Solar Plexus level.

Finally the decision to raze a captured merchant ship dropped me into the Sacral level of the Simulation where one has an almost complete lack of spiritual power. I was then hit by a storm (not a coincidence) and perished before I could return to my beloved.

The lifetimes between the Sam Bellamy lifetime and the one I'm currently in have largely been about paying back the giant karmic debt from the Samuel Bellamy life.

This fall was the ultimate lesson of this lifetime. At no point during this fall did I consider myself evil. I was always doing what I thought was right at the time. The takeaway from this experience and the successive karmic recovery was how easy it is to get mixed up down here and completely lose track of truth. This tough lesson has ultimately made forgiveness in successive lifetimes easier.

When the lifetime was first recalled I was romantically entangled with a beautiful young lady. The mind immediately made the error of thinking she had been Maria Hallett in the early 1700s. But as God has a sense of humor, the real Maria Hallett was actually an ex-girlfriend of mine whom I'd shared an overwhelmingly loving but extremely tumultuous relationship with.

It was only days later (not a coincidence) that the aforementioned ability to calibrate using a pendulum appeared and I quickly ascertained the truth. The current romantic relationship collapsed and the relationship with the woman who was Maria Hallett in the 1700s bloomed again, as loving and tumultuous as ever. Through a lot of pain on both ends, the karma was resolved. Both myself and the former Maria Hallett were free to spiritually evolve without the karmic anchor which had weighed us both down for hundreds of years.

When one begins recalling past lives or doing past life research, it becomes very clear that souls tend to travel through time and co-evolve together in different bodies and scenarios. It also becomes clear that often your adversaries are also your greatest loves on the other side. I like to call these "soul frenemies." You show up in each other's lives throughout time when a difficult lesson must be learned and often play an adversarial role for the benefit of both. This is most efficiently done with a soul that you love dearly deep down. The former Maria Hallett has been in my life for over 2600 years and is a love of the highest order.

This book also largely stands on the shoulders of the late Dr. David Hawkins in whom a similar relationship exists. The former Maria Hallet tended to show up when a star-crossed romance was needed for a difficult soul lesson. Dr. David Hawkins tended to show up when a fierce adversary was needed, and we often found each other on opposite ends of a war. Other souls from the Sam Bellamy lifetime have been encountered in this current lifetime.

Shortly after recalling the Sam Bellamy lifetime, acquaintances in this lifetime were intuitively recognized as the same souls I'd encountered during it.

Paulgrave Williams, who'd helped me in the Samuel Bellamy lifetime happened to be a friend in this lifetime also (tested true).

A minor acquaintance who had always given me the willies and an unexplainable eerie feeling was revealed to be the infamously sadistic pirate Charles Vane.

I noticed an immediate affinity with a student who had a positive personality and wonderful sense of humor who often found himself in trouble, but never with me. He was intuitively sensed as a member of my crew in the Sam Bellamy lifetime (tested true). He was now a more evolved version of the person I'd shared a ship with during the early 1700s, but core characteristics and even mannerisms were in common. Karmic research has revealed that in my years of teaching, four other pirates from my crews have miraculously shown up in my classroom as students (tested true).

Two cousins whom I was very close to growing up (one a merchant marine captain) and lost touch with after the Angelic spiritual experiences put my world upside down were remembered as people from the Sam Bellamy life. This actually provided an interesting conversation starter to get back into each other's lives. In the first time seeing one of these cousins after the karma of the Sam Bellamy lifetime had been processed, we took her boat out onto the ocean and I had one of my first pleasant days on the ocean in over 300 years. Our common grandfather was an Angel in a human body (tested true).

In this lifetime I was an officer in the US Navy. By no fault of the US Navy or the people around me, this was the darkest period of this life. Part of this darkness was a subjective paying back of karma from the Sam Bellamy lifetime (tested true).

Negative experiences on the ocean and on boats have been common in this lifetime.

The lifetime directly after the Sam Bellamy lifetime I set out on a ship at the age of fifteen, which sank almost immediately as my karma associated with the sea at the time was truly horrific (tests true).

My trips to Cape Cod of Massachusetts in this lifetime were never enjoyed, even if I was visiting the cape for an enjoyable purpose like a engagement party or a family vacation.

If one is interested in learning more about Sam Bellamy's life, my two recommendations are the two main sources I was drawn to.

The aforementioned Netflix documentary *The Lost Pirate Kingdom,* comes out of 'Heart' level and gives an enthusiastic fun look at the era. Minor historical inaccuracies exist, but are nothing to get our panties in a twist about. The documentary was blast to watch and captures the overall feel and history of the era extremely well.

The book, *Memoirs of Captain Sam Bellamy* by John Boyd comes out of the reasonable Throat level. This book represents the best effort one can make to accurately tell Sam Bellamy's story using historical evidence.

The Ego Program:

Angelic Takeaway: We all have a cute pet which follows us around wherever we go. It lives primarily in the Root and Sacral chakras and is the remnants of our animal consciousness from prior stages of evolution. It is the program which helps us interface with physical reality. It is the primary cause of suffering, but once understood one can have fun with it and realize it's just a survival program. Don't let it bite the mailman.

At the onset of the evolution of life on Earth, life would have been very simple and consisting of single-celled organisms. Due to a lack of complex biological machinery and the harsh conditions of early Earth, the consciousness of these organisms would be programmed for survival only, and would need to seek energy outside of itself for sustenance while avoiding a host of dangers.

This is the evolutionary roots of the ego program, the code we use to interface with this Simulation. A single-celled organism would have a very primitive ego program wired for survival only and wouldn't have the capacity for higher logic, love, spirituality, and would live a very simple existence completely in the lower regions of the Root chakra level of the Simulation.

These evolutionary roots of the ego still linger in human existence and is the dominant part of the psyche when operating from the Root or Sacral levels of the Simulation. It seeks to acquire energy outside itself and functions completely inside the partically constructs of the Simulation, lacking higher intelligence of its own. It was and is a necessary step in the evolutionary process, but after a certain point in evolution, its limitations become apparent. The eastern concept of enlightenment is the escape from the clutches of the ego program (tested true).

The important thing to realize about the ego program is that it is not the real you. It is just computer code you use to interface with this Simulation. The real you exists as a soul or a wave far above it. At the evolutionary stage of most of the readers of this book, the ego is simply a program that helps keep you alive in this dimension inside an animal body. This is even a subtle illusion, as our moment to moment existence is dependent on divinity, the ego is just extremely good at taking credit and congratulating itself (tested true).

Any manipulation of the body or processing of the physical senses happens through the animal software of the ego. Even though it's not the real you, you are still responsible for getting it trained, not letting it control you or pee on the carpet. This is a gradual process that takes many lifetimes.

The ego program provides fear-based data to the soul which is useful in the animal world when trying to survive, but often counter-productive in the modern world as it's not necessarily aligned with ultimate truth and can be wrong.

If on a dark path at night, the ego program may attempt warn the soul of a danger lurking behind a tree. It may be wrong nine out of ten times but the soul will be thankful for the one correct warning.

However in the complex modern world, these fear-based reports may be problematic if focused on the results of an academic test already taken or what a potential romantic partner is up to a Friday night.

Native Americans and some other cultures grasped that we do indeed have an animal interface. They refer to this as our spirit animal. Souls in human bodies are often souls that have graduated from the wild animal world but still have a bit of the wild animal essence from their earlier animal stages of evolution. These characteristics survive and manifest in certain traits associated with common lines of animal evolution (tested true).

My spirit animal is a wolf. In my personal narrative I recount a story of how I found this out while in Las Vegas. Many of my personal characteristics bear resemblance to this. I'm protective of those I love, value freedom, will fight if backed into a corner, and get along well with dogs. These traits are in accord with others who consider their spirit animal a wolf. I've also always enjoyed wolf art and have very vague memories of being in a wolf-like body many eons ago.

In reality, we live in a divinely perfect reality where all karma is flowing perfectly, and God is creating ever more beautiful things through his Angels. Unfortunately the ego notices none of this, because it is concerned with keeping the physical body alive. It can only draw energy by creating problems that need the soul's attention.

The absolute worst fear of the ego program is an enlightened soul that is happy, no matter what is going on. Interfaced with a soul like this, It would have no way to distort reality to create an illusion of a problem. Enlightened beings often disturb typical earthly beings when they reveal they have no preference for the life or death of the physical body. The illusion that life is actually dependent on the 'alive' status of the physical body is the ego illusion that underlies them all (tested true). In the chapter called "Laws of Conservation" I talk about the law of conservation of life, which tells us our core essence is actually invulnerable to the ups and downs of physical existence.

The ego program does all its enormously complex functions in about 1/10,000th of a second (tested true). The picture of reality that we see and feel with the body's senses is the ego's distorted problem-laden version of reality. Just beyond it, existing just before this 1/10,000th of a second gap is a beautiful reality, stripped of all distortions and illusions.

The acronym "EGO" stands for "edging god out." We all find ourselves in a divinely perfect Simulation which is evolving us exactly as it should. When fully interfaced with the divine, reality is beautiful and nothing is sought from the external world of the Simulation. The ego survives by distorting reality to create an illusion of a problem, which is how it siphons off energy to stay powered.

The tiny soul inside a single-celled organism would be perfectly happy to sit at the bottom of a pond just soaking in the essence of the universe. However, life insists on evolution, and in order to do that it must seek outside itself to keep the Simulation moving. The primitive ego of this tiny organism completely in the Root chakra level of the Simulation would create an unpleasant sensation called pain when the single celled organism was lacking food, and a pleasant sensation called pleasure when the organism found food. This creates movement in the Simulation so it can serve its evolutionary purpose of evolving higher life forms called Angels (tested true)

As life evolves, these ego programs get more and more complex. Behaviors to avoid pain and feel pleasure become complex survival behaviors. As life advanced and the earth got more crowded, a set behavior was coded in to avoid enemies. Hence, the primitive 'flight or fight' response.

Souls experiencing life in these simple organisms would have slowly increased in awareness and eventually be able to occupy the higher levels of the Simulation. Here they learned how to function with others, create tools, and eventually learn computer programming to create their own Simulations.

The ego functions a bit like a set of slider bars distorting reality so that the soul moves around and does things in the Simulation in order to evolve further. Remember the Simulation is actually perfect and would chug along fine with or without our help, but in order to keep the individual soul evolving, the ego creates the illusion of problems to be fixed.

Karma plays out as egos with opposite distortions tend to come into contact with each other and souls often alternate in ego distortions between lifetimes. In back-to-back lifetimes I fought in the Crusades as a Muslim and a Christian. In these two lifetimes I had opposite ego distortions in regards to religion (tested true).

This is a super simplified version of the ego slider bar with no pre-programmed data.

EGO: Interface with physical reality

No Ego Position

Evolution	———————————	Creation
Democrat	———————————	Republican
Optimism	———————————	Pessimism
Patriotic	———————————	Unpatriotic
Anal-Retentive	———————————	Disorganized
Controlling	———————————	Libertarian

Here is the ego slider bar that I was programmed with as a result of my childhood experiences and previous life karma. As I've aged, these sliders have gradually slid towards the middle of these bars, leading to less ego distortion. Following the Buddha's middle path leads to less and less ego distortion and was the core of his teachings (tested true).

EGO: Interface with physical reality

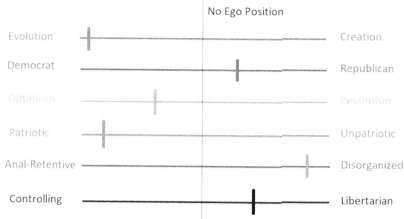

In my youth, I favored science over religion and was a strict evolutionist. I was raised in a family that leaned slightly politically right. I was generally optimistic, patriotic, disorganized, and had a libertarian 'live and let live' attitude which was common in the geographical area of Maine I grew up in at the time.

While using my phone's built-in photo editor I noticed that it utilizes slider bars. Here are three pictures of my dog from three positions on the same slider bar. Three different people may look at my dog and see the same image three different ways.

Aside: Psychic ability and ego distortion.

The dog pictured above called Buddy has a common genetic defect common in Labs, which causes their hunger switch to not turn off so they are always hungry. This dog has leveraged this defect into genuine psychic ability, in which he seemingly magically senses food.

Whenever anyone thinks of eating, Buddy shows up like a genie with a smile on his face in that room. I've conducted crude tests, simply holding in mind the image of food, and Buddy magically appears. My more skeptical dad has observed this too, but always seems to have some scientific sense-based explanation of how buddy just knew food was about to be consumed. Our different conclusion on buddy's ability based on the observation of the same reality is an example of different ego-distortions. My ego trends more towards abstract spiritual reality and my father's more towards concrete sense-based reality.

End Aside.

Part of the fundamental programming of the Simulation is to draw opposite ego positions together to balance karma. In the lowest levels of the Simulation this often results in war. A bit higher it results in romantic love, as two opposite egos come together to balance their extremes. Sexual orgasm feels good because one is temporarily feeling reality with less ego distortion, as two opposite ego programs temporarily cancel each other (tested true). At the highest levels, souls see their personal ego distortions, and mutual cooperation is agreed upon in order to evolve. This is actually a higher form of love than romantic, and without the fireworks and drama.

A helpful technique that is recommended by multiple spiritual teachers is giving the ego a name and viewing it as a helpful pet needing to be trained, which isn't far from the truth. I've named mine 'Scooby' after the famous cartoon dog. It has a mischievous sense of humor, means well, and would rather hang out in the van and let others do the real work.

Scooby has a deep seated sense of rebellion. Whenever an authority figure has told it that something was absolutely unacceptable, it became the exact thing Scooby wanted to do. This is simply Scooby's way of responding to force and balancing its karma.

A principle of this book is "force creates counter-force." The harder an external authority has tried to exert its authority over Scooby with force, the harder Scooby pushed to break free. Many egos have this trait, which is why authoritarian governments always fall eventually.

If you are a scientist, one could think of Scooby as the part of my consciousness associated with my physical body and animal instincts. It is mostly centered in my brainstem. It is not me, but part of me while the physical body stays alive.

If in private contemplation or with developed spiritual friends, this technique of naming the ego in order to train it and eventually dis-identify with it is very helpful. If interfacing with the general public, it will likely get you diagnosed with a multiple personality disorder.

To function optimally in a worldly capacity, an ego is needed even if one understands it isn't the real 'you' but just a fancy survival software package.

Seeing reality as it is would simply overwhelm many souls with its beauty so it is filtered through an ego that only seems to note things that agree with its pre-existing ideas about reality and current stage of evolution. There is no point in trying to teach first graders college level calculus. Temporary peak spiritual experiences called 'Satori' are sneak previews of a higher level of the Simulation which provide a soul with a direction for evolution. These are karmically earned (tested true). My spiritual experience in December 2019, which was a genesis of this book, was a sneak preview of direct experience of Crown chakra level of the Simulation, which had only been experienced sporadically to that point in life.

As one evolves, one learns that dropping all ego positions does tend to make you seem a bit odd. There are certain ego positions that virtually all people considered sane by the world tend to have. "Being rich is better than being poor," "The physical body is important," "Death of the physical body is bad," and so on.

With nuance, one learns to tentatively accept these common ego positions, at least for the purposes of everyday conversation, without assigning them absolute reality over oneself. Part of spiritual evolution in the higher levels of the Simulation is learning to act in a way that does not increase the fear and worry of those around you.

The weirder folks reading this who enjoyed socializing with other weird kindred spirits may have played Dungeons and Dragons. It is a tabletop role-playing game where players create an imaginary character, and play this character in an imaginary world. The world is controlled by a player called the Dungeon Master (DM), using a fairly complex set of rules and dice.

A useful analogy for the nerds who have played and enjoyed this game (including myself) would be that the soul/wave is the 'real' you, corresponding to the human player sitting at the table playing the game. The ego is the set of programmed characteristics corresponding to the imagined character being played in the game.

The Angel Training Simulation we all find ourselves in is controlled by a set of rules called physics, like what is laid out in the rulebooks for the game Dungeons and Dragons. In this analogy, the Dungeon Master (the player running the game) corresponds to God, which is perhaps why my ego absolutely loved this role. When playing Dungeons and Dragons, like video games, one is engaged in a Simulation within a Simulation.

Teaching:

Angelic Takeaway: Optimal teaching looks very different depending on what level of the Simulation the teacher and students are operating from. No simple black and white pedagogy will completely solve our education issues. I wish I had the answers, but I do not. Though generally successful and popular in over a decade teaching, many personal difficulties associated with my speech impediment, autism, and rapid spiritual evolution hardly made me a teacher to be emulated. I do know that the people who are least likely to have the answers to our educational problems are the people claiming to have all the answers to them.

Here is a brief view of what teaching high school physics tended to look like when I was operating from various levels of the Simulation. Though I describe myself, these teaching traits were observed in others.

Root: No extended period of time was spent teaching here. Normally, this occurred when I was extremely tired or had a severe emotional or mental disturbance. Teaching from this lowest level of the Simulation was characterized by desperation, as one is relatively powerless in this state. There was not enough energy available to hold the students' attention or project knowledge in any meaningful way. Most available energy was used to hold one's own psyche together and handle basic classroom tasks. In this state, neither I nor the students really wanted to be in the room.

Sacral: A bit of energy was available here. This was never a permanent state where I taught from, but from here there was enough energy to go through classroom rituals and get through a lesson plan ineffectively. In this tribal state of mind, one holds a class together by demanding absolute compliance to classroom traditions like 'no talking' and 'binders out on desk.' In this level of the Simulation there isn't enough energy present enough to hold student's attention, so one must do the next best thing: demand that they look like they are paying attention.

Solar Plexus: When I began teaching, I often operated from this level of the Simulation and elements of this style have survived as I've evolved. In this level, there is a lot of physical energy, along with a bit of spiritual energy to project one's power. This is still a very physical level, so transmission of complex intellectual information isn't optimal here. In my case, what seemed natural here was using one's energy to be an alpha and get compliance using a combination of respect, threats, and rough humor. You can generally get compliance at this level if you are the perceived head of the pack.

Heart: Teachers at this level tend to be cheerleaders for the education process, and in many ways, it is the optimal level for a high school teacher. In this level of the Simulation, a teacher really wants to do what's best for the students and school, although disagreements about what's best still occur at this level. At this level, one needs less force and discipline. The abundant positive energy available is generally attractive to others, and voluntary compliance of students is not hard to come by. The energy of teachers at this level screams: "Be positive, enthusiastic, and pay attention to me, and your life will be amazing." When operating from this level of the Simulation, I loved spirit days and anything that I perceived to be helping the students.

Throat: This is likely an optimal level of the Simulation for a university professor. Here one is most interested in transmitting knowledge in the most meaningful, creative, and efficient way possible. However, an issue with being at this level is one can easily start talking over the student's heads and discipline and behavior can become an issue, particularly if one has students who are not inherently interested in learning. Teachers at this level have a lot of power available to hold the attention of students who are interested in learning but using force and discipline begins feeling very unnatural here.

Third Eye: One is now interested in creating a fun, loving, and supportive environment. In this level of the Simulation one is quite literally in love with life, so by the laws of the Simulation one tends to be loved by life. A teacher here depends on students resonating with this lovely energy, but when a troubled student cannot, the use of discipline and force on the troubled student is extremely uncomfortable. This, and the fact that one's aura is feeding energy to the students makes keeping an orderly classroom difficult. However, if one has an inherently high energy class then magic happens on a regular basis. The more mundane activities associated with teaching, like grading and paperwork, become a low priority as one realizes that one's most important role in the building is to be a source of energy. Sadly, the bureaucracy of education rarely recognizes this and tends to not see the value this level of the Simulation brings to the education process.

Crown: I believe we will begin seeing more teachers teaching from this level of the Simulation as time moves on. Here, one recognizes that the wavy energy one is projecting is actually more important in the long-run than anything partically going on.

A nice role for teachers operating from the Third Eye and Crown levels may be running Gifted and Talented programs, which are currently drastically underutilized in American Education. Gifted and Talented students need less direct instruction, as I've found gifted students actually learn better on their own, but a wise, high-level energy to guide them would be of enormous assistance.

Students are various vibrations:

Here are general traits of students operating from the various levels of the Simulation. This is derived from personal experience, both during my education and being a high school teacher for over a decade, observing students vibrating in the different levels of the Simulation.

Root: Students operating from this level often deal with a number of personal problems and rarely are academics high on their list of priorities. These students will exert effort if the teacher makes them feel safe and loved. Admittedly this is a bit difficult and energy taxing as students at this level tend to be perceived as problem students. This level of the Simulation is largely run by pleasure and pain impulses, so candy was an extremely effective motivator for students at this level. A 'sackcloth and ash' extremely dark sense of humor, which tends to put off the higher level students, is a good way of connecting with them. It tends to relate better to their actual life experiences.

Sacral: Academics are not natural in this vibration but come easier than at the Root Level. These students seem to benefit the most from praise as they tend not to get it often. These students also enjoy learning experiences that relate to their pack. They enjoy seeing videos and movies where the people in the video look and act like people in their pack. For example, I observed here that a science video featuring a nerdy white guy would work far better for the white students at this level than the minority students at this level. High-minded academically minded activities don't work well with this level of the Simulation in general.

Solar Plexus: One can be a good student here but it requires a lot of effort, as diving deep into academics isn't really natural in this level. Learning experiences that show a direct application to the world, along with hands-on activities such as labs, are most successful with these students. I found these students enjoy competitive learning experiences such as review games or building competitions. In my years as a vocational high school teacher, many students at this level already had a career mapped out in a nice blue-collar trade, such as plumbing or construction. So, a "C" was fine with them.

Heart: These students tended to get the high grades, especially if high grades were a prerequisite to their life's goal. These students tend to be very goal-oriented and often have a lot of activities going on outside the class. This level is broadly optimal for worldly functioning, so these students are often well-rounded and get pulled in many directions: sports, student government, and extra-curriculars. Students in the level of the Simulation tend to be popular and well-liked.

Throat: These were the students who comprehended the class material the best and would challenge the teacher if they sensed something wrong was being taught. Most would get high grades without too much effort, but the grade they got was secondary to actually learning. Here, learning is natural and is done for its own sake. Gaining knowledge is enjoyable for these students, and if a class is not meeting their expectations, they will concentrate their learning elsewhere. Gifted and Talented programs and enrichment activities greatly benefit these students.

Third Eye and Crown: Having a student in your class at these levels is a divine gift, however grades are largely irrelevant to them. At this level, whatever grade the Simulation brought their way was fine. Though rare, the students I had over the years floating in these high levels tended to be "B" to

"A-" students. They learned the basic class material easily, but were hardly concerned with their grade at all. They seemed to sense what the universe had in store for them so they only needed a grade high enough to meet that requirement.

They were a pleasure to be around (which helped their grade in an indirect way) but were unwilling to force anything. For example, they'd often skip an assignment they already knew how to do. They tended to avoid what they considered busy work so that they could concentrate on their real passion.

Dealing with students at different levels of the Simulation is a core challenge teachers deal with. The optimal learning experience for students at different levels of the Simulation is vastly different. Oftentimes students from the lower levels will present more discipline challenges and as less energy is available to them, they will drain more energy from a teacher. On the other hand, students at the higher levels will be more likely to resist forceful authority and question teachers who are not challenging them.

Even at a vocational high school, I saw massive effort to try to force every child down a college prep academic pathway. The heart was in the right place, but it often was not of optimal benefit to the majority of the students.

The main problem in American education as I see it is the layers upon layers of well-meaning bureaucracy that tended to laden teachers down with paperwork and administrative tasks. This shunted energy away from actually teaching and interacting with students.

The excess bureaucracy in education 'misses the forest through the trees.' Optimal solutions to problems in American education involve simplifying and eliminating regulation and bureaucracy rather than increasing it, which is what is happening now (tested true).

Simplifying things and reducing regulation in education will mean certain 'bad' things will happen but it will also mean 'good' things can happen with greater velocity. These good things include getting rid of ineffective teachers, dealing properly with troubled students, adjusting school practices to the modern world, and allowing the teachers to teach the students in front of them, and not some idealized group of students who only exist in the head of some academic or government bureaucrat.

Angelic Calculus:

Angelic Takeaway: If you slept through math class in high school or have never heard the word calculus, this may be a chapter to skip. The message of this chapter stated as simply as possible is: as life evolves, it views reality through more and more nuanced lenses, which allows it to predict future trends better. Calculus provides us a convenient analogy for the logical mind to understand it.

If one is familiar with a basic mathematical function, one will know that a simple graphed function has multiple derivatives.

A very basic review of calculus:

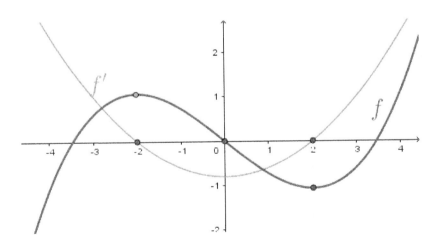

In this function, the f function represents the position of an object. Fancy math magic gives us f' which represents the rate of change of the position function or its velocity. A further derivative would be f'' which would represent the rate of change of the velocity function or the acceleration of the original function. A further derivative would be f''' and would give the rate of change of the acceleration function and would be the jerk of the original function. Each additional derivative provides a more nuanced understanding of the behavior of the function. If you are confused, you probably got laid in high school.

These basic calculus concepts that your underpaid math teacher taught you provide an interesting analogy for how to view the various levels of perception arising from the different levels of the Simulation. Each higher derivative provides a further out, more nuanced view of a function, much like each higher level of the Simulation does.

With the addition of each derivative, we get an exponentially richer view of what a mathematical function is doing. Evolution of consciousness works in a similar way. As a soul evolves and each new level of the Simulation opens up to it, it gains access to higher views of reality.

Each higher level of perception sees further into the future, as the energy from the higher levels ultimately controls the lower levels. Generally the lower levels of perception give a clear, short-term assessment of events, which are accurate at a local level. The higher levels will provide clearer, long-term universal assessments, as they are seeing a more fundamental reality more in tune with God. An animal operating from the Root and Sacral chakras would understand its immediate surroundings enough to hunt in the forest, but wouldn't see the hurricane approaching like the meteorologist operating from the Throat chakra.

An entity that only has access to the Root chakra level of the Simulation would only notice the immediate position of things with respect to its own survival. Minimal memory and future planning exists. Therefore, one could call this very simple perception like that of an insect or reptile.

Root perception = f

With further evolution, an entity gains access to the Sacral level of the Simulation. The entity can now analyze social situations and judge both its own and other's survivability, based on its position within a pack and the pack's strength relative to other packs. Basic analysis of the past and tentative predictions about the near future open up here, as well as a more complex perception of life.

Sacral perception = f + f'

Further along the evolutionary tree into the Solar Plexus level the Simulation, an entity can sense individual power beyond simple appearances and think in terms of self-interest projected a long time into the future. Basic spiritual power becomes available here, even though it is mostly relegated to the physical domain. A basic intellect also opens up here, giving the entity the ability to put things in proper working order, strategize, and do long-term planning.

Solar Plexus perception = f + f' + f''

When an entity evolves into the Heart level of the Simulation, it realizes that love is more powerful than anything below it. In the long run, love will beat any of the survival strategies or skills derived from the lower levels of the Simulation. An entity is better able to predict the outcome of events, as one now begins to understand where true power in the Simulation flows from.

Heart perception = f + f' + f'' + f'''

Eventually, even Heart perception will show its limitations and an entity will evolve into the Throat level of the

Simulation, where a true intellect is formed. One can now analyze massive amounts of intellectual data and arrive at correct conclusions. Humans in this level of perception tend to be educated, and are able to see things that others simply do not have the tools to see. Scientists at this Throat level seem to have magic at their disposal which the lower levels are unable to comprehend. Historians at this level are able to predict world events with an uncanny accuracy, as trends tend to repeat themselves.

Throat perception $= f + f' + f'' + f''' + f''''$

Eventually even the limitations of even the greatest intellects are exposed, and entities develop the ability to sense quantum vibration. One is able to sense how fast something is vibrating on a quantum level, which tells the actual spiritual power of an entity. In the long-run, the quantum vibration of a person (their vibe) is more important than any of their purely physical characteristics or circumstances, as revealed by the lower perception levels. Some of your weird spiritual friends likely talk about the vibes in the room because they are feeling this level of perception.

Third Eye perception $= f + f' + f'' + f''' + f'''' + f'''''$

Finally, evolution reaches the point where it has entities directly able to feel the divine power source running the entire Simulation via the Crown chakra level of the Simulation. Ultimately it becomes obvious that everything is being energized by the divine. One can see that in the very long run, divine Will prevails, even if all other levels of perception point the other way. This level of privileged perception goes beyond and outside the bounds of normal perception.

Crown perception $= f + f' + f'' + f''' + f'''' + f''''' + f''''''$

Oftentimes, artificial substances will increase the level of perception at the expense of another. In the ultimate sense of things, none of the levels of perception are strictly better than another. Valuable lessons are learned at every level of perception. This is similar to the fact that very few math teachers told you that the second derivative of a function is better than the first derivative of the function, unless you are trying to argue that a wrong answer is right on a test.

As beings evolve, they slowly develop a more and more nuanced perception as they evolve into the Angelic ranks. The struggle to understand reality inside this often-confusing Simulation seems to encourage the development of the nuanced higher levels of perception. It's often the failure of one level of perception which encourages the development of the next higher (tested true).

Spirituality and Video Games:

Angelic Takeaway: If a loving parent asked me for my advice on whether they should allow their children to play video games and I was absolutely forced into a binary answer, it would be 'No.' However reality is more nuanced than that, and I'd hardly wish that I was deprived of the joy of beating all my friends in Mario Kart, Tetris and not losing my virginity till twenty-six due to the long hours playing through the wonderful 80s and 90s era role playing and strategy games.

Video games were a major part of my personal development, and a dominant part of life for a large portion of it. Many of my important lessons in this life were learned from them, and one of the main ideas of this book is that we currently find ourselves in an Angel-evolving Simulation. This idea would never have even formed had it not been for the medium of video games.

The great spiritual teachers of the past never talked about Simulation theory simply because video games and computers were not available during their time; their followers would have no context in which to understand it. A wonderful Bible story would be the night Jesus and the apostles enjoyed a fun night of turning water into wine during a wild night of Mario Kart. Unfortunately, Uemura Masayuki (the inventor of Nintendo) would not be born for nearly 2000 years.

Even though video games will always occupy a loving place in my heart and I still enjoy talking about them and occasionally playing them, they have played a much smaller role in my life since October of 2019. It was an online discussion with other spiritual video game nerds where we discussed the downside of video games on our spiritual development that caused me to temporarily stop playing them. This turned out to be way easier and more rewarding than my wildest imagination would have anticipated.

It was not a coincidence that only a couple of months later in December of 2019 that the mind-blowing Angelic experience discussed earlier in this book would occur.

When calibration became available to me, I was disappointed to find the overall energy of video games a bit lower than I thought. Very broadly speaking, they do tend to hamper spiritual growth for the following reasons.

- They re-enforce the ego's assertion that it is in control. My favorite games were always those with clear-cut rules, where I knew I'd eventually win given enough time. Having minimal consequences for failure was also a big plus. Unfortunately our reality is not this simple, and one must deal with mistakes and failures without absolute guarantees of victory. My ego enjoyed the escapism and quasi-security that video games provided from a reality that was more complex, and oftentimes harsher.

- They are at their core a Simulation and as we are already in a Simulation, one may be wise to question the wisdom of going into a Simulation within a Simulation. Once again, my ego enjoyed the escapism that they provided from the Simulation that God already had me in.

- Our psyches at their core do not differentiate between experiences that happen inside a video game and what happens in real life (tested true). This can cause confusion.

I recall playing the fun romp of a video game called *Simpsons Hit and Run* where one drives around the town of Springfield in various vehicles, crashing into anything in sight with no consequences.

I had been playing it all day, and realizing the sun was going down. I had very little food in my apartment, so I decided to make a very quick drive to the grocery store. This way, I could enjoy the rest of the night driving cartoon cars without hunger.

Running out to my car to minimize my time away from the game, I absentmindedly drove across the lawn of my apartment complex where kids often played on my way to the road. This was a perfectly acceptable action in the game but not in real life. No one was hurt and the police were not called, but it was hard to ignore a lapse in my reality matrix this big. Extremely violent video games do indeed make their players more violent (tested true).

That being said, they can be an enjoyable part of this reality if handled with a bit of care. Here are a few of my classic favorites that can be enjoyed without too much spiritual danger.

Final Fantasy 4,6 and *7*: These three RPGs that were released during the golden-age of this series are three of my favorite games. They are all available for the newer gaming mediums, including phones. All three storylines explore complex themes that will likely have a positive effect on a developing psyche. Though it's probably more efficient to read a book, a parent could feel comfortable if they see their child playing one of these and not cooking crystal meth.

Tetris: My ego wants to brag that in college I got 4598 lines in a mere thirty minutes and eighteen seconds in Tetris 64. I challenge any of you imposters to beat that!

This simple puzzle game has no violence, and is easy to learn but tough to master. Playing it in moderation will have a positive effect on one's intellect, and again, it's better than cooking crystal meth.

Mario Kart: This series of racing games teaches us the important lesson that the best player does not always win. Though not deep, it's a game that an entire family can play together and the youngest kid might occasionally beat the bullying older sibling. The game involves items that provide advantages in the race; the players in the back get the best items and the player in the lead often gets stuck with nearly worthless banana peels. This provides a light-hearted fun experience that is healthier than cooking crystal meth.

Civilization series: Name one other way to experience the joy of being nuked by Gandhi. This series of games allows one to experience building an empire from the Stone Age to the Space Age. One can learn patience, strategic thinking, and even a bit of history by playing these games. Many similar games known as 4x strategy games will provide a similar experience. My favorite ones tend to take place in the future in space. My ego needs to brag about being one of the handful of beings smart enough to beat *Master of Orion 2* on 'impossible' against seven opposing computer-controlled civilizations. Did this accomplishment get me very far in life? Nope, but I could've been cooking crystal meth.

States of Matter:

Angelic Takeaway: Many things discovered in conventional science point to concepts involved in the evolution of consciousness. As one heats up matter, it tends to move from a solid state to a liquid state, and finally to the very flexible gaseous state. The evolution of consciousness mirrors this, because souls have less restrictions and more flexibility as they gain access to higher levels of the Simulation.

Here is a basic high school chemistry review. There are three fundamental states of matter: solids, liquids, and gasses. In this analogy I relate the physical property temperature to the amount of life essence in a person, place, or thing.

If you had a chunk of ice (H_2O in solid state) and took the temperature, you would see something below 32 degrees Fahrenheit, 0 degrees Celsius or 273K. The properties of the ice would change subtly as you changed the temperature; for example -20 degrees Celsius to -10 degrees Celsius. (If you are a proud American who does not understand the Celsius scale and love the good old American Apple Pie Fahrenheit scale, simply use a temperature translator that can be easily found on any search engine.) From here on out will use the Celsius scale primarily simply because its numbers are cleaner.

If you continued to add heat, at about 0 degrees Celsius you would see a drastic change in properties as the ice transitioned to liquid water. Now you could vary the temperature between 0 degrees Celsius and 100 degrees Celsius with relatively subtle changes in property. Again, at 100 degrees, the liquid water would transition to water vapor (H_2O

in gaseous state) and would show dramatically different properties.

Some scientists even say that there is a fourth state of matter known as plasma. Plasma could be likened to the extremely high impersonal levels of the Simulation above the Crown level that go beyond the scope of this book.

Now let's relate this basic high school chemistry to the Levels of the Simulation.

States of Matter of Water; Chemistry	Levels of the Simulation	Numbers on Hawkin's Scale	Colors on Spiral Dynamics Scale	Languaged Characteristics
Temperatures <0°C Solid	Root and Sacral	<200	Beige, Purple	Wild/Ego/Animal
Temperatures 0°C - 100°C Liquid	Solar Plexus, Heart and Throat	200-499	Red, Blue, Orange	Human/Mind
Temperatures >100°C Gas	Third Eye and Crown	500-799	Green, Yellow, Turquoise	Angelic/Spirit

Plasma (extremely high temperature)	Levels above Crown	800+	2nd Tier Colors	Godliness/Avatars

You might observe that the lower wild/egoic frequencies aren't strictly worse but simply life with a lower quality of "life essence" (heat in this chemistry analogy). Arguing that one level of the Simulation is better than another tends to start sounding like arguing over whether water vapor is better than ice. However, if I'm dying of thirst, I'd heavily prefer liquid water over any of its other forms. All the levels of the Simulation serve an important role in the overall thrust of life.

Life gets more peaceful, loving, and happy as one evolves up the levels of the Simulation. The majority of people attracted to the book will be interested in evolving up the levels of the Simulation.

Music:

Angelic Takeaway: I've found music is one of the most efficient ways to alter one's energy. I've also found the background music played in my classroom one of the most effective ways to manage the energy of a classroom.

Wonderful music comes out of all levels of the Simulation. Here is my brief subscription of music from each level of the Simulation:

Root: Much of this music comes out of high-crime, inner-city areas and promotes hard drugs, rape, crime, and the lowest levels of human expression. It also comes out of very primitive areas and features a very simple structure. Normally this music tends to have a negative effect on one's life, but perhaps serves some value I don't yet understand. Teaching in an inner city school I observed that this was often the music popular with my students.

Sacral: Lots of simple folksy music, some country music, and some soft drug music often comes from this level. It is usually very specific to a certain pack or group. It tends to play on the difficult parts of life and is normally locally popular, but not popular on a worldly level.

Solar Plexus: Empowering music often played at sporting events. Bon Jovi, Rush, Michael Jackson and Village People are all examples. Most music that reaches the highest levels of popularity comes out of this level. It's not particularly deep spiritually but has a positive physical vibration so it gives energy rather than takes. Most people find it enjoyable.

Heart: Mostly feel good and do good music: Light Christmas songs, light church songs, Cyndi Lauper, Billy Joel,

Elton John, and Hall and Oates are examples. This music has a distinctly positive vibration and tends to pull one into the Heart level of the Simulation, which is an enjoyable place to be. It tends to avoid the darker issues of life. People can use it to recharge physically and spiritually.

Throat: Throat music positively stimulates the mind. Examples are 2Cellos, Hans Zimmer, John Williams, Two steps from Hell, Abba, Simon & Garfunkel along with most classical music. This music stimulates the mind and will provide the positive energy required to contemplate the deeper issues of life. This music puts one in resonance with the scientific Throat level of the Simulation in a similar way that good education does.

Third Eye: This is music which carries a loving, peaceful vibration. Beatles, Air Supply, Lindsey Stirling, Taylor Davis, Rebecca Tripp, Celtic Woman, Katherine Jenkins, Andrea Bocelli, Diana Ross, and Celine Dion are examples. This music is highly energetically recharging, tends to put one into a high state, and helps one resonate with the Third Eye level of the Simulation.

Crown: Music which carries a divine vibration and was written as tribute to God. Examples are the great church choirs, cathedral music, Robert Gass and the classic Christmas carols such as "Silent Night" and "What Child is This." This rare music helps one resonate with the highest levels of the Simulation available on Earth. If one's goal is to move up the levels of the Simulation this is the music which provides the greatest assistance in that endeavor. However, it's probably not optimal to listen while operating heavy machinery or trying to focus on the mundane physical tasks of this world.

Music, as with all art, should not be judged based solely on the level of the Simulation that it comes out of. Artistically well-done music comes from all levels of the Simulation and plays different roles in the panorama of life. Most music in practice comes from multiple levels of the Simulation simultaneously, and the artists mentioned above all have individual songs from different levels of the Simulation, but I attempted to pick artists whose overall vibe captures a certain level of the Simulation. A future book will be devoted to the energy of music alone, but this chapter was included as a broad introduction.

Movies/Series:

Angelic Takeaway: Movies are an entertaining and efficient way to educate a soul from any level of the Simulation. My observation as a teacher showed that some of the most effective things that I did involved the showing of 'sciency' movies. A dream is to create education courses based on popular entertaining movies.

Movies, as with all art, come out of every level of the Simulation, and their artistic merits should not be judged on the level of the Simulation they come out of. A great horror movie allows one to process fear from the Root and Sacral chakras but would not be good in an academic environment where the Throat and Third Eye chakras dominate. A faith-based movie might be great for spiritual development but might be a bit dull for most parties.

Here is a brief description of movies coming out of various levels of the Simulation:

Root: Movies that promote bare survival, base human characteristics or display the worst aspects of the human condition. *American Psycho, Pulp Fiction, Fight Club, The Nightingale, Porn* and most horror movies are popular examples. Coming out of this level of the Simulation does not imply that they are not well-done on an artistic level, but watching them clearly pulls the soul in a certain spiritual direction.

Sacral: These movies often focus on certain subcultures (religious, racial, or economic groups), fear, and pride. They include distortions of reality and often have chauvinistic elements. Examples are *American Pie, Napoleon Dynamite, Fast and the Furious, 300,* most pot-head comedies, and many simple, locally-made films. These movies are generally designed to appeal to certain subcultures but can be popular on a large scale if they successfully capture the plight of a certain group or provide a flashy entertainment experience.

Solar Plexus: These are empowering and entertaining movies. They sometimes may not deal with ethical gray areas in an optimum fashion, but generally show a higher level of the Simulation triumphing over a lower level of the Simulation. In popular language, this is good triumphing over evil. Examples are both *Top Gun* movies, many classic action blockbusters, most *Marvel* movies, most *Star Wars* movies, *Braveheart, The Goonies, A Few Good Men, Footloose, 47 Ronin,* and *The Patriot.*

Heart: These are movies that promote a positive message. These movies have heart, encourage viewers to be "good people," and promote positive values. They tend to be more ethically nuanced than the levels below it. Examples are most faith-based movies, *Karate Kid, A Dog's Purpose, Charlie Wilson's War, Bill Durham, Dead Poet's Society, Mr. Holland's Opus, Good Will Hunting, The Green Mile, Shawshank Redemption, Avatar,* and the *The Lord of the Rings* films.

Throat: These are movies that are intellectually stimulating and dig into a very complex societal issue. Common examples are: most historical documentaries, *Imitation Game, Apollo 13, Bohemian Rhapsody, Interstellar, The Martian, Stranger than Fiction, The Soloist, Seabiscuit, Gravity, King's Speech,* and *Last of the Mohicans.* Movies of this level encourage development of the intellect and explore moral gray areas in nuanced, sophisticated fashion.

Third Eye and Crown: These are movies which successfully integrate many vibrations and leave the viewer often with a deep wavy/spiritual lesson. Movies and shows that are able to pull this off are quite rare and are very valuable to watch if one desires to move up the levels of the Simulation. Good examples are *The Chosen, Lincoln, Life is Beautiful, Gladiator,* and *The Green Book.* A movie that carries a large component of these levels and still holds entertainment value are of immense value to human society.

I found movies to be incredibly effective educational tools, from both a teacher and student perspective. However, the obvious weakness of using movies as a teaching tool (which actually applies to all methods of education to some extent) is discerning what energies the students are actually absorbing. I saw many good teachers over the years, despite good-intentions, teaching their students destructive philosophies that were even often endorsed by certain political entities.

Another issue with movies, like people, is that the energy never comes out of just a single level of the Simulation. Movies are complex pieces of art that must impersonate life in the Simulation, which means that they integrate many different aspects of reality. Using my calibration technique I found a way to summarize the overall energetic gist of a movie using fifteen numbers that can be derived by calibration. A future book will concentrate on energetic breakdowns of this type. This fifteen number system can be used to describe not only movies and shows but also music, people, places, and concepts.

Here is the basic template where I use it to analyze the great historical movie *Lincoln* as an example:

Chakra/Level of the Simulation for *Lincoln*	Percentage Aligned	Energy Level
Crown	5	720
Third Eye	8	620
Throat	39	560
Heart	18	340
Solar Plexus	10	320
Sacral	13	300
Root	7	270
Overall		490

Abraham Lincoln was an Angel in a human body (tested true) and this movie is aligned with truth on all levels of the Simulation.

The scale which I use to measure energy of each of the chakra is similar to the number scale Dr. David Hawkins used. The energy of each level of the Simulation is measured on a scale where 200 is the neutral point. An energy level below 200 means that the handling of that level of the Simulation in the movie or show was not aligned with reality. An energy level above 200 means increasing alignment with absolute truth. Once an energy level goes over the 500-600 range we are then in the enlightened truth range.

The movie reaches an above 200 energy level for all levels of the Simulation, so there is not much inaccuracy or damaging propaganda in the movie. The very high energy found at the top three levels shows us it contains extremely high truth and alignment with divinity.

By percentage the movie's highest alignment is with the Throat level the Simulation as the movie looks primarily at the passing of the Thirteenth Amendment from an intellectual point of view. Though not the main point of the movie, incredibly high levels of truth are conveyed from a Third Eye and Crown point of view. This is mostly portrayed through Daniel Day Lewis' divine portrayal of Lincoln, who was a man of great faith, humor, and wisdom.

At the bottom is an overall energy rating. A good interpretation of this number which is arrived at by calibration is similar to asking the Angelic kingdom, "What is the overall energetic impact of the movie when all the energies of all the levels of the Simulation are taken into account?" This movie has a 490 rating, which is about as high as you find in a popular entertaining movie. A rating below 200 in this overall energy will tend to lead one away from truth, and a rating above 200 will tend to lead one towards it. However, none of these numbers correlate with the artistic integrity of a movie, and numbers are pointers to reality, not reality itself. Do not confuse the map with the territory.

Another movie about an Angel in a human body was *Gandhi*, and I've energetically broken it down in a similar fashion:

Chakra/Level of the Simulation	Percentage Aligned	Energy Level
Crown	8	630
Third Eye	11	300

Throat	34	460
Heart	25	290
Solar Plexus	7	280
Sacral	8	320
Root	7	290
Overall		450

This movie is about the famous Indian sage Gandhi. When broken down by percentages, it is far more highly aligned with higher chakras than the lower ones. This means one should not watch this movie expecting great action sequences or sex scenes (not that there is anything specifically wrong with those scenes).

This movie is aligned with truth across the board, as its energy is above 200 in every level of the Simulation. The 630 Crown chakra energy shows that the film successfully captures Gandhi's divine connection. Its overall energy of 450 shows that spiritually speaking, it's of immense value to watch.

Both these movies about Angels in human bodies show the downside of their fight for social change and do not sugarcoat history. Movies that sugarcoat history or portray an overlay dark version of history tend to have a Throat alignment of under 200. Both these films have high Throat chakra alignments, which one could interpret to mean 'historically accurate.' Either of these films could find a place in an integrous History, Social Studies, or even spirituality class.

War Movies and Shows:

War tends to have a bad reputation in the spiritual world and probably deservingly so. However some important spiritual lessons are only available in war and much higher insight can be gleaned from it.

Having served in the military in this life and fought in many wars in past lives, I've found war and the divine masculine generally underrepresented in spiritual literature. One need not comb ancient war histories for a taste of this divine masculine spirituality but can get it from many popular movies and series. Here is a sample of a few war series and movies aligned with divinity.

HBO miniseries:

	Band of Brothers		The Pacific	
Chakra/Level of the Simulation	% Aligned	Energy Level	% Aligned	Energy Level
Crown	5	440	5	360
Third Eye	10	360	10	370
Throat	15	250	14	260
Heart	29	500	30	500
Solar Plexus	21	270	17	250
Sacral	11	310	12	320

Root	9	300	12	300
Overall		330		310

These two miniseries cover the major warfronts of America during World War Two. They have a similar energetic profile, but both series are aligned with reality in all levels of the Simulation. Both series show good leadership, bad leadership, and ugly leadership. Though not the main point of either series, they both show the divinity that shines through war if one is looking for it.

Both series are highly aligned with the Heart at an energy of 500. It shows the love that occurs between combatants under terrible conditions. It is a different kind of love that shows up in your typical romantic comedy, but extremely powerful and tear-jerking nonetheless.

Mel Gibson War Movies	Brave-heart		Patriot		We Were Soldiers	
Chakra/Level	% Aligned	Energy	% Aligned	Energy	% Aligned	Energy
Crown	3	470	3	450	4	470
Third Eye	11	240	9	250	8	240
Throat	10	310	11	300	11	300
Heart	21	340	20	330	16	310
Solar Plexus	17	210	15	230	16	250

Sacral	16	190	19	210	22	210
Root	22	250	23	240	23	240
Overall		250		240		250

The three films energetically broken down above star Mel Gibson and have a similar energy profile. All three have Mel Gibson playing a military leader with a deep faith in God which he is extremely good at portraying.

The three films are quite violence heavy, so they should be avoided by very sensitive audiences. However, the violence isn't of the quality of aimless violence one may find in a grotesque horror movie, but used to show the real brutality and nature of war.

All three movies could be considered loosely based on historical events, and all three are extremely successful in capturing the overall energetic environment of the period (tested true).

All the above war movies and shows are all aligned with higher levels of the Simulation and successfully show that God even shows up in war.

The Chosen:

The Chosen		
Chakra Level of Simulation	% Aligned	Energy Level
Crown	13	840
Third Eye	22	470

Throat	11	330
Heart	12	670
Solar Plexus	24	290
Sacral	14	320
Root	4	390
Overall		500

I had a lukewarm relationship with Christianity early in this lifetime as I identified with agnostic beliefs and philosophy through my first twenty-eight years. My intellect ignored it in order to focus on other issues early in life, but upon revisiting it later, I found many of its core tenets and principles had largely disappeared from society. But these were things that society desperately needed back. An advantage of exploring Christianity later in life with a developed intellect was that I was able to separate the wheat from the chaff, as well as avoid some of the lower level dogma that often gets associated with Christianity.

If one can get through the chaff then the beautiful essence of truth of this great religion shines forth. Unfortunately many people, particularly those who had a bad experience with Christianity at a young age, tend to focus on the chaff and miss the wheat completely.

This gem of a show reignited my interest in the Christian faith. It portrays the life of Jesus and his disciples and the challenges they faced. The creators ingeniously split the difference between biblical accuracy, time-tested truth, and entertainment value, giving it a high overall energy level of 500.

This is an incredibly high overall energy level for this medium of art.

The character Matthew in the show *The Chosen*, brilliantly portrayed by actor Paras Patel, lives with an autistic-like condition. The historic Matthew was indeed autistic (tested true). This is an example of an interesting detail that gets included when a show is aligned with the high truth of the Crown and Third Eye level of the Simulation. Important elements can be included that could not be derived from historical record alone. People involved with the show indeed had some higher insight.

Science Movies:

Since I just gave a nod to Christianity, I figure these may appeal to the other side of the fence with these two science movies, both of which I've used successfully in my physics classes. Highly-evolved people can enjoy both the gifts of science and the gifts of faith.

Both of these science movies have a large alignment in the Throat level of the Simulation, which will stimulate the mind and aid in an educational context.

	Interstellar		*Martian*	
Chakra/Level of the Simulation	% Aligned	Energy Level	% Aligned	Energy Level
Crown	3	210	0	x
Third Eye	4	400	0	x

Throat	44	330	57	280
Heart	20	500	21	340
Solar Plexus	12	220	7	170
Sacral	7	320	7	300
Root	10	400	8	210
Overall		360		270

Interstellar has a higher Simulation alignment than is typical in science movies as it goes a bit spiritual at the end (for which it's often criticized). This spiritual alignment is not common in science movies but it is pulled off well and adds a dimension of reality often missed in the genre. This is despite the fact that the movie's main focus is mainly on logic and science from its 44% Throat chakra alignment.

Its two highest energy levels come from the Heart and Root levels of the Simulation. The movie demonstrates the power of love, as indicated by the extremely high 500 Heart energy level. The 400 Root energy level is extremely high for this level of the Simulation. Normally the Root deals with survival of an individual, but this movie transcends individual survival and explores the deep issues dealing with balancing the survival of a race versus the survival of individuals. This is dealt with in a masterful way with an interesting plot twist.

Spoiler Alert: Angelic interpretation of *Interstellar.*

Throughout the movie the characters reference mysterious beings from a higher dimension. These beings could easily be interpreted as Angels or more evolved future versions of humans. At this level of evolution life would be almost primarily identified with the wavy unified universe. They would have access to all time and space but would not be grounded enough in the partically universe to pinpoint the details needed to save humanity. Hence these beings were able to create the higher dimensional wavy construct inside the black hole but still needed Cooper's partically help to navigate to the appropriate time-space partically details.

Also the Angels simply saving humanity would likely be karmic violation as it would nullify humanity ultimately saving itself and fulfilling the evolutionary purpose of the Simulation. The final scenes point to the fact that it was ultimately the Love between Cooper and his daughter that allows this dimensional bridge to occur. This portrays a high truth that love is indeed the link between the partically and wavy universes (tested true)

Spoiler Safe.

Interestingly *The Martian* has no alignment with the highest two levels of the Simulation but a ridiculously high 57% alignment with the scientific Throat level of the Simulation. If one is looking for Angels and meditation lessons, this probably isn't the movie for you. However, it is a true science movie as that is where most of its energy is contained. The book which the movie is based on has a similar energetic alignment across the board.

One factor that accounted for the amazing popularity of this science book and movie was its 21% strong, feel-good Heart alignment. In both the book and movie, it is obvious the characters care for each other, which lifted it above the level of a conventional, boring linear science media.

I believe the second factor for the popular appeal of the book and movie may have come from its negative '170' Solar Plexus alignment. Without giving spoilers, the main characters (led by Matt Damon playing a particularly lovable rogue) display a distinct lack of integrity. There are many swears, breaking of NASA policy, and abundant politically incorrect jokes. Though I don't recommend this movie be shown as a morality lesson, it does successfully make science fun.

The mix of science, heart, and mischievous humor works together to create a movie and book which balances education and entertainment well. At an overall energy level of 270, one should not interpret it as high divine truth, but it's well enough above 200 to feel confident that it broadly leads one in the correct direction.

Non-Sciency Movies (that worked well in my entry level of science classes)

	Men of Honor		Ford vs. Ferrari	
Chakra/Level of the Simulation	% Aligned	Energy Level	% Aligned	Energy Level
Crown	3	210	3	280
Third Eye	4	250	7	580
Throat	9	260	12	270
Heart	7	310	8	270
Solar Plexus	23	430	34	300
Sacral	28	250	22	240
Root	26	250	14	340
Overall		250		400

These are two movies that I've also successfully shown in my science classroom because it hits on a very specific part of my curriculum. Both movies teach some very valuable 'non-science' lessons, and are extremely entertaining to watch.

The movie *Men of Honor* tells the story of Carl Brashear, the first African American US Navy Master diver. During a struggling period in my second year of teaching and the night before starting a buoyancy unit, my Angels arranged for me to stumble upon this movie. Upon finishing up a dry pre-planned dry buoyancy lesson early the next day, I started the movie with a class who had expressed a lot of interest in the Navy. To my surprise, this movie provided much more value to the students than my dry buoyancy lessons ever could have. Miraculously, the events of the movie lined up perfectly with the bare-bones lesson plan I'd design for the cycle. It was almost as if Angels had planned it (because they did). Showing this movie would become one of my most successful and favorite educational activities over the next decade.

In addition to teaching basic buoyancy, this gave me a context to tell many of my Navy stories and discuss racial social issues, which a science teacher rarely has the opportunity to talk about. It contains some pretty painful racism at the start of the movie, but it gets resolved and ends on a happier high note. It shows that despite difficulties down here, good always eventually triumphs over evil.

The movie aligns positively above 200 across the board. It has an extremely high 430 Solar Plexus energy level as it brilliantly portrays the virtues of grit, determination, and hard work. Though never diving too deep philosophically or scientifically, the movie has worked extremely well over the years, particularly with lower-level students with whom traditional lecture was ineffective. Though I never kept statistics, a higher-than-expected number of my students found themselves in the Navy, and I believe this movie played a small role in that (tested true).

Ford vs. Ferrari tied into my velocity, acceleration, and friction curriculum. It tells the tale of the rebellious but extremely talented Ken Miles, brilliantly channeled by Christian Bale. It is a well-rounded story with humor, education, and is aligned with the highest levels of the Simulation.

The movie's primary alignments are with the bottom three physical levels of the Simulation. Movies with high components in these levels tend to be the most popular and enjoyable with the wide audiences, as they are down-to-earth. As many of my classes were inclusion (students at very different levels), this movie provided a good educational experience to a large number of students. The primary plot of the movie revolved around cars, mechanics, and racing, which could be related to basic physics concepts.

My favorite parts of the movie were when Christian Bale (as Ken Miles) describes the advanced meditative state he'd enter when racing. These short but brilliant passages about meditative states, along with Christian Bale's acting during the driving scenes, were the primary factor in the movie having a rather ridiculously high 580 Third Eye alignment. This is something one would never expect to find in a film primarily about racecar driving. A sneaky Angelic throw-in!

The movie's energy is above 200 across the board with an overall energy of 400. It provides a well-rounded view of reality, which is of great value for anyone to watch, especially given its entertainment value as well.

Negatively aligned movies/shows

	Game of Thrones		Inglorious Basterds	
Chakra/Level of the Simulation	% Aligned	Energy Level	% Aligned	Energy Level
Crown	2	170	0	x
Third Eye	9	190	0	x
Throat	10	210	0	x
Heart	5	70	1	150
Solar Plexus	23	190	10	210
Sacral	27	170	11	100
Root	24	180	78	30
Overall		180		50

By sheer number, the amount of movies and series with a negative alignment (represented by an overall energy below 200 on the scale I use here) outnumber movies and shows with positive alignment by a fair amount (tested true). Therefore, someone should not expect a positive educational experience watching a random selection of movies and shows. However, if one picks the movies and series they watch with a bit of intelligence and spiritual discernment, then it can be a positive educational experience.

A negative energy alignment does not mean they are not well done artistically, or even give an important human message. However, an individual or society emulating the behavior displayed in a negatively-aligned movie or series will lead to dark places over time. Sadly, this subconsciously happens far more often than people realize.

I chose the fantasy series *Game of Thrones* and Quinten Tarantino's film *Inglorious Basterds* as examples of negatively aligned pieces of art to discuss. I enjoyed both; they are extremely well-done on an artistic level, leading to a good deal of popularity.

Game of Thrones is a series based on books by author George R. R. Martin. This popular series portrays a brutal medieval world where noble families fight for power and the Iron Throne. The movie has an extremely low seventy Heart alignment, because the world that the series takes place in is basically heartless. This opens the door to tell a tale where brutality and cold-heartedness reigns.

Not aligned with ultimate truth, the overall energy of the show comes out at 180. However, according to my calibration research, this was the approximate energy of the world during the Dark Ages. If fantasy elements such as Dragons and White Walkers are taken out, the show portrays a somewhat accurate depiction of life during the Dark Ages (tested true).

This show is extremely entertaining to watch, but one should guard against unconsciously taking on the energy of the show or emulating the behaviors of characters or society in the show. This is easier said than done, as one will subconsciously absorb a bit of the energy just by watching.

The show may serve some light educational value in that it does energetically portray what life was like in the Dark Ages. If interpreted correctly, it acts as a cautionary tale against regressing back to this lifestyle. However, my observation shows that the glamor the show projects onto the violence, brutality, and cold-heartedness tends to encourage society's regression rather than advancement.

During my first viewing, I was enthralled with the film *Inglorious Basterds*. I had just gotten out of the military and was operating from a low energy level with a strong sense of American patriotism. This artistically stunning film with an extremely low energy level of fifty hit all the right buttons with my psyche at the time.

Quintin Tarantino films tend to come out in this very low range of energy. They are known for violence and shock value, and lack any alignment with the higher levels of the Simulation. Quintin Tarantino has a talent for sensually stunning pieces of art that tend to highlight the worst in human nature. During certain stages of my spiritual evolution, I enjoyed his work; however recently I've found myself unable to resonate with the films and notice the low feeling after taking them in.

My calibration research shows that it is indeed impossible to watch gruesome films that glorify the worst in human nature without absorbing negatively-aligned energy. However, my research also shows that these films serve a value in the universe that my earthly mind does not completely comprehend. This Simulation does exist for the purpose of evolution, and perhaps absorbing the energy of these films and then eventually transcending it serves a valuable long-term spiritual lesson, as it did with me. They may also provide a steppingstone out of the extremely hellish levels of experience.

Simulation Hypothesis:

Angelic Takeaway: We live in a brilliantly-programmed Angel-evolving Simulation. One wins the Simulation by learning one's lessons, evolving in order to serve God optimally, and not creating further negative karma for yourself. This earns you entry into the Angelic ranks. Trying to exploit the Simulation for personal gain results in perpetual frustration. The Angels who programmed this Simulation are way more evolved than any of us. They ensure that everyone gets what they need for their optimal evolution and that good always triumphs over evil in the end.

Before this chapter, I should mention that I describe this reality as an Angel-evolving Simulation in this book. Simulation theory has not traditionally been mixed with spirituality, because the spiritual masters of the past or the people they were talking to did not have access to computers or video games to create a frame of reference in order to explain reality using Simulation theory. This does not make the essence of their teachings any less right or wrong. The fisherman and goat-herders Jesus was talking to had never even heard of a computer.

Older spiritual teachings often describe this reality as a dream. This metaphor is just as applicable as Simulation theory. One can understand the core concepts of this book having never touched a computer or video game by just thinking of the lower levels of the Simulation as a deeper state of sleep or a deeper layer of the dream.

Whether one views this reality as a Simulation or a dream, some key commonalities exist:

- Both present this reality as a temporary experience and one comes back to reality when the Simulation or dream ends.

- The figure in the Simulation or dream in which one identifies with is not the real you. Remember the true self is a wave, not a particle (tested true).

- Both have the potential for a divine creator. Whether one believes God designed the Simulation or that this is God's dream, it ends up sounding about the same in the end.

Whichever metaphor is more comfortable for you is fine, but one should guard against the common error of 'confusing the map with the territory.' Whether logically thinking of this reality as a dream or Simulation, it is wise to remember that it is metaphor that points to ultimate truth, but isn't the ultimate truth which defies all attempts at verbalization. One can get lost in concepts in the Throat level of the Simulation and never transcend to a higher level.

A new way of conceptualizing the universe is the Simulation hypothesis, which is the broad proposal that all of our existence is a computer-simulated reality.

Over the years I've investigated this hypothesis from different vibrational viewpoints. Many books have been written on this and many videos have been made. Most of these come out of the Throat level of the Simulation.

I like that it provides a way of explaining some of the more abstract concepts of our reality better than was possible before the world directly experienced the computerized world of Simulations and video games. This hypothesis is great for explaining certain aspects of this reality, such as the relationship of the soul and body, and the relative reality of the physical/partically Simulation.

However, it's dangerous to take the hypothesis too seriously. The book *My Big Toe* by Thomas Campbell gives a very good humorous look at the Simulation hypothesis that goes into way more detail than I will here, and avoids the trap of 'confusing the map with the territory' as he states this specific error in his introduction. A thorough reading of this work (highly recommended) written from the reasonable Throat viewpoint points one toward the higher levels of the Simulation, and encourages one to transcend the programming of the Simulation rather than just get stuck deeper in it.

What proponents of Simulation theory omit is any concept of divinity or a way out. I was a bit taken aback by a recent conversation with a friend who is a computer programmer and an avid student of Simulation theory. This conversation took a dark turn, as he described us as being stuck in this Simulation and probably trapped for all eternity infinite layers down (meaning in a Simulation within a Simulation within a Simulation, etc.).

His thinking, though intellectually-sophisticated, reminded me of the inner dialogue going through my head during the spiritual low point of this life stuck in the spiritual depths. A property of the lowest regions of the Simulation is that time slows down to such an extent that it seems infinite. I could sympathize with him, but ended the conversation as he was bumming me out. I pray for him regularly.

An artful masterpiece of a movie called *The Matrix* presents the Simulation hypothesis in an exciting way that was comprehensible and enjoyable to a large percentage of the population. However, it clearly confused the map with the territory and missed the concept of divinity completely.

Spoiler Alert:

When we first meet the main character Neo, he is in a very partically Simulation. After he escapes the partically Simulation, he finds himself in an even more grim partically world. The storyline of the movie is thought-provoking but clearly presents a picture quite opposite to reality. Anyone who actually went through a spiritual awakening or already has a large piece of themselves in the higher levels of the Simulation will attest to this.

End Aside.

If we assume that we are indeed living in a programmed Simulation, some advanced wavy concepts about our reality become more comprehensible. One concept is the Heisenberg uncertainty principle.

If we assume this Earth is a Simulation written by a being with higher intelligence, wouldn't it make sense that no character in the Simulation could 'break it?' That is what the Quantum Mechanics concept of the Heisenburg uncertainty principle points to.

As stated earlier, the Heisenberg uncertainty principle is a law in Quantum Mechanics that limits how accurately you can measure two related variables. Specifically, it says that the more accurately you measure the momentum (or velocity) of a particle, the less accurately you can know its position, and vice versa. Stated slightly simpler, our knowledge inside the Simulation has some hard limits.

Just so my ego gets its name in this book, I'd like to present the **Faulkner uncertainty principle.** It states:

"A higher level of the Simulation or level of consciousness cannot be proved using the tools of a lower level of the Simulation or level of consciousness" (tested true). In other words every level of the Simulation has to be completely convincing as a reality.

Every Soul in the Simulation is free to have the evolution experience optimal to it without outside interference. Forcing a soul to have an experience in a level of the Simulation not optimal to its growth carries severe karmic consequences. This is why divine help only appears when prayed for as the Angelic kingdom is not allowed to to force anyone from their current experience even if that experience looks grim (tested true).

That a higher level of the Simulation cannot be proved by a lower level of the Simulation is the reason why psychic research tends never to be as conclusive as the researcher may have wished. It tends to point to the existence of a higher level of the Simulation but never conclusively proves it. Purely logical thinking or endeavor will never produce an air-tight case for God or the Third Eye and Crown chakra levels of the Simulation. A bit of faith is always required to ascend.

If we assume God created this Simulation, and rumor on the street is that He is pretty smart, then one can assume He wouldn't create a Simulation that would allow itself to be broken.

The Faulkner uncertainty principle, stated another way, is that the experience of the Simulation cannot be ruined for a low-level player by a high-level player. The principle actually protects the entire structure of the Simulation.

The higher levels of the Simulation are protected, as younger souls will never stumble upon something that would allow them to ascend too fast and have far more power than they could handle responsibly. Many great books have been written about the higher levels of the Simulation, a few of which are mentioned in the recommended reading section of this book. However, simply reading any of them will not allow ascension into the higher levels of the Simulation without a bit of faith and internal work. If such a book existed that conclusively proved all the precepts of God and spirituality, we'd all become rapidly enlightened and this Simulation and all its drama and evolutionary purposes would lose steam in a hurry.

For a number of years, I made it a personal crusade to find a video that would demonstrate to my students the existence of a reality beyond the simple mundane. Although no matter what video I found, whether it was an *America's Got Talent clip,* a magician demonstration, or a Quantum Mechanics talk, I'd always have a student present a viable case on how it was faked or invalid in some way.

I could've saved myself years of frustration realizing every level of the Simulation sees its own version of reality and that is exactly what is supposed to happen. By showing these videos, I provided a pointer to a higher level of the Simulation for the students who were ready for it The students who weren't simply found a way not to believe it. Turns out, things in the Simulation are working just fine.

This principle also protects the structure of the lower physical/partically levels of the Simulation. Imagine a flying Angel Jesus coming down with the ability to launch fireballs at the gates of Rome while casting magical healing and strength-boosting spells on his disciples. He could magically turn the world over in a matter of years with this much physical power. This may seem an interesting plot for a sci-fi film, but this would've wrecked the structure of the Simulation. Who is going to believe in physics anymore if Jesus is flying around and breaking every rule of them?

Many of the famous saints and spiritual masters of all time did indeed have miracles flowing through them (tested true). However these miracles existed in the quantum realm where they were both believable and not believable at the same time (tested true). Besides a small number of people blessed enough to witness them personally (which was by design), the rest of the population was free to make up their minds about it.

I imagine a funny conversation between two goat herders in 30 A.D. discussing a rumor of Jesus' miracle of the fish. One goat herder might be ready for a spiritual leap and take the rumor on faith (besides, he knew Simon Peter personally). The other skeptical goat herder would point to the fact they probably just hit a very dense school of fish, and that the witnesses were all tipsy because of Jesus' water to wine magic trick. Both goat herders would be free to make their decision, and end up in a level of the Simulation optimal to their soul's evolution.

One of my favorite attempts to almost prove the existence of the higher levels of the Simulation is the book *Proof of Heaven: A Neurosurgeon's Journey into the Afterlife* by Eben Alexander. This book was written by an intelligent, scientifically literate western medical doctor who had a near-death experience, and ended up seeing a very wavy, heavenly level of the Simulation.

The book corresponded personally with my limited satori experiences or peeks into higher reality and I recommend it to anyone interested in this area. In this book he succeeds brilliantly on an objective level in that he was able to explain his experience and what he experienced in a way that appeals to a western scientifically minded person in the reasonable 'Throat' level of the Simulation. However, due to the limits of the Faulkner uncertainty principle, he is unable to provide absolute scientific proof of this reality as his book is still very highly reliant on his personal first-person subjective experience.

I loaned Eben's book to a student who seemed generally interested. After a few weeks had passed and I asked the student about the book, he replied in an apathetic tone, "He made it all up." Note: He never returned the "made up" book.

I feel readers of this Eben's book who have already experienced bits of the higher levels of the Simulation will sense its wonderful truth, enjoy the experience of reading it, and absorb its wisdom. A more skeptical scientist-type reading this book who went into the experience demanding absolute mathematical/scientific proof of life after death will probably be disappointed. Either viewpoint is fine, but the first viewpoint is more fun at a cocktail party.

This Simulation we all find ourselves in simply won't let itself be broken by any individual character in it. A few historic characters such as Jesus and Buddha came about as close as one could. If in the hypothetical scenario where Eben had been allowed to bring a video camera to the heavenly dimension, provide in-depth interviews with all the Angels, and provide a mathematically-conclusive theory of everything to everyone's satisfaction, then the skeptics would have a field day proving the video was all special effects. Thank God for the skeptics because if they did not succeed, everyone would lose interest in whatever experience or lesson they were having down here in the Simulation, which seems completely real to them by design.

I've never played a video game with a button that said "Push to break this game, for not only yourself, but all others." It is clear we are all experiencing this reality on different levels. The immature ego might assume that breaking the reality of this Simulation and sending us all to eternal paradise might be in the highest good, but it's also clear that souls are evolving optimally here. The need to experience duality and the divine mix of good and bad that occurs serves a higher purpose.

Aside: Worst Purchase Ever.

Older nerds may remember a device in the early 90s called the Game Genie. When this device came out, my Nintendo career was in full-swing and I was the first chubby little nerd in line to get one. The device was hooked up to Nintendo game cartridges, and then one could enter codes to change the parameters of the game.

At first glance, this seemed like a wonderful thing. On the surface, only having a limited number of lives and not being able to defeat an enemy in a single hit seemed like a limitation that would be fun to transcend, and beating the game would be extremely easy. Unfortunately, I quickly realized that the programmers of all these Nintendo games had given their games certain parameters and limitations for good reasons.

I found that when one made this cheating easily available, the game lost its challenge and the game would quickly lose its luster. It was quickly discovered that performing well in a game due to intelligence and perseverance was its own reward, and the ability to easily enter a code to perform well in a game was vapid at best and indeed broke the game.

In online competitive games, hackers, those players who have realized ways to cheat and make themselves appear better at the game than they actually are, generally have a poor reputation among the other players who are playing the game the way the programmers intended. Maybe the programmers of this reality are even smarter than programmers of your favorite online game. Hacking to destroy the relative reality of this Simulation is regulated by the Faulkner uncertainty principle. No level of the Simulation can destroy the experience for another level without permission. The programmers of the universe (Angels) are simply too smart to let any individual break it.

End Aside.

My ego would love a cheat code that gave me unlimited money, a private tropical island, and a job where I was just told I was right all day, but this would ruin my own soul's personal evolution, which I suspect is way more important than any tropical island.

One should remember that the ultimate point of the Simulation is to learn lessons and evolve, not to win or go on a crusade to fix a Simulation that is actually doing exactly what it was designed to do. One should remember all the actual power and energy is in the hands of the Angelic, who could be thought of as the programming team of the Simulation. The powerless demonic players tend to be lost in the details trying to win and exploit the rules of the Simulation, to keep the other players down and themselves temporarily on top.

The first commandment, "Thou shalt have no other gods before me" exists to help us avoid getting lost in the Simulation and losing one's grip on divinity. Following this commandment gradually moves one up in the Simulation, and breaking it seems to cause one to sink down in the Simulation (my first twenty-eight years of this life).

I observed a rough analogy of the Angelic-demonic game occurring while I was immersed in another game. For many years I played the card-collecting strategic Simulation called Hearthstone by Blizzard Entertainment. One can always question the wisdom of going into a Simulation within a Simulation, but overall I found my years playing the game fun escapism. It enjoyably developed my intellect with its simple, but surprisingly deep strategy.

During this chapter in this life in which I played the game, I spent a moderate amount of time playing daily and a small amount of real-world money, which resulted in me spending most of my time occupying the middle ranks of the game (not with the noobs, but never competing for a championship). I look back at my experience in the game as a broadly positive experience.

Over the course of my time playing the game, I made a quasi-friend who was another player who occupied a higher rank than me. Our friendship, which never went beyond chatting over text, took on a bit of mentor-mentee feel as he spent far more time in the game than me. I enjoyed the help.

My mentor helped me in the game, which was one of the reasons the friendship was maintained. However, he was very negative, used abundant profanity, was always angry, and often kept me chatting or playing the game with him longer than I would've preferred.

The whole time I played the game, I maintained a job in the 'realer' world as a high school teacher while he was unemployed and lived in a family basement. He took his rank in the game very seriously, as it was very clear that the poor soul had very little power or influence in the 'realer' world.

Having a bit of status in a Simulation was what his poor soul grabbed onto for scraps of happiness.

The mentor had a talent for exploiting the rules of the game for cheap victories, and always knew the available ways to bend the rules and cheat. Along with the immense amounts of time that he spent playing the game, he stayed highly ranked until the programmers (Angels in this analogy) would close down his cheating loophole.

I remember some very unpleasant profanity-filled rants when the programmers of the game would release a software patch that made the game fair again. He claimed to write the programmers of the game angry emails, that I suspect were never seriously read.

I'd imagine the programmers at Blizzard were well-paid, and their title of programmers of a successful game allowed them to occupy a comfortable position in the world (real power). They had very little to gain by reading the profanity-laced angry emails of unemployed players.

I stopped playing the game in October of 2019 after a conscious choice was made to focus on spiritual growth instead of gaming, but I did not leave the game in anger. A few months earlier, my mentor had left the game in an angry fit. This was after programmers had once again released a software patch, which disallowed one of his particularly annoying ways of achieving exploitive victories in the game. I don't suspect the programmers or other players in the game lost too much sleep.

I felt the visceral frustration of my mentor as he called the programmers of the game terrible things, but seemed to be figuring out real-time that he had no real power in the situation; him leaving the game would only affect him.

This crude analogy goes to the core of the Angelic-demonic interactions. One side simply has power and the other side does not. The demonic live an existence of perpetual frustration, as their schemes for quasi-power never work out in the long run. I recommend one pray for these souls but do one's best to stay out of their way.

When interacting in this Simulation, keep in mind that:

The partically/physical level of the Simulation world has no power on its own or of itself (tested true).

Any out-picturing of the partically Simulation is simply to evolve our soul or true self and has no reality within itself. The more highly evolved a soul is, the more one can roll with the ebbs and flows of the partically Simulation. It is eventually realized that nothing purely physical is permanent, so in the big picture, its importance pales in comparison to the immortal life of the soul.

Reality Explained Like an MMORPG:

Angelic Takeaway: If one prefers real world interaction and has never heard the term MMORPG, this is a chapter one can easily skip. If one understands the functioning of this Angel-evolving Simulation, one can not help but notice the parallels between these fun Simulations within a Simulation. I write this chapter in hopes that the readers will resonate with the analogy and take this Simulation a bit less seriously. The more seriously one takes a video game or this Simulation, the more one is bound by it (tested true).

MMORPGs (Massively multiplayer online role playing games) are games where nerds around the world utilize the internet to control a computer-generated character inside a fake computer-generated world. Characters in the virtual world are free to interact, talk, work together, or fight. *World of Warcraft* and *Guild Wars* are popular classic examples.

In most of these games, all the characters exist in the same world and are free to interact with all the other characters. Generally, players of similar skill and power tend to interact most often. Characters of vastly different power levels interacting together tends to not be as fun.

Most MMORPGs have controls in place to minimize the interaction of characters of vastly differing power levels. This is similar to how players in this Simulation tend to interact most commonly with players operating from the same level of the Simulation. This is commonly called the law of attraction in spiritual circles.

A person accustomed to meditation in nature would be uncomfortable at a party with gangster rap playing in the background, but most party-oriented people would likely be bored or uncomfortable meditating in a natural setting.

As mentioned earlier, a lot of the friction and drama of this world occurs when players at different levels of the Simulation interact. However, this serves the ultimate evolutionary purpose of this purgatorial Simulation.

If one has played a MMORPG (Massively multiplayer online role playing game) then one has perhaps noticed some similarities between that simulated reality and this Angelic-simulated reality.

A similarity between most of the MMORPGs I played and this reality is that it is obvious that we are not all playing the game with the same goals. This occurs in this Angel-evolving Simulation because we are all in vastly different stages of soul evolution. It occurs in MMORPGs for similar reasons, but mostly people are playing the game for different reasons.

If one plays modern MMORPGs they will notice some people will be interested in playing the game exactly the way the programmers (Angels of the MMORPG) intended. Some players will be interested in having a character whose combat abilities are maximized so they can kill things (mainly other players). Some players are interested in collecting the in-game currency and becoming rich. Some players want to find ways to exploit the rules to maximize their position within a fake world. Some players are just interested in chatting with people around the world. Some players may be looking for love. Some players are just interested in making their player look nice by buying exotic skins and decorating their in-game house. All these modes of gameplay are fine. A bit of turbulence is encountered when people playing the game in different ways encounter each other, and that sounds an awful lot like this Simulation.

Another way of looking at the different levels of the Simulation is to identify the game they are actually playing down here.

Root: Pleasure vs. Pain game (basic survival).

Sacral: My Tribe vs. Your Tribe game. (Many modern online games are well set up to play a version of this game.)

Solar Plexus: Win the individual game while following the rules.

Heart: Be a positive presence in order to make the Simulation enjoyable for others.

Throat: Learn how the details of how Simulation works so you can explain it to others and have fun within it.

Third Eye: Spread love and joy in the game while enjoying the humor of it all.

Crown: Correct major bugs that are ruining gameplay for everyone. Monitor the game to make sure everyone is evolving and correct major power imbalances.

Here are some favorite in-game hangouts/activities for the various levels of the Simulation:

Root: Liquor stores, all-you-can-eat buffets (these first two were my favorites when operating at this level) jails, street fights, and isolation.

Sacral: Ethnocentric areas, arguing about politics online.

Solar Plexus: Sporting events, gyms, work.

Heart: Churches, charity runs and events, schools.

Throat: Libraries, universities, laboratories.

Third Eye: Tend to go wherever they are needed to maximize the amount of love and energy in the game.

Crown: Once physical death is realized as a 'so what,' many of the amusements of this dimension lose their luster. Time is preferred away from too much physical action so one can enjoy their state of bliss and do their job.

As mentioned earlier:

The partically/physical simulated world has no power on its own and of itself (tested true).

This is important to remember because it helps one from getting too lost in the details of the Simulation. One is really a wave, and this partically Simulation and physical body are just add-ons. One hopefully realizes in an MMORPG and in this Simulation that the character one is playing will eventually need to be put aside.

If one is familiar with MMORPGs or video games in general, here is a rough translation guide.

Disclaimer: some nuance of meaning lost in translation.

Physical Reality = Computer code

Ego/Physical body = Game Character

Soul/Wave = Player

Mind = Controller

Old Soul = Player who has already completed multiple play-throughs

Natural Disaster = Challenge Scenario

Belief System = Optional App

Genetics = Character Stats

God = Game Designer

Fight = Battle Scene

War = Multiplayer Battle Scene

Logical Debate = Special battle mode unlocked by high level players operating from the Throat level of the Simulation

Injury = Temporary Stat Loss

Death = Respawn

Reincarnation = Restart

Racism = Terrible Gameplay

Love = God-Mode Unlock

Hobbies = Side Quests

Reiki = Healing Spell

Meditation = Self-Healing Spell

Hypnosis = Mind Suggestion Spell

Fashion = Worthless In-Game Purchase

Education = Useful In-Game Purchase

Lover = Tight In-Game Alliance

Bad Karma = Bad Luck

Good Karma = Good Luck

Alien: Character From a Different Game

Angel = High-Level Player

Archangel = Higher-Level player

Guardian Angel = Higher-Level friend

Soulmate = Friend you've played another game with before

Non player character = souls operating in the 1st and 2nd levels of the simulation

Tabletop Role Playing Games = Going a layer deeper into the Simulation with effort

Video Role Playing Games = Going a layer deeper into the Simulation without effort

Science = Cheat Codes

Car = Fast Travel Spell

Airplane = Very Fast Travel Spell

Astral Travel = Teleport Spell

Taxes = Subscription Fee

School = Tutorial

Healthy Food = Stat Boosts

Junk Food = Stat Decreases

Drugs = Illusionary Stat Boost

Angry People = Hostile Characters

Vibe = Character Level

Soul Evolution = Level Up

Infant = Noob

Dog = Slightly lower-level friend with super high smelling and sensing stats

Bully = Really low-level player with a high strength stat.

Celebrity = Mid-level player with high charisma and appearance stats

Scientist = Title awarded to players who have unlocked the entire logical skill tree

Purgatory = Earth Game

Heaven = Good Ending

Hell = Bad Ending

Magic = Hidden Power

Insect = Really Low-Level Opponent

External Reality = Low-Level Opponent

Demon = Mid-Level Opponent

Ego Shadow = High-Level Opponent

Universal Source Code:

Angelic Takeaway: This Simulation has a core code with God ultimately at the top. Higher-level programs manage the big picture issues of the Simulation. These programs pass energy down to lower-level programs, eventually stepping down until one finds programs that run the simple critters enjoying their existence eating weeds and poop.

God() {

Archangel Level { Big_Picture_Simulation_Executive_Function()

 Crown Level { Simulation programming()

  Third Eye Level { Simulation energy distribution()

   Throat Level { Simulation knowledge holding and distribution()

    Heart Level { Animal_world_executive_function()

     Solar Plexus Level { Animal_error_correction()

      Sacral Level { Animal_social_norm_managment()

       Root Level { Animal_survival() }}}}}}}}}

This is a hypothetical program structure for the Simulation which shows the higher levels of the Simulation as nesting the lower levels of the hierarchy. If one understands the concept of nested hierarchies in programming, one can see that the function of the lower levels of the Simulation are completely dependent on the higher levels.

A theme of this book is that the Angelic always wins in the end and if one is familiar with this programming structure one can see the futility of function nested inside a higher function struggling against the higher function. This is the sad futility of an ardent atheist struggling against divinity. An entity misbehaving in the lower levels of the Simulation is really only hurting themselves as the higher levels can simply cut off power to the lower level entity.

The late Joseph Chilton Pierce, in his book *The Biology of Transcendence*, observed the dominion of someone in a higher level of the Simulation (which he called unconflicted behavior) over someone operating from a lower level. He does not use the Simulation terminology that I do, but both metaphors point to the same fundamental truth (tested true).

Divine energy flows from the higher levels of the Simulation to the lower levels of the Simulation. If a higher level of the Simulation is healthy, it corrects errors in the levels below it. An error in a higher level tends to compound as it flows down the levels of the Simulation. On an individual level, a positively aligned Crown chakra corrects the errors in the lower chakras over time, but a misaligned Crown will compound errors in the lower chakras over time.

Another key element to this Simulation is that time lag increases exponentially as one falls through the levels of the Simulation. At the higher levels of the Simulation, delay between something appearing in one's consciousness and then manifesting in physical reality is extremely short. Each layer down in the Simulation sees an exponential increase in this time lag (tested true). This is why a criminal operating in the lower levels of the Simulation is often able to go many years, or even an entire lifetime without karma catching up with him or her. Higher level entities notice very little difference between their thoughts and external reality.

The calibration process and similar processes such as divination that appear magical are ways for the higher levels of the Simulation to pass important data down to lower levels of the Simulation. This is similar to the way an operating system on a computer (higher level) communicates with an application (lower level) running within the operating system.

Rising up through the levels of the Simulation is analogous to rising in altitude on a plane. Rising up a level of the Simulation involves lots of adjustments to one's being, their relationship to their surroundings, and one's role in the Simulation. One's reality will change quite dramatically, and life becomes temporarily chaotic as the final pieces of karma from the lower level come up to be cleared. A plane is often steady and stable when cruising at a constant altitude, but temporary turbulence is felt when the plane begins to rise.

As stated elsewhere, when one endeavors to rise through the levels of the Simulation, karma from the lower levels of the Simulation rapidly surfaces to be processed. When I had my Angelic experience in December of 2019, I naively thought I was spiritually in the clear, but the reality was opposite. Over the next years, concurrent with COVID-19 my karma rapidly rose to the surface to be cleared. This showed up in my life a bit like the turbulence I've felt on a plane that was rising.

Whenever I've moved up a level in the Simulation in this life, I have also met with a strange resistance from the group I was interacting with at the time who were functioning on the previous level. I tended to react negatively to this resistance, but now it just seems natural. When one moves up a level in the Simulation, one is free from the restrictions of the lower level of the Simulation and one's individual perspective changes dramatically.

The people whom you were close to on the lower level of the Simulation tend to feel abandoned. A small part of the karma of moving up a level of the Simulation is to make this transition as kind as possible to friends on the lower level. Oftentimes a life change like moving to a new area or changing job is a convenient way for the Simulation to allow us to move to a new level without guilt.

I observed this quite often teaching in an urban high school. When I had a student actively pursuing a more comfortable life outside of their native urban area, they'd encounter resistance from acquaintances in their urban area. This is a well-observed phenomenon when gang or cult members try to leave the pack.

As I've personally encountered this resistance in a number of different contexts, I've learned one should try not to view this resistance with hostility, but simply see it for what it is: love. Your former lower-level associates are temporarily losing you. Unfortunately, soul evolution marches on, and one is generally surprised how quickly new soulmates and friends are found on the new higher level of the Simulation.

First Level of the Simulation: The Root Chakra (Broadly Masculine)

Angelic Takeaway: The lowest level of the Simulation is associated with the Root chakra. One wields little actual power from this level, as its purpose is to keep the physical body alive which isn't even the real self. Reptiles and simple forms of life occupy this level so it was a necessary stage in evolution. Pain and pleasure nervous system impulses control life at this level.

Evolution starts at this level as tiny organisms and simple reptiles. Entities operating from this level of the Simulation are run by their pleasure and pain inputs and lessons at this level revolve around nuances surrounding this. It eventually evolves to the point where one can function within a pack, which is the next level of the Simulation: the Sacral level.

Humans operating from this level of the Simulation live an almost completely partically/animal existence. Empathic folks feel an energy of desperation and danger around this level/vibration. As life is run by pleasure and pain impulses, there is almost no inherent morality. One should not expect an alligator to follow the golden rule if one jumps in the water with them.

Most of us temporarily fall back to this level when dealing with survival situations, a traumatic event, the downside of chemical abuse, or even lengthy depressions. I believe this could be described as human consciousness with no bells or whistles. Simple survival is the top priority.

In the ancient world, you would have found quite a few humans operating from this level living a primal hunter-gatherer lifestyle. You still find large amounts of people at this level in the poorer areas where drugs, crime, and apathy rule the streets and culture.

In this life I've regularly seen groups temporarily occupy this Root chakra level. At jobs when bad news would come down the chain of command, people (including myself) would go into a temporary, whiny Root energy. One would feel cut off from help, like a particle cut off from its wavy power source.

Some people find this level temporarily enjoyable due to the temporary adrenal gland rush. This is often the motive for dangerous hunts, daredevil stunts, or watching dark or scary movies.

In the human world, this vibration is often perceived as bad, useless, or at its worst, evil. I think 'extremely selfish' is the most accurate phrase, as this is simply how life behaves at this level of evolution. It's only dangerous when given worldly power, like the leadership of a large organization or a weapon. However, every vibration of life serves a divine purpose. This might be the perfect level for a Neanderthal learning how to make tools and mastering the basics of physical reality.

Also well-known in twelve-step communities such as Alcoholics Anonymous, it is often at the lowest points where one can let go and completely surrender to God. This results in an extremely rapid climb up the levels of the Simulation.

Here is a personal experience of this vibration:

After a night of heavy drinking (not a recommended action) I awoke at 3 a.m. with a severe headache. The only thought that my compromised psyche seemed to be able to process was that I was thirsty, craving salt, and miserable.

I stumbled clumsily down my staircase. All my effort was put into walking the body. There was no higher consciousness or deep thinking going on, no contemplation of the meaning of life or higher mental function.

I found a bottle of Gatorade and chugged it so fast, half of it ended up on the front of my shirt. Still craving salt, I went to my refrigerator and found a jar of pickles. I struggled to open the jar because the concept "lefty loosey, righty tighty" was beyond me. Just wanting salt, I drank the pickle juice, leaving the pickles. After the juice was drained, the jar was dropped, and pickles and glass went all over my floor. Feeling careless and with biological needs met, tiredness returned. I stumbled back upstairs and fell into a dreamless sleep.

About seven hours later I woke up and headed downstairs to find the mess from the night before: pickles and glass all over the floor, a puddle of gatorade, and a refrigerator which was never even closed. This was a temporary experience of the Root chakra level of the Simulation. It was enough consciousness to satisfy physical senses and perform very basic human functions, but no higher functioning available.

I experienced this level in a very sheltered environment during the first seven years of this life, but with strong support from my highly energized Third Eye and Crown chakras. I needed to re-align with this level so I relearned survival in physical life after I'd completely given up in a previous life during a slow, gruesome death in the Vietnam war.

Modern expressions of this level look like apathy, drug addiction, homelessness, mental illness, and physical sickness.

Evolution: This vibration of consciousness began to show up when machinery complex enough to be capable of self-awareness showed up in early life. Most reptiles and insects operate from this level of the Simulation. This may be the vibration of life where one learns the basics of using one's individual intelligence for the purposes of bare survival.

Subjective First-Person Experience: Experience in this band of vibration occurred in my early life in a pleasant, sheltered way and then again during my low point of this life in my twenties when I struggled to survive in an apparently loveless world while heavily addicted to alcohol.

One feels completely cut off from any assistance from the wavy universe or any concept of love or divinity. One feels alone and one feels powerless to change the situation. The lower parts of this frequency band are experienced as hellish.

The point of this book is not to instill fear, but if I must do it once, it will be with this statement: Do not even mess with the things that send one's soul to the lower parts of this level. The suffering one endures is not even comprehendible from the perspective of the higher chakras. Follow the ten time-tested commandments and don't play with the demonic!

Soul Lessons: Soul lessons at this level are the basics of individual basic survival, managing pleasure and pain nervous system responses. Eventually when one has a tentative hold on individual survival or paradoxically when one's individual survival is threatened, one begins to see the value of others, which leads one to the Sacral chakra level of the Simulation.

Second Level of the Simulation: The Sacral Chakra (Broadly Feminine)

Angelic Takeaway: This level of the Simulation appeared on Earth when animals complex enough to function in packs appeared. The game Follow the Leader was likely invented at this level. This level is far advanced over the one below it, but is still run by a simple 'safety in numbers' principle. When stating unpopular opinions, expect attacks from packs of entities operating from this level of the Simulation.

At this level of the Simulation life is still very simple, but it now learns to work with others in groups, often called tribes or packs.

At this level, one has a tribal mentality. Empathic folks feel an energy of fear around this vibration. At this vibration, one has risen above bare survival of the physical body and feels an urge to form groups to increase survivability. The solution to the fear of this level of the Simulation is safety in numbers.

The rules, traditions, opinions, and superstitions of one's pack are followed with an almost religious zeal at this level. It is common to think that anyone not following the ways of the pack should be kicked out or members of opposing packs attacked. Modern human packs love to do this online through social media.

A person at this level born into a strong family structure tends to view their immediate and extended family as their pack. If born into a weak family structure, the person tends to seek a pack externally. This can be a political group, social group, or gang.

At this Sacral level, one still feels very much like an alone particle. There is a weak connection to the wavy universe, just strong enough to rise above mere individual survival by bonding with others into a tight pack structure. Military training programs often play to this level, encouraging units of trainees to function as a pack.

Superstition is common at this level of the Simulation as one's worldview is not complex. One tends to have a magical view of life and one's pack leader is the primary source of truth. Many people in western world, educated in the basics of the scientific method, have trouble understanding this level. The relationship between cause and effect, which a lot of educated folks take for granted, is very weak here. During the COVID-19 pandemic, much superstition from this level replaced rational science and spiritual values from the higher levels.

When someone uses the term "sheep" in a derogatory way, they are often describing someone operating from this level of the Simulation. An entity at this level does not have the complexity to form an individualized worldview, so the pack's views are unquestionably their views. In the higher Simulation levels, one's intelligence increasingly produces a personally-formed worldview, but at this level, one's pack is often their primary and only source of truth. This is not bad or evil, but simply representative of a certain stage of evolution. However, some human packs who deviate too far from logical truth can end up doing things that could be interpreted as evil by most of society (gangs, Marxists, Nazis).

Modern Expressions: Gang members, isolated cultures, fundamentalist religions, politically-correct crowd.

Evolution: This stage of evolution showed up when early humans began forming into tight tribal/pack structures. Survival was much more efficient in packs and allowed for some specialization. This resulted in humans producing some of the first music, art and technology.

Subjective First-Person Experience: Experience here was generally unpleasant for this soul. I did not feel the self confidence that manifests in the higher levels. I tended to be a strict rule follower of whoever I perceived as the strongest member of the pack I was in. I did this due to an almost complete lack of personal power; it was simply the best tool available to counteract fear and obtain a semblance of security. In this level of the Simulation, survival seems completely to be based on the power of one's pack and one's position within it.

Soul Lessons: Basic socialization. Using basic intelligence to increase one's position within the pack and defend one's pack against enemies either real or imagined. Eventually as one tentatively masters life within a pack, the evolving psyche will seek individual expression. It will then strive to break free of overly restrictive pack structures and enter the Solar Plexus level of the Simulation, where real spiritual power first appears.

Political Correctness:

Angelic Takeaway: Shit, Boobs, Merry Christmas, and AMERICA FUCK YEAH! If you were offended, kindly skip this chapter.

One of the more troubling things for society that I've observed coming out of the Sacral level of the Simulation is political correctness. It is often mistaken for proper manners, but in reality it's a way for tribes or packs of people to outlaw certain forms of expression that are not advantages to their group, tribe, or pack. Over time it leads to major distortions of truth, which leads to human social disasters.

The Sacral level of the Simulation isn't necessarily aligned with truth. Entities vibrating in this level of the Simulation follow the quasi-truth of their individual group, tribe, or pack. Once a group begins to use political correctness to promote its agenda, it spreads like a plaque throughout the members of the group, tribe, or pack unchecked at a horrific cost to society.

I recently met a gentleman who took a great interest in the fact that I'd begun to remember past lives. The conversation was going very pleasantly until I talked about one life as an African American.

During this life I was extremely patriotic (just as in this one), but ended up dying in a war for a country that at the time was unappreciative of my sacrifice. One of the main lessons from this life was to learn some of the nuances and plights of being a minority.

While describing this life I used the term 'black' to describe myself. To which, the gentleman interrupted me and told me to use the term 'African American.' He told me his reasons for this and why he found the term 'black' offensive. I did not strictly disagree with him on any particular point, so I let it go and continued the conversation.

A few moments later, I accidentally used the term 'black' again, to which I was scolded and given the same litany of reasons of why the term 'black' was offensive. The conversation now continued a bit under tension. Shortly after, in large part due to my limited language ability, the term 'black' came out again. To which he gentleman responded with a great deal of anger and I was called racist.

Now frustrated that I felt like I was being forced to use a seven-syllable phrase where a one-syllable word got the core idea across fairly well, I ended the conversation and have not interacted with this gentleman since.

I've also run into similar instances with the LGBTQ+ community.

If my physical body were examined by an elite team of medical doctors they would likely conclude two things:

- That if forced into a binary decision about my sex I would need to be called a 'male,' as I have a penis and most of the traits associated with males

- Although a male, my body has an unusually high amount of feminine traits that manifest physically, emotionally, mentally, and spiritually.

As a child in a traditional environment I learned to hide my more feminine traits, but as I've gotten older I've slowly become more transparent about them; I've realized in most cases they are an advantage and not a disadvantage. At no point in life have I had strong opinions on either side of the LGBTQ+ political issues, despite often being someone treading the line between masculine and feminine energies.

About a decade before the writing of this book, I made a great friend whom I was able to have deep philosophical conversations with. We agreed fundamentally on most major issues affecting humanity.

As the years have passed, this person became very active in the LGBTQ+ community. I was generally much more concerned with other aspects of life, so I was unable to keep up with increasingly complex issues that he was becoming further involved in.

My limited language ability caused me to often slip up in language with this person, which tended to cause offense. Over time this person found me increasingly offensive, and I found it less enjoyable to talk to this person; I simply could not dodge the minefield of topics and words that offended him.

There is no longer any contact with that person, which is a bit sad given the once enjoyable friendship.

My autistic condition limits my language ability, which makes following the ever-changing language rules of political correctness particularly difficult. However, my autistic condition allows me to cut to the essence of things. This condition was shared by one of my historical heroes, Winston Churchill (tested true).

Churchill was unpopular in Europe during Hitler's rise, as he clearly saw what Hitler was at his core. But as Hitler was popular in Europe, Churchill's politically-incorrect criticism of him made him even more unpopular.

Pre-World War Two Europe was a good example of political correctness run amok. As the bureaucracy of Europe became more complex, the mistreatment of the Jewish people became a politically correct thing to do. A minority in Europe saw why this was wrong, but they were simply far outnumbered. This is the danger of letting Sacral pack truth replace actual truth.

When Hitler began his invasions and his true colors were revealed, Great Britain turned to Churchill to save them from disaster. Churchill, who was an Angel in a human body (tested true), was able to draw a desperate defensive line down the English Channel and prevent Hitler from ever conquering his island, even though he was desperately outgunned militarily. This saved the world many years of great suffering (tested true).

Unfortunately, Winston Churchill fell from political power after the war's conclusion, due to his tendency to say politically incorrect things.

Whenever I've observed a word or concept banned from proper public discourse, the word or concept moves into the shadows away from the public eye and propagates in a more negative form. Wild conspiracy theories draw power in the shadows when the human pack bans their expression in public. If one finds a certain form expression forcefully opposed by the human pack, it may be worth investigating the reason for this. It is often the most taboo political discussions that are the most critical for society to engage in (tested true).

Though I do not advocate that absolutely no controls be placed on what is acceptable to say in society, political correctness is fundamentally flawed not due to its intention, but with the results it actually produces. When any group tries to force language or ban a concept from the world, karma dictates that an equal and opposite reaction force is automatically produced. Conflict and war tends to be the eventual result of these opposing forces.

In the long run, political correctness always produces the exact opposite effect of its original intention (tested true).

Third Level of the Simulation: The Solar Plexus Chakra (Broadly Masculine)

Angelic Takeaway: This is the level of the Simulation where true personal power first appears. If you need something fixed around your house, find a person operating from this level of the Simulation. This level forms the brick or mortar of the world. Integrity, hard work, and standing up for what is right is born from this level of evolution.

One should note that this is the first level of the Simulation where an entity wields spiritual power of actual significance. This means the entities' consciousness has an effect on the Simulation beyond what it is physically doing alone. It is also the first level where one can alter their existing ego programming, and not simply be subject to the programming of their external environment. This ability to alter one's inherent programming increases exponentially every level from here on up.

One now begins to perceive a bit of wavy reality instead of just partically appearance. This gives this level an inherent sense of right and wrong. In the first two levels one must be taught that stealing is wrong, but at this level, one will intuit that stealing is wrong, although mistakes and temptations will still occur.

While operating out of the Sacral level one tends to follow a pack. At this level of the Simulation there is now enough energy flow and intelligence to attempt to lead a pack or seek individual security or glory. Empathic folks tend to feel safe in the presence of this vibration.

This level is also the dividing line between where life moves from exploiting life to survive to supporting life to survive. This is the first level where one serves life. Below this level entities survive by killing, eating, or exploiting other life forms.

However, nuance is needed. Wolves tend to operate in the Sacral level of the Simulation and live by hunting, catching, and eating other animals.

From a limited lens, one could say the wolves are hurting the rabbits by catching and eating them. However, the wolves, by catching the slower, less intelligent rabbits more often, actually serve the rabbits' evolution through natural selection. If one looks beyond simple appearance, it becomes clear that all life is serving all life in a beautiful process of co-evolution and creation.

Intelligent animals kept as pets generally have access to this level of the Simulation. Dogs, cats and horses are often observed to have a mind of their own, which is their Solar Plexus exerting its individual will for the purpose of its evolution.

People living at this level try to put the world in right order. If one needs a mechanical object fixed, this is the level one should seek out. Part of my autism is I seem to have a little less of myself resonating at this level than normal, so I have always struggled with mechanical objects. I often marvel at this level's ability to put anything back together.

A concept that comes from this level is hard work. This level tends to instill this concept into the youth for the benefit of all society. A telltale sign of a person operating largely from this level is a strong work ethic and a nose-to-the-grindstone attitude. People operating primarily out of the Solar Plexus work the long hours and do the difficult jobs for society that no one else is willing to do.

However, hard work should not be confused with the ultimate spiritual truth. If that were the case, people working sixteen hours a day and refusing to take time off would be the happiest, most successful people on the planet. In general, they are not.

Hard work is a nuanced concept when accomplishing goals. Writing this book required occupying a nuanced position between extremes. At times I needed to force a tired body to write and edit, but I also needed to honor divine timing and let it flow when it was ready to come through.

Long-term goals and education become viable realities at this level, and one now has the discipline and morals to show up to a job everyday. Showing up to an integrous job every day, even if one is imperfect and mistakes occasionally made, magnetically pulls the lower levels of the Simulation into the Solar Plexus Level (tested true).

There is enough energy available to be a winner in sports, have the best-looking house in the neighborhood, or even be the boss at work. Lives at this level are rarely perfect, and the lessons the Angels give an entity at this level revolve around testing one's integrity against temptations.

Modern Expressions: Blue collar workers, salt-of-the-earth people, martial artists, soldiers, motivational speakers (those who encourage success and effort).

Evolution: This stage of evolution showed up with the first great military rulers as now this level of the Simulation had built things worth ruling. The empire of Rome seems to represent the pinnacle of a society run by this level.

Subjective First-Person Experience: Unlike the lower vibrations, one feels a bit of innate power here. Because of this, one is interested in rising to the top of whatever social system one finds oneself in. Being competitive is very natural at this level. One tends to be happy when one is winning and not happy when one is losing. Due to my personal genetics, I tended to win in academics but lose in sports. This resulted in a very mixed experience at this level. The quasi-happiness after a win or accomplishment never seemed to last.

Soul Lessons: By aligning with integrity one realizes one is aligning with the power that runs the entire Simulation. Being one's best, prioritizing long-term goals over short-term goals, the value of hard work, and rule by both power and force are all soul lessons at this level. Eventually, one realizes that dominating others by force and winning does not lead to lasting happiness. With legitimate spiritual power, one begins to feel karmic blowback when one abuses it. Therefore one begins to seek higher truth and a softer way of being, which leads to the Heart chakra level of the Simulation.

Fourth Level of the Simulation: The Heart Chakra (Broadly Feminine)

Angelic Takeaway: This is the level of the Simulation where some of the nicest people in the world operate from. Worldly power accumulates here, as functioning in the physical world is optimal. Entities have a lot of spiritual power, but they do not float so high as to lose their worldliness. It is tough not to follow a person operating from this level when they have a cause which has ignited their spirit.

Entities at this level of the Simulation are run by goodwill and tend to follow the prevailing good causes of society. True personal and romantic love arises at this level of the Simulation.

However, sometimes what is actually good for society is more nuanced than this level of development realizes.

Even greater spiritual power appears at this level of the Simulation; humans at this level tend to be the movers and shakers of society. A house built by a person in the Solar Plexus level of the Simulation will be reliable and functional, but a house built by this level will have artistic flair and a special charm.

At this level, the soul searches for ultimate truth and serves something higher than itself. Empathic folks feel a sense of goodwill when in the presence of this level. Individuals at this level are very interested in doing good in the world. When this level finds a good cause, it serves it undyingly. This level will typically try to improve the experience of those around them, unless the person holds an ideology which conflicts with their higher truth.

Many basic spiritual practices such as Reiki and meditation begin to appear at this level of development, as the soul now has enough power to make them work. Lower levels often attempt them but give them up as futile, because there isn't enough power available to collapse the wave function into the desired result.

This level is often found in teachers, religious leaders, and high-ranking military members. Teachers in this level of the Simulation tend to be at every school event and are popular. Religious leaders at this level draw followers due to their enthusiasm. Military members at this level are the true engine that makes the whole system run and keep morale up during the tough times.

Individuals here have a good deal of positive energy and charisma; this gives them the ability to draw people to their causes. When meeting someone at this level, it is very clear they are serving something greater than themselves rather than just their individual self. They tend to get what they want through a combination of spiritual power and good worldly functioning, which are both strong at this level.

How someone operates from this level of the Simulation is highly context dependent. One is an effective cheerleader for prevailing good causes in one's society. Teenagers born into traditional America with a strong Heart vibe express the all-American stereotype: well rounded, high-achieving students who strive to be of service.

Political division still appears at this level. When born into a conservative area of America, this level supports law and order, business initiatives, and financial prosperity. If born into a liberal area, it supports education, social causes, and equality.

From my personal experience, this seems to be the level where functioning in the physical world is optimal. One has enough spiritual power to support what is perceived as the highest good, but one is still grounded enough to not be floating in the clouds with Angels most of the time. There is enough positive energy available to project one's will into the world, but one does not get caught up in the head as often. This tends to be an issue for the next higher Throat level.

World religions, integrous governments, integrous corporations, and strong social organizations tend to have large vibrational components at this level.

Modern Expressions: feel-good movies, liberal religions, loyal servants to integrous organizations, Chinese fortune cookie messages, leaders, motivational speakers (those who encourage goodness and service).

Evolution: As the great military empires such as Rome began to crumble under their own weight, the great religions tended to fill the power vacuum and began to create a society that transcended the "might makes right" ideology.

Subjective First-Person Experience: With the competitiveness and violence of lower levels under control, one can now seek big-picture truth. One finds happiness in self-improvement, which allows one to be of service to the world. This level is the easiest to function at on a worldly level, as one is generally enthusiastic about life but tends not to go against one's prevalent societal culture.

Soul Lessons: Search for more permanent truths and be of service to the whole. This level sees the world through a 'positive vs negative' lens and strives to support that which they consider positive. However what needs to be learned at this level is that what is true good is more complex than what the soul initially thought. After perhaps supporting a couple of causes that were not truly as good as one believed and facing the karmic backlash, the strict lines of 'positive vs. negative' may become a bit more nuanced. One then strives for a higher truth, developing one's intellect and respect for the scientific method in the Throat chakra level of the Simulation.

Fifth Level of the Simulation: The Throat Chakra (Broadly Masculine)

Angelic Takeaway: Do you read a lot? Do you enjoy long conversations of intellectually nuanced topics? Do you find it a bit difficult to find satisfaction in the more shallow aspects of life? If you answered 'yes' to these questions, welcome to the Throat chakra level of the Simulation, which is the level that this book is largely written from.

A telltale sign of a person operating from the Throat chakra level of the Simulation is their living space or tablet is often filled with books, the majority of which have been read. The main responsibility of this level of the Simulation is to attain, retain, and transmit holistic knowledge to the rest of the Simulation (tested true).

Empathic folks immediately recognize this level as a reliable source of truth and wisdom. A person operating from this level of the Simulation is likely knowledgeable in a very wide array of human endeavors. At this level, one's true higher self is now developed enough to think independently and provide intelligent solutions to human problems that the lower levels of the Simulation are unable to see. Many technological advancements come out of this level.

Humans at this level are the keepers of truth for the world, and can be counted on to do the reasonable thing. Where the Heart level seeks absolutes to believe in, the Throat level sees intellectual nuance and avoids extreme positions. This level will often take an unpopular political position because it sees the higher truth. Its intellectual integrity demands it.

Aside COVID-19.

At the onset of the COVID-19 pandemic, I saw a social environment in my area where the Heart and Throat levels of the Simulation were working in relative harmony. In March 2020 when this mysterious virus hit, the people operating from the Heart tended to support the greater good and strongly supported restrictions in order to 'stop the spread.' The Throat level, however, looked at the situation through a deeper lens. Though not blatantly disregarding caution against the virus, they questioned the wisdom on enacting restrictions, which often had a bigger downside than upside.

This led to a split between the Heart and Throat levels which has not yet fully healed.

End Aside.

Someone vibrating in the Heart level of the Simulation may have the positive belief system "Every person in my country deserves food and shelter." They will then enthusiastically support this cause by whatever means available to them. Someone who's evolved to the Throat level will respect the inherent integrity of this belief system, but will also realize that it must be balanced with many other factors, such as health of the economy, military strength, infrastructure, education, and so on.

Many famous scientific discoveries came from this level. This level is willing to go against the grain if it sees an opportunity to support a higher truth, a way to advance society, or even personal gain. A voice vibrating at this level of the Simulation has enough power to shift scientific paradigms. Many of the famous scientists of history operated from here.

Nikoli Tesla, Isaac Newton and Albert Einstein are classic examples.

Modern expressions: Scientists, libraries, some universities, democracies, capitalism, motivational speakers (those who encourage study and achievement).

Evolution: The bubonic plague exposed the limitations of religious leadership at the time, which was largely in the Heart level. It was the Throat level and the arising intellect that ultimately provided a reliable defense against the plague. Shortly after, the free-thinkers, scientists, and artists of the renaissance began to wield major societal influence. Education and intellectual development began to gain widespread societal support.

Subjective First-Person Experience: This is a very pleasant vibration and a major component of this book. In the Throat level, one is very happy alone with a good book or intellectually-stimulating activity. One desires to learn the mysteries of the universe. This level loves to wrap one's mind around things. In the Heart level, one desires to be of service to the world and therefore tends to be very involved in the world. In the Throat level, one tends to take a step back and look at life through a wider, more intellectually rigorous lens.

Soul Lessons: Develop one's intelligence and ability to look at the world rationally. This involves learning the logical fallacies. One learns to take a bird's eye view of the world and use one's intelligence to accomplish things that seem impossible to the lower levels of the Simulation. Eventually, one evolves to a point where there appears a desire to escape the cold world of the intellect and seek a more loving, holistic way of life in the Third Eye level of the Simulation.

Note: An early error I made when first exposed to the scales of consciousness was confusing people operating from the reasonable fifth level of the Throat level of the Simulation with a high IQ. I've since found there was actually very little correlation between IQ and the level of the Simulation a person is operating from.

I was blessed with a high IQ in this life, and the same IQ functioned while operating from every level of the Simulation. Here is how a high IQ functioned at the different levels of the Simulation, in my particular case:

Root: I spent little time working, while spending most time intoxicated, eating, and sleeping while minimizing interference from the people in my life and the authorities. If one doubts the intelligence that can spring from this lowest simple level of the Simulation, I'd encourage you to visit your poor pothead friends and see the technology they have rigged up to get the chemical THC into their brain most efficiently.

Sacral: I liked to defend my pack and argue while not contributing much to whatever walk of life I was in. I had a talent at working my way into a high position in whatever pack, group, or tribe I found myself in. I enjoyed complaining about how the other packs were ruining my life in a quasi-logical way, using logical fallacies quite effectively.

Solar Plexus: I put my intellect to work trying to minimize body fat percentage while maximizing muscle. Due to genetics, I was never overly successful. I was very financially responsible and frugal at this level, saving money and investing well. I performed the day-to-day duties of life integrously and sought to advance my position in the world.

Heart: I put my mind to work doing my best to improve the quality of life of those around me and contributing to the success of whatever organization I was in. Worldly functioning was the optimal here, and I had a positive impact wherever I was. However, I often confused what society thought was best for myself and others with what actually was best for myself and others. A subtle, but important difference.

Throat: I read a lot and was interested in the pursuit of knowledge. I would never be interested in a specific field for very long, as I was more interested in a holistic understanding of the world. The high IQ was of most service here, as it was a prerequisite for many of the societal positions typically reserved for people operating from this level.

Third Eye: I wanted to find the most efficient way to increase the energy level wherever I was and make those around me feel loved. The intellect was utilized exploring the world of spirituality and science through books, movies, and experience.

Crown: One is generally very uninterested in using intellect, as in these high levels, a meditative/prayer state is far more natural. Intellect was utilized to explore the world's great spiritual teachings and aligning itself optimally in the service of God.

The Logical Fallacies:

Angelic Takeaway: Often proper logical thinking is more nuanced than what one originally believed. It is easy to fall for false arguments that utilize the logical fallacies. These are arguments that sound convincing but actually invalid. Believing them may eventually have you trading your retirement for a bag of magic beans.

The Throat level of the Simulation is generally well-respected by society. People who operate here develop most of the technology of the planet and are the keepers of wisdom for the human race. However, only about 10% of the human race operates from here, even though a much larger percentage of the population thinks that they operate from here.

The lower levels of the Simulation see the power and prestige associated with this Throat level of the Simulation and will try to impersonate it. If one has ever stumbled into a social media political argument, you will probably find many people pretending to be logical members of the Throat level who quite obviously aren't. When separating the folks operating in the Throat level of the Simulation (people you should probably listen to) from the folks operating lower levels (people you probably shouldn't listen to) it helps to have a working understanding of logical fallacies.

Logical Fallacies are arguments that sound convincing but are actually based on faulty logic, and are therefore invalid. Having a working understanding of them will help you resonate in the Throat level of the Simulation, fix some programming errors in your thinking, and probably most importantly, recognize when someone is trying to feed you invalid information. Studying the great books of the western world (with the exception of Marx) gives one a taste of reason and logic without the logical fallacies.

Books written by people more knowledgeable than me on the subject have been written, however, here are a few logical fallacies I've observed commonly used to distort reasonable discussion in society.

Straw Man Fallacy: This is when someone attacks a position or argument which does not exist. I see this happening quite often in online political discussions where the political left attempts to project an uncaring, racist attitude on the political right, and the political right attempts to project a fiscally-irresponsible, anarchist attitude onto the left. In some cases these attitudes exist in reality, but it's not typical among the reasonable population.

For example, a very liberal friend after seeing *Top Gun Two* made an out-of-context comment that the strong minority and female representation must have pissed me off.

This was an attack on a position I simply did not hold, as a day before I'd commented to a friend that the increased minority and female representation was an improvement over the first *Top Gun* (which despite this minor flaw is still the greatest movie of all time).

I've also observed people of faith get attacked for the most illogical actions and beliefs of people of their religion and people of science attacked for people claiming to be scientifically minded but actually aren't.

False Cause Fallacy: Oftentimes people will compare the correlation of two things (things happening together) with the two things causing each other.

For example, I could observe that the number of pirates off the coast of America has been steadily decreasing while our national debt has been steadily increasing, and then errantly conclude that pirates were keeping the national debt down.

Most often in the practical world we see this used to defend errant political policies. Observations of positive trends to defend an errant policy which just happened to occur concurrently are examples of this logical fallacy.

Two trends can rarely be correlated together in isolation, particularly with large economies. An economy has the potential to thrive, especially if it has positive momentum, despite a single bad policy being forced. Be cautious of people trying to isolate correlations in defense of pre-planned arguments. Everything ties together in an infinitely complex divine tapestry.

Ad Hominem Fallacy: This is where logic is essentially ignored and the speaker is attacked directly. This happens a lot in modern contentious political races. For example, an integrous statesman operating from the reasonable Throat level of the Simulation gets his or her logical policies attacked by a lower-level candidate because of a tiny slip up during college.

This tends to be a way that the lower energy side of an argument avoids a direct confrontation with the truth. In a direct, fair confrontation, truth will beat non-truth 100% of the time (tested true). The lower levels of the Simulation tend to demonize the higher levels in order to keep a temporary power balance in their favor, even though it's never maintainable in the long-run. A politician who runs a campaign centering primarily on attacking the other side is rarely equipped to lead (tested true). The way of love and truth always eventually prevails (tested true).

Sunken Cost Fallacy: If one has a predilection to gambling, this is one to be cautious about. Oftentimes when we've already poured resources and effort into a faulty endeavor, there is temptation to keep charade going in order to at least break-even. This is because we errantly place value on the lost resources.

I recall in middle school (still very underdeveloped at the Throat level) playing a Nintendo role-playing game called Dragon Warrior Three. Late in the evening, I wandered into the game's casino with a purse full of gold, (the game's currency). An early losing streak had me obsessing with just to get back to my starting point. The mind made the error of thinking the gold already lost and the time already invested had actual value, so I was on the verge of a big winning streak. Unfortunately the 1s and 0s on the Nintendo processing unit could not keep up with my thinking. I spent the night stressed out and the next day tired due to falling for this logical fallacy.

This fallacy tends to play on a person's pride which comes out of the Sacral and Solar Plexus levels of the Simulation. For example, this happens when someone buys a stock at $20 a share and it drops to $15. Despite signs the stock will continue the fall, the person holds onto the stock, or perhaps even buys more in a futile attempt to get back one's lost money. The person's mind on some level still values the stock at $20 a share which is errant.

This error has been made personally in this life with relationships. Previous energy and time invested in a relationship was over-valued, and the relationship was held onto long after it had served its purpose. Suffering usually resulted for both parties.

On a macro-scale, this could look like a political policy having a negative effect on society, but the social policy continuing to be pushed in an attempt to prove it works. I painfully observed this in education.

Bandwagon Fallacy: Just because everyone is thinking a certain way does not mean it is correct or logical. Most human souls in this Simulation are not operating from the higher levels.

This fallacy has grown more common in past years, and I believe it is partly owed to the nature of search engines and social media. A wrong idea begins popping up first on search engines and people's social media feeds it. Suddenly, everyone is talking about this false idea as if it is reality. A large percentage of the human population operates largely from the Sacral level of the Simulation. From this level, whatever the pack is saying must be the truth.

Something to keep in mind is that only about 10% of the human population is operating primarily from the reasonable Throat level. One should be cautious about accepting ideas simply because they are popular. A fallacy of all levels of the Simulation is assuming others see the world largely the way that you do. I've watched over and over again in this life as reasonable people are surprised when they observe that the majority of the population is not.

More time could be devoted to these but the purpose of this book is to help people evolve past the Throat level of the Simulation, not get further entrenched within it. On a practical level however, the logical fallacies are useful and practical to understand when arguing with your racist co-workers.

Sixth Level of the Simulation: The Third Eye Chakra (Broadly Feminine)

Angelic Takeaway: Though relatively uncommon in the human race at this time, many know someone operating from this level of the Simulation. They can be seen floating through life blissfully with very few problems. Major vulnerabilities still exist here, as one is still affected by the vicissitudes of life despite seeing life through rose colored glasses. One learns here to love the majestic lion without trying to get in its cage and share a burger with it.

In this level of the Simulation it becomes obvious that love is more powerful than anything below it. It becomes obvious that one's happiness is directly related with how loving one is.

At this level of the Simulation one is quite vulnerable. A relatively small portion of the world resonates here but one still interacts directly with the world. A major lesson of this level of the Simulation is to learn to use one's Third Eye, discern essence, and see into the deeper truth of things (tested true).

Many of the great spiritual masters of the past taught the way to enlightenment which broadly means resonating with the Crown level of the Simulation or higher. However, only a small percentage of the world is interested in these levels or even knows of their existence. Only one person in tens of millions is interested in enlightenment, as that is generally not the main point of this partically Simulation. One should not be surprised that people vibrating at these levels are incredibly rare. However, that makes their input extremely valuable.

My spiritual research has shown that the Third Eye level of the Simulation is a realistic and practical spiritual goal for the majority of humans on Earth at this time. One only needs to commit to being unconditionally loving and committing to seeing things as they are to begin resonating here. One has happiness and significant power here.

However, as one evolves toward this level, one finds being unconditionally loving more difficult and nuanced than anticipated.

First, as one rises through the levels of the Simulation, negative karma from the lower levels is activated to be experienced out so lessons are fully absorbed. This often results in a bit of temporary suffering.

Second, one learns that although they do indeed love everything, not everything is loving back, at least in the way one perceives love. At this level, one sees reality through rose-colored glasses, and forgets one is not actually living in a celestial realm. There are entities in the Simulation that do not have your highest interests at heart. The true meaning and nuance of the statement 'trust in God but tie up one's camel' is comprehended.

This level contains genuinely loving and wise people. Empathic folks will immediately feel the love and wisdom of anyone vibrating at this level. At this level you love others, and so by laws of the Simulation, you tend to be loved back. People at this level are very connected to the wavy/spiritual universe, which gives them a very loving, peaceful, but powerful way of being in the world. As long as trouble is actually recognized, they have the power to deal with it easily.

A weakness at this level is political naivety. In this loving bubble, one tends to expect the world to be loving and will often promote extremely progressive political causes, which make sense in their reality. However the percentage of people operating from this level of the Simulation is a minority. Oftentimes from this privileged mindset, one does not realize that most of the world lives in a very different reality. This level's murky dealings with the lower levels of Simulation can create some serious societal and political problems, as their realities are extremely different.

Most people love being around this level, as the aura projected from this level fills the room with a pleasant energy and feeds all the positive energies in the room. Integrous people have nothing to fear from entities at this level, as they are indeed safe.

Many people experience shades of this level of the Simulation. Because it feels exponentially better than the levels of the Simulation below it, people tend to re-seek the feeling. A downside of this phenomena is addiction. Marijuana increases the feeling of the Third Eye chakra and pull a person into this level of the Simulation temporarily. However, karma dictates that the high obtained from the Marijuana must eventually be balanced by an equal and opposite low.

Modern Expressions: Spiritual retreats, most churches and monasteries, genuinely loving people, a high energy party.

Evolution: As science and industry from the reasonable Throat level created a more wealthy and complex world, many humans were left behind. The world quickly became a smaller place for hunter/gatherers, the uneducated, and people without access to financial resources. The 1960s in America saw a large influx of the Third Eye level, with cultural phenomena such as The Beatles and peace movements. They encouraged the creation of a more loving, equal society but also brought with the challenges associated with this level. This level improves society, as long as it does not idealistically attack the lower levels of the Simulation that actually understand their function better than entities at this level. The great spiritual master probably does not understand the finer points of building a house or fixing a car.

Subjective First-Person Experience: Where one tends to be considered a bit odd by the world in the Throat level of the Simulation, public functioning becomes difficult at the Third Eye level, even though the experience is extraordinarily pleasant. One is simply in tune with the universe and wishes to stay there. Intellectual activity, natural at the Throat level, is now less natural. Meditation, gratitude, prayer and love become higher priorities than any type of striving.

Soul Lessons: Becoming a powerful, loving presence in the world becomes one's primary goal. Here the classic Buddhic Third Eye opens, which gives one the ability to sense the quantum vibration of an entity and provides a deep connection with the realities of truth and love.

However, when all one sees in oneself and others is love, one does tend to get taken advantage of. Eventually the soul strives for a deeper energetic connection to the 'all that is.' Eventually, one feels a pull to evolve into the divine Crown level of the Simulation.

Introduction to Witches:

Angelic Takeaway: I mentioned previously the spiritual vulnerability that exists in the higher levels of the Simulation. My introduction to witches is how I learned this lesson viscerally. I realized that my humorous image of witches from the movie *Hocus Pocus* needed a bit of refinement.

As previously mentioned, in December of 2019 I was blessed with an Angelic experience that changed my reality in an irreversible and wonderful way. The immediate effect of the experience was an almost complete immersion into the blissful Crown level of the Simulation, which led to me temporarily ignoring all six of the lower level chakras and letting them all de-energize. This can lead to major spiritual vulnerabilities, which the following chapter documents.

In the high levels of the Simulation one now experiences spiritual reality viscerally. Everything is beautiful. One's thoughts and consciousness have an obvious effect on the reality around them, and in my case, I had a direct line of communication with God and his Angels.

In my life prior to this experience, I'd been reading and hearing about spiritual reality for about a dozen years. Now almost without warning, I was living it.

Over the years I'd had a close spiritual confidant who identified herself as a witch. Meeting her after my linear left-brained early life, I initially thought the idea of witches a bit silly. This was until I saw a bit of what she could do, her relative spiritual sophistication, and her amazing connection with nature.

Prior to my Angelic experience, I'd always viewed her as a spiritual mentor. I got the impression she was always humoring my curiosity about spiritual matters and saw me as stuck in my head (she was not completely wrong).

After my Angelic experience, my friendship with her bloomed. She was one of the first people that I confided the experience to, and she was a help in explaining what had happened to me.

She also had an attractive daughter closer to my age who also identified as a witch. Over the years I'd always had a slight crush on this daughter, but got the impression she saw me as a bit of a spiritual neophyte (she was not completely wrong).

After the Angelic experience, I noticed the daughter's reaction to me alter drastically. She had a gift for sensing energy and it was now clear to her from my aura that I was no longer a spiritual neophyte.

The beginnings of a romantic relationship bloomed, as we were able to have deep spiritual discussions; she actually helped me write some of the very early versions of this book.

However, despite an incredibly strong attraction, the romantic aspect of the relationship was awkward. There seemed to be very strong forces of attraction and repulsion acting simultaneously.

At this point in my spiritual evolution, it was obvious to me that my sense of spiritual power and joy came directly from God. She did not feel the same way and was hostile to any discussion of God. Over time, I learned not to mention God and just stuck to topics in our discussions that we were both comfortable with.

I've since learned that many people prefer not to go into the concept of 'God.' This is actually quite natural at certain stages of evolution as different aspects of reality are being explored. Although downright hostility to God tends to be a warning signal.

I was resonating blissfully in the Crown level of the Simulation at the time, but with all six lower chakras misaligned due to neglect. As a result, I was seeing all reality through a very rosy and loving lens with all defenses down, so no topics seemed off-limits (particularly where an attractive woman was involved).

With God off the table, the nature of both our relationship, discussions, and spiritual research got steadily darker. At one point we were writing a chapter for my book together on demonology.

Note: All work on this book done during this period has been deleted permanently.

I recall being at a party near her house where axes were being thrown during the height of our entanglement. I'd been at this house and had resisted throwing axes, as it did not seem like an activity in line with my spiritual path.

However tonight a very dark energy ran through me as I hit perfect bull-eyes with the axes, despite no experience whatsoever. On my way home from the party, I howled like a wolf in my car.

This darkness eventually culminated in a night so dark and ghastly that a verbal description is not possible. I will not go into the details, as I don't even want to run the tiniest risk of the energy of that horrific night splashing onto a reader. Needless to say, my spiritual mentor Dr. David Hawkins' advice on how to handle the darker parts of reality was 'don't go there' was finally comprehended. Though I'd intellectually absorbed this advice, this night sunk this lesson in viscerally.

Even though this night was probably the darkest of this lifetime, there was a bright side. As soon as I realized the hellish pickle my foolish ways had gotten me into, I began praying fervently to any heavenly body that would listen. They are always are listening.

At this point, a series of miracles (word not used lightly) rapidly transformed my reality. By grace I got out of the incident with minimal long-term harm. This involved three Angels in human bodies whom I'd never met before that night, who seemingly showed up just when they were needed (tested true). I was also blessed in this lifetime with a support system of wonderful human beings, including my parents who helped me out of that night.

This incident highlights the spiritual vulnerability that can exist in the highest levels of the Simulation unbalanced by the lower ones. One lives in blissful reality where love is the only power in the universe, and one's needs all seem automatically met. This can cause one to trust everything and let one's guard down, which can lead to quite serious spiritual error.

With maturity in the higher wavy levels of the Simulation, everything still seems loving. With increased wisdom, one tends to see everything for exactly what it is. One realizes that one can love the alligator from afar and and even pray for its highest good without swimming with it.

Seventh Level of the Simulation: The Crown Chakra (Broadly Masculine)

Angelic Takeaway: A very small percentage of people on the planet operate from this level of the Simulation. They play a very important role in helping bring divine energy down onto the planet, but they are not particularly good for operating heavy machinery or acting normal at parties.

This is the level of the Simulation where divine energy channels directly to a person. One has a feeling of invulnerability here, as it becomes clear that the true self is under God's mighty protection; only the limited physical body is vulnerable. It is not uncommon to hear people from this level of the Simulation say they have little or no preference for the life or death of the physical body. This can sound disturbing to the average person, but it's no more drastic than a video gamer saying they have little or no preference for the death of the character in a video game.

This level of Simulation (and especially those above it) are rarely seen by the public. This happens for a number of reasons:

- Entities that are allowed to operate at this level of the Simulation have earned their wings, and leaving the body becomes an open option. Many take this option as depending on context, their evolution may be more efficient elsewhere.

- The distribution of consciousness on the planet is roughly the shape of a pagoda, with many entities towards the bottom and very few near the top. There have been periods of history where no living being had significant access to the Crown chakra level of the Simulation on the planet. These typically resulted in dark ages.

- At these high levels, a simple life in the countryside where one can quietly exert a positive influence on the collective consciousness is far preferable to a life with a lot of worldly complexity. Most entities at this level that choose to stay in physical form leave the world of conventional endeavor. After my Angelic experience in 2019, this was a temptation, but I had societal obligations I wished to honor, many people I loved, and some major karma left to balance, which required continued interface with the world.

When I first read Dr. David Hawkins from the Throat level, I had trouble comprehending why he thought these high-level entities not doing anything were so important to the collective consciousness and the world. One techy way to perhaps think about it is that these entities are divine Wi-Fi extenders. They channel wavy energy onto the planet and angle it to where it is most needed. Personal credit isn't important at these higher levels so it's often easier to do this work anonymously. One realizes at these levels that one is ultimately only accountable to God and no other people.

Note: It is not a coincidence that 'angle' and 'angel' are spelled and pronounced almost the same (tested true).

One may have noticed that the seven levels of the Simulation discussed in this book alternate between masculine and feminine. The difference between masculine and feminine was discussed elsewhere, but a quick summary is that they are perfect reflections of one another. The Masculine sees life in terms of a vertical hierarchy and with certain things more desirable than other things, valuing truth. The Feminine sees all things as equal in a horizontal hierarchy and values love. Both sides have their weaknesses and strengths, and the Simulation flows most optimally when the two are in tune.

The below graphic also demonstrates the relationship between the Masculine and Feminine and provides a possible interpretation of the Holy Cross.

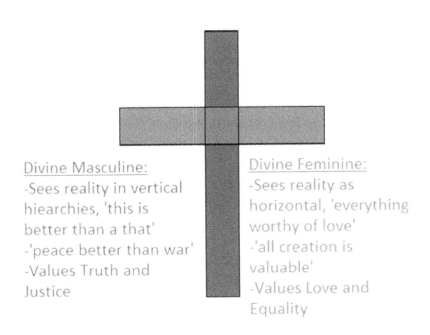

Divine Masculine:
-Sees reality in vertical hiearchies, 'this is better than a that'
-'peace better than war'
-Values Truth and Justice

Divine Feminine:
-Sees reality as horizontal, 'everything worthy of love'
-'all creation is valuable'
-Values Love and Equality

In spiral dynamics the higher levels of the Simulation are labeled second tier and are observed to be higher octaves of lower levels of the Simulation. This is an observation that both Claire Graves (the founder of spiral dynamics) and I had in common. This is similar to a way a musical instrument can play the note of 'c' in low octave or a higher octave, but a talented musician still hears them all as a 'c'.

I've eliminated most of the material from this book where I attempt to explain levels above the Crown chakra as they are outside the context of most human experience and just refer to all the levels above the Crown chakra generically as the Crown chakra.

Here I'll briefly discuss these non-personal higher levels of the Simulation and how they are higher octaves of the personal levels of the Simulation discussed in this book. The names I've given these higher levels were handed to me by the Angelic kingdom, which I used heavily in an earlier version of this book. The properties of these higher levels are broadly agreed upon in spiritual literature but the naming is not at this time due to the rarity of their discussion.

The Crown level, which channels divine energy into the physical body, is concerned with vibrational survival of human society. It is a higher tier of the Root level, which is most concerned with the survival of the individual body. Entities operating from the Crown level of the Simulation sense the divine essence of entities very well, which tells how much life energy an entity contains. The Crown tends to be most concerned with the survival of human society as a whole, and the Root with the survival of individual humans. Both the Crown and Root levels are broadly masculine.

The Eighth Holistic level of the Simulation sees humanity as a single unified organism with our individual bodies as cells in that organism. This is a higher Octave of the tribal Sacral Level. The wonderful movie *Avatar* artistically portrays a race with a large component of this Holistic nature on a higher tier than many tribal Sacral societies. The Sacral level sees the necessity of individual bodies bonding and working together, but the Holistic level sees the necessity of life being energetically connected. Both levels are broadly Feminine.

The Ninth Power Level of the Simulation is a higher octave of the Solar Plexus Level. The Solar Plexus level contains the masters of fixing physical things and putting the partically universe back into working order, where the Power Level contains masters of fixing spiritual things the putting the wavy universe back into working order. As energy flows from divinity down the levels of the Simulation, putting the wavy universe back together automatically corrects the partically universe over time. I discuss this idea further in the chapter "Angelic Electrical Engineering." Both the Power level and Solar Plexus level are broadly masculine.

The Tenth Celestial level of the Simulation shares similarities with its lower octave cousin: the Heart level of the Simulation. Both have an optimistic nature and are enjoyable places to hang out. Where the Heart level serves the partically universe and has enough power to pull physical entities together into a loving bond, the Celestial level serves the wavy universe and has enough power to pull the divine masculine and divine feminine aspects of the Simulation together in a loving bond. Both the Celestial level and the Heart level are broadly feminine.

The Eleventh Akashic level of the Simulation stores all the knowledge available in the Simulation in spiritual/wavy form. The Throat level of Simulation contains entities that store the information of the Simulation in limited partically/physical form. Both the Akashic level and the Throat level are broadly masculine.

The Twelveth Heavenly level of the Simulation is the loving operations center of the spiritual universe, where Third

Eye level of the Simulation is its lower octave physical version. They both seem to have the responsibility for vibrationally holding all life together using the power of love but from wavy and partically perspectives respectively. Both the Heavenly and Third Eye levels are broadly Feminine.

Levels likely exist above these twelve, but whether they can be accessed from the earthly levels of the Simulation or verbalized is questionable at this time. Reading about the highest choirs of Angels might give one insight into these highest levels.

The lessons from Quantum Mechanics teach us that the partically world is a projection of the wavy world. An early title for this book was *Waves Create Particles,* as it became obvious that divine energy flows into the wavy universe first, then from the wavy universe into the partically universe. 98% of the world subconsciously operates with this principle backwards. They believe that spirituality arises from a sort of physicality, which can be a costly error. I made this error for the first twenty-eight years of this life which left me in the spiritual pits. A section of the partically world that voluntarily cuts itself off from its wavy divine power source begins to slowly crumble (tested true). History shows it again and again!

That 'waves create particles' is an obvious experiential reality from the Crown level perspective. The high levels tend to see everything as radically what it is at its essence. Some people highly respected by society are spewing nonsense, and some very wise people are being ignored or shunned by society. This results in a cryptic sense of humor, which plays on the difference between the way things are and the way things appear that most have trouble understanding. Particularly in the lower levels of the Simulation, there is a significant difference between the way things are in reality and the way things appear in the Simulation.

As energy flows from high levels of the Simulation into the lower levels of the Simulation, keeping the Crown chakra healthy both on an individual and collective level is very critical to the health of the entire Simulation. A healthy higher chakra will tend to correct imbalances in lower chakras over time (tested true).

It is often puzzling and funny to view the world from the wavy, high Simulation level perspective and wonder why society misses things very obvious to the wavy point of view. The rare wavy beings that have talked publicly tended to make statements that are simple and to the point, yet often sounded like riddles or paradoxes to the common person.

Dr. David Hawkins had a characteristic chuckle that you hear a lot in his lectures. This is simply him seeing a paradox that is not entirely resolvable in simple language terms.

Humor tends to be a juxtaposition of the reality of two different levels of the Simulation to resolve a paradox. Laughter is a mini-seizure as the soul attempts to resolve a paradox between various levels of the Simulation in its own programming (tested true). One can often resolve more paradoxes watching a talented stand-up comedian than attending a class taught by a humorless but intellectually erudite professor.

Entities vibrating in these wavy levels respond to the needs of the whole and feel less attached to any individual entity. This is similar to how a talented surgeon might realize that lacerating a patient's skin and killing individual skin and blood cells might be necessary to save the life of the entire body. A challenge/lesson of the Crown level is that these entities view humanity as a single organism and individual bodies as cells in it. Challenging decisions arise where one finds they love all the individual cells, but some of them are clearly cancerous.

One tends to assume others live in a reality like them and they see the world through their individually-colored lens. Eventually it becomes obvious how different the realities we find ourselves in actually are. A common error of the higher levels is assuming others share your positive spiritual values and ethics.

Modern expressions: Oftentimes people operating from the Crown chakra are the lovable oddballs of society. Some of the great comedians operate from this Crown level, which is why they have a talent for making humorous observations that are not obvious to others but help others resolve paradoxes in their consciousness. People operating from the Crown chakra level of the Simulation can make good leaders, but they will very rarely seek out the position as this requires more worldly functioning. Most folks operating from these higher levels tend away from busy human life, as it's clear at these levels one's power flows directly from divinity and restores faster when not occupied by earthly business. At this level it makes sense why the Buddha left society to meditate under the Bodhi tree.

Evolution: It is hard to ignore that Bubonic Plague which highlighted the weaknesses of the feminine Heart level and allowed the reasonable, masculine Throat level to surface in the renaissance. This was the last time a new masculine-slanted level of the Simulation broke into society on a grand scale.

Now the COVID-19 pandemic most certainly showed us the weaknesses of feminine systems built on love and unconditional trust. I'm seeing signs of the masculine Crown vibrational level breaking through in many areas of society simultaneously, as people hunger for the truth and divine security that this level can bring to the table.

We need not replace the lower level systems that are functioning fine, but supplement them with the vibrational support of the Crown level. A quick glance at the evolution of societies shows that systems collapse before an evolutionary leap happens. You don't build a new house on top of an old house, you must tear the old one down. Society is not collapsing but making way for more advanced levels of the Simulation.

Soul Lessons: When viewing things from a wavy perspective, one develops an odd sense of humor that points out the difference between the way things appear and the way things are. Learning to control this sense of humor and respect life at whatever level it is evolving at is a constant lesson of this level. One also sees that everything is simply experiencing the effects of its own karma. This concept in particular must be told to people with care, as telling someone in the depth of terrible suffering that they are experiencing their own karma, though true, is often out-of-context in the moment.

Everything is living its perfect karmic destiny. There is very little need to fix anything or view a lower levels of the Simulation as wrong. God and His Angels have this Simulation under control despite surface appearance.

It also becomes obvious here that using force techniques to fix the problems of another level of the Simulation often makes the original problem worse. A principle of basic physics is "Force creates counter-force." Forceful measures create counterforce, which means a lot of noise and messy karma flying around in all directions.

Spiritual Aspirants of Various Levels:

Angelic Takeaway: There will likely never be a spiritual teaching which will completely satisfy everyone is this purgatorial Simulation. A major reason for this is that we are all operating from different levels of the Simulation and have a mix of energies unique to us. Part of the advantage of this Simulation is that by putting all the levels of spirituality together in one place, every soul has a choice as to which direction to evolve. This Simulation provides a smorgasbord of spiritual paths.

Spiritual Aspirants take on different qualities depending on the level of the Simulation they operate from, and below I explain broad qualities of each level. I make specific reference to people at a bi-annual *A Course in Miracles* retreats, which I attended for a number of years, as they were frequented by a wonderful cross section of people at various stages of the spiritual journey. In this life alone I've personally displayed characteristics of each level, and it's worth noting that most people will display a mix of the various levels, as most aren't operating from one level exclusively.

Root: This survival level tends to seek spirituality which is inherently negative, such as voodoo and curses, as a way to desperately seek influence. Since true spiritual power is basically absent from this level, anything done from this level will come with a severe karmic blowback on the entity (tested true). The spirituality from this level is generally viewed as evil from the perspective of higher levels, but it's simply how life behaves at this selfish level of evolution. It is naive to think that a reptilian-level consciousness has a built-in benevolence. This benevolence is often taken for granted by people operating from the Heart level or above in the Simulation.

Sacral: This level tends to have a magical view of life, as the cause-and-effect connection and intellect that the higher levels of the Simulation take for granted isn't yet well developed. Some New Age Fairs contain large amounts of spirituality from this level, which has a magical feel but is often not actually effective. This spirituality is often taken up to be part of a crowd or pack. While at this level I was most interested in magic, as it's easy to accept without a well-developed intellect asking pesky realistic questions. Generally lacking the discipline to follow an integrous spiritual program, this level tends to grasp at quick physical results. For a light-hearted, funny look at spirituality from this level, check out the episode "The Gang Gets Extreme: Home Makeover Edition" from Season Four of the irreverent comedy *It's Always Sunny in Philadelphia*.

Solar Plexus: Here is the level in which true spiritual power first arises. At this level, people have often just begun the real spiritual journey and are looking for something concrete to do in the physical. At the spiritual retreats I attended, the people at this level were often eager to help with the logistics of the event by moving chairs and tables around, coordinating schedules, and making sure everyone knew when the meals were. In my recommended reading section I mention *The Disappearance of the Universe* by Gary Renard, which I describe as a blue collar introduction to *A Course in Miracles*. This book was extremely popular with this crowd. The 365 day program laid out in *A Course in Miracles* seems extremely helpful at this level as following it requires discipline which tends to be strong at this level.

The folks at this level would often begin the retreats tentatively with physical affection, but by the end would be the most anxious to give good-bye hugs. As this Solar Plexus level tends to be evolving into the Heart level, this shows progress.

Heart: The Heart level of the Simulation is generally seeking ultimate truth, and is enthusiastic about the truth they are pursuing. During my first retreat I gravitated to this group, as they usually had the most active lives outside the retreat and were a joy to be around. Being naturally positive and charismatic, this group loved to share wonderful stories about how the *A Course in Miracles* changed their lives. This group tended to be the cheerleading section for *A Course in Miracles*, which provided the foundational positive energy for the retreats.

However this group tended to interpret A Course in Miracles as 'the' ultimate truth, and would be dogmatic about it. I remember drawing a bit of hostility from this group, questioning the accuracy of certain passages. However, by the end of these weekends, these members would often bring up paradoxical philosophical issues showing that they were moving into the deeper Throat chakra.

Throat: During most of my time at the retreats, I was hanging out with this group as they were interested in the deep philosophical discussions that I was interested in having. A group of us would get up early every morning and engage in humor-filled, very open discussions about spirituality and the other books we'd been reading. We all tended to leave with a reading list as we all read widely, and were anxious to share the best reads that we had stumbled upon. The group also had a very politically incorrect sense of humor, so we had our best discussions early in the morning before the more well-mannered people attending the retreat or the monks running the monastery got up. At the end of the weekend we'd sometimes report an extra layer of perception and an increased ability to feel energy. This is the natural evolution from the Throat level to the Third Eye level.

Third Eye: By the end of my time at these retreats I fell into this smaller group. Eventually it begins to dawn 'that the map was not the territory.' I was now less interested in talking about things with the intellect and being in one's head. I was now more interested in experientially living the reality *A Course in Miracles* was pointing to and sharing direct examples of this. This group was more interested in walking, listening to music, and enjoying the energy of the retreat. Some of our more famous presenters were from this group, and they were extremely humble about their role. Some of the most loving souls I've encountered in this life were in this group. At this level, supernatural abilities seem to begin to arise. These are known as Siddhis in the East. Among the people at these spiritual retreats at this level, I met a healer who miraculously fixed a few of my physical problems, and a psychic who spooked me at first with her uncannily accurate reads of my life and energy.

Crown: People from this level of spirituality are quite rare. From this level it is obvious everything is being run by divine will or an impersonal field. Everything is one, and no individuals strictly exist. A challenge at this level is putting one's observations in linear logical language that makes sense to others. Language is inherently dualistic, so holistic waviness will never fit cleanly into language's limited box. Spiritual masters of this level have written some of the greatest spiritual books and have founded the great world religions. However, from this level it is often easier to remain anonymous, unless one has a specific soul purpose which requires entering the public eye.

Managing people from the different levels of the Simulation:

Different levels of the Simulation are motivated by very different things. Though I'm clearly not an expert in management, here are some of my observations of people at different levels of the Simulation in a workplace. I've often observed organizations wasting valuable resources using motivational techniques not suited well for the Simulation level of most of their employees.

Root: People in this level of the Simulation generally do not make good employees, not because they are bad people, but because they are normally struggling with many issues, including addictions. The complexities of a modern workplace tends to overwhelm them. These employees often need tough love, and the expectations of these employees need to be clearly stated. My common thinking at this level was along the lines of: *What do I have to do in order to meet the bare minimum requirements of this job so I can put as little time and effort into this job and keep collecting a paycheck?*. This level is most motivated by pleasure (food rewards) and pain (direct punishment).

Sacral: People in this level of the Simulation value safety, security, and belonging. Honoring rituals and traditions such as birthdays is important to this level. They tend to value feeling like they are part of a pack. Instilling a sense of pride in the job, company, or organization helps retain employees at this level. Parties and outings where employees feel part of a group is effective at this level. Superstitions and logical fallacies can accumulate at this level, so a good manager should be aware of this. There is generally a desire to see non-conformists punished.

Solar Plexus: People in this level of the Simulation like to feel a sense of power and importance. Motivational speeches which honor the greatness of the organization and the individual are popular with this level. Jobs which show a concrete result such as assembly or construction are suitable for this level. Keeping the organization's operation center in good physical shape (not a lot of broken stuff) is also valuable in retaining employees at this level. Having dead weight employees who do not contribute to the organization will anger this level.

Heart: People in this level of the Simulation want to feel like they are doing something good in the world, and don't like situations where they are forced to act against their ethics. Seeing that their organization is making a positive contribution to the world is very important at this level. Outlets for their natural positive energy and enthusiasm are highly valued by this level. Teachers at this level tend to love spirit days where fun can be had with students and they can dress creatively.

Throat: People in this level of the Simulation want intellectual and creative flexibility. They want to know their ideas and intelligence are respected. Being put into a rote position where there is no room for creativity or intellectual development will generally cause this level to leave a job. Monetary incentives and flexibility are far more important at this level than speeches, events, emotional support, or parties. These employees are very valuable to an organization, but often they will have many interests outside of the job.

Third Eye: If one is lucky enough to have a person from this level of the Simulation in their organization, they must realize that this person wants to feel part of a loving community, and that the organization is putting love and positive energy out into the world. This level is happy even in lower positions and generally won't strive for a high position, but it's often prudent to put them in one. However, this level generally does not want to be in a position where they need to discipline other employees or be a bad guy. This level will consider the energy of the environment more important than the physical characteristics of the environment.

Crown: The people in this level of the Simulation rarely interact with the world in a traditional way. However, they can be happy in any position if they feel God requires them there. Money and traditional motivators are generally very unimportant to people at this level, as their motivation is almost completely an internal drive to serve God. Their energetic role is often far more important to the organization than their physical role, and these people will probably find very unconventional but more efficient ways of doing their job. A good organization will recognize this and give them flexibility. A person at this level will also have a positive effect not noticed by most. Their energetic aura will be quite large and powerful, and lower troublesome energies will find their presence very uncomfortable (tested true). Simply having them in the building will help keep energetic pests away and boost the positive energies around them.

Employees are best managed by people either in the same level of the Simulation or a single level higher. Employees being managed by a manager in a level below them tend not to work out well. Managers two or more levels higher than the employees they are managing will have a hard time relating to them, as their realities are too different.

Racial and Social Issues:

Angelic Takeaway: Every level of the Simulation tends to experience and view racial and social issues in a different light. Each level presents solutions that would work well if it was the only level of the Simulation. However tension is created when all the different levels and with their own perspectives are squished together in this purgatorial dimension. Optimal solutions will take all levels into account.

A hot topic political issue in our society is the issue of race and social discrimination. A large part of the confusion again seems to be the different levels of the Simulation viewing the same issue and having vastly different interpretations and potential solutions for the issue.

Here is roughly how the various levels of the Simulation view racial and social issues. These observations are derived from personal experience, observations and calibration research.

Most racial problems arise from the lower levels of the Simulation and tend to be underestimated by the higher levels of the Simulation. Therefore, no easy 'one size fits all' approach will completely eradicate these issues. Humor, spirituality, and basic morality are the best defenses against it (tested true).

Root: One tends to have their hands full just surviving in the complexity of the Simulation and dealing with the many difficulties at this level. This level is generally uninterested in complex social issues as the lessons on this level revolve around managing pain and pleasure inputs. However, the desperation of this level can make it explosive, as this primitive level is the most likely to use violence and is the least likely to be able to control it. When social issues become violent, it is often initiated by a soul operating from this level of the Simulation.

Sacral: True racism is mostly found at this level. I wouldn't call it evil, but simply the animal instincts of this level of life doing what it does. Someone at this level believes others who look or act different from their tribe or pack must be an enemy.

Solar Plexus: Racial and social issues begin to be resolved at this level of evolution and I've seen the most practical solutions come from this level. Sports and rough humor tend to be the most effective as solutions at this level. The great football film *Remember the Titans* about the racial integration of high schools has one scene where two alpha males of different races chant "left side, strong side" while hitting each other. The players in the movie also make many subtle racial jokes as a way of bonding. This humor is also appreciated and effective in difficult military situations where all the races in a unit feel the same difficulties.

Though these solutions may be viewed as low-class by the higher levels, I've found them to be more effective in practice than the more intellectual erudite solutions that come from the higher levels. Higher isn't strictly better.

Heart: This level has the greatest tendency to directly oppose racism and get politically involved. It is also the most effective at dealing with these issues on a political level. However at this level, 'racism is bad' can be a strong belief, but oftentimes it can miss subtle energetic nuances where opposition to racism must be balanced with other societal factors. The need to balance these other factors is generally better understood at the higher levels.

Throat: Here one is interested in the mind and intellect, generally having bigger fish to fry. From this reasonable level, the idea of judging someone by their outward appearance is illogical. I've found this level tends to acknowledge the problem but often seems more interested in other issues.

I recall during the 2016 presidential election in the United States, the race-related news events made race a very touchy uncomfortable topic at my urban high school. During this time I saw groups tended to re-segregate according to race, as different racial groups viewed the race-related news events very differently.

A huge exception existed however. There was a large group of students who were operating from the Throat level of the Simulation and fans of competitive strategic card games. I was personally a fan of the competitive card collecting game Hearthstone during this period, so there was a natural affinity with this group. They would often play in my room after school as I was still largely operating from the Throat level at the time, so my classroom was a comfortable energy for these students. I noticed in this social subgroup, players of different races and social backgrounds mixed and intermingled completely freely. I don't ever recall the topic of race specifically coming up when this vibrational subset of students were alone.

At this vibration, one is interested in whatever they are pursuing in their mind. At this level, the race of another person is a 'so what.'

A danger here is that at this level, one does not tend to draw race issues into one's direct experience, so it's easy to find oneself in an ivory tower out of touch with the world as it is. This occurs to an even greater extent at the higher levels.

Third Eye: At this loving level of the Simulation, social discrimination rarely enters one's experience on a personal level, but one notices it in society. This high level tends to have a murky history in dealing with the issue on a political level.

From the point of view of this loving level, racism is abhorrent and simply shouldn't exist. It is sometimes difficult for someone with a highly energized Third Eye to understand why a high vibrating person is being mistreated simply by the color of their skin. The Third Eye level lives in a reality where one loves everyone and receives love back, so the core reasons for racism are often difficult for them to grasp. As a result, they often present society with solutions that work good in theory but not on a practical level.

The solutions that tend to come from this level involve unconditional love, listening to each other's feelings, and group hugs. These solutions are wonderful and have their place, but most hot-bed race relation issues play out in a very different reality, where attempting a group hug might get one shived.

Crown: At this level, race and physical appearance is viewed as almost irrelevant. Confusion arises as to why people operating in the lower levels of the Simulation are infatuated with the issue of race at all. It is obvious at this level that every soul is living out their karma in a perfect process. Therefore, people in this level are fairly uninterested in the issue, and only takes a hard stance if living in an area where the issue is explosive. Famous and overwhelmingly successful Indian sage Gandhi's occasional mistakes often came from underestimating how vehemently people operating from the lower levels of the Simulation took their racial and religious biases, as he didn't see the world through that lens (tested true).

Police:

Recent controversies in society have centered around police. In this life, my interactions with police have been overwhelmingly positive. This is despite the fact that my reason for interacting with the police was not always positive.

I have at best a poor understanding of how police spend their time and the ordeals they go through, so do not want to present myself as having the answers to a complex societal issue.

However, one thing I have observed is that often police get stereotyped. Some recent events have caused many to form negative stereotypes of police; 'all police are racist' and 'all police are lazy' are common stereotypes. Also occurring, and in some ways almost as damaging, are the positive stereotypes in which the police receive unanimous support from certain segments of the population despite errors clearly being made.

We've all made errors no matter our profession, and police work is a particularly hard job where important decisions need to be made in fractions of second, oftentimes while the officer is in a way of direct physical harm.

To avoid stereotyping officers, it might be nice to remember that this profession, like all others, has people operating from all levels of the Simulation. Negative stereotypes unfairly portray integrous officers doing a great, if imperfect job, and positive stereotypes often provide a shelter to the officers who are operating from the lowest levels of the Simulation and whose power should be limited. I've observed these characteristics from officers operating from various levels of the Simulation.

Root: These police officers get into police work for the feeling of power, as at this level of the Simulation, the soul has very little access to it. When in the job, there is a tendency to abuse power and have a lack of the social nuance needed to handle the difficult aspects of the job, which often deal with complex gray areas. There are also addiction issues at this level.

Sacral: A characteristic of this level of the Simulation as mentioned earlier is racism. It is not strictly the fault of these souls, but simply how life operates at this level of evolution. In the Sacral level, one's fellow police officers are often part of one's pack, so unethical officers are often defended past the point where it is logical. Citizens who are perceived as outside the pack tend to be treated unfairly. The majority of the problems associated with the police come from this level. Although from an evolutionary standpoint, police work might be an optimal situation to learn the common life lessons presented at this level of evolution.

Solar Plexus: Many police officers seem to operate primarily from this level. This level is the brick and mortar of the American Police force. Keeping tight law and order is natural at this level of the Simulation. As a police officer ascends through levels of the Simulation, I suspect you'd see increasingly complex social nuance and understanding as to where one should best place their energy. For example, a group of kids smoking marijuana in a basement party on Friday night, while hardly ideal, is probably not where the officer's energy is best placed when more dangerous and violent crimes are likely being committed.

Heart: These police officers tend to take on a larger, more social role, often spearheading social outreach programs. In this level of the Simulation, officers are no longer satisfied just meeting the bare-minimum requirements of the job but want to support the larger good of the community. The enthusiastic energy at this level makes them great for this role.

Throat and higher: Oftentimes you find this level in more highly specialized roles where their intelligence and energy can be better utilized. It bears a reminder that the higher levels of the Simulation are not strictly better. I would've performed better chasing criminals and interacting with the public in the Solar Plexus level than the more bookwormy Throat version of myself.

At a spiritual retreat, I met a man whom I enjoyed talking science and philosophy with. He was operating from the intelligent Throat level of the Simulation. He had actually left the police force and was working as a security guard at a prestigious university. Though he made less money than he did as a police officer, this allowed him to hang out in his natural Throat level of the Simulation. He did not have to deal with as many chaotic confrontations with the lower levels, which would be unnatural from this level.

Transcending Linear Causality:

Angelic Takeaway: Alternate chapter title: Learn to function in the Third Eye level of the Simulation if one is currently hanging out the Throat level of the Simulation. One gets more chicks.

The entire reasonable Throat level of the Simulation and the world of traditional science is built upon is the principle of Causality (tested true). Causality is the physical observation of something causing something else. The lower five levels of the Simulation including the Throat level are bound by causality, but one is continuously released from it as one evolves higher (tested true).

The whole system of logic and science is built upon it so it is heavily reinforced by society, especially in the educated world. The issue is that the concept of causality holds no absolute reality, but are habits of the Simulation (tested true).

An unstated goal of large parts of the education system is getting people to function in the Throat level of the Simulation. Teaching a person to think logically in terms of causality will help someone resonate in the Throat level of the Simulation, which is of great value in the physical Simulation. This is why societies that educate their youth are far more successful. At the time of the writing of this book only about 10% of the human race have reliable access to this level of the Simulation, so these humans are of enormous value to the race as a whole.

However, causality, which is boon to most of the world, becomes an obstacle if one wishes to advance their consciousness into the Third Eye level of the Simulation. To do this, one must break the cause and effect relationships which dominates the consciousness of people operating out of the Throat level of the Simulation.

A sign one is evolving out of the limits of causality, words like 'tend' and 'seem' begin to feel more natural as one realizes the limits of strict black and white thinking.

A basic principle in physics is that positive charges attract negative charges, and that negative charges attract positive charges. Reading the previous sentence, one may wonder which charge attracts which. The reality is they attract each other with an equal force.

An even higher understanding is that no direct relationship exists between the particles; they are all just being moved by the will of God alone. Don't tell a chemist this unless you want a really funny look.

If protons (positive charges) are separated from electrons (negative charges) by a barrier, eventually they will attract and line up against the barrier like so.

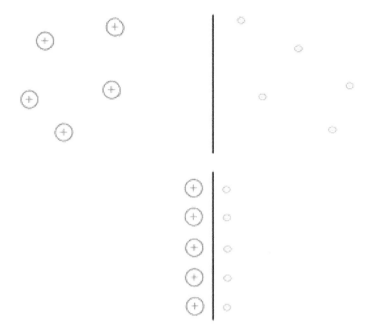

The positive charges didn't attract the negative charges, and the negative charges didn't attract the positive charges. The higher power of karma attracted them to each other in order to balance the karma of the universe (tested true).

Karma attracts opposite charges. For example, if in a past life you financially drained and then brutally broke the heart of a lover, your soul takes on a karmic charge. In a future life you are likely to attract a lover who will financially drain you and brutally break your heart.

The law of gravity states that all matter attracts all matter. The force of attraction between two objects is governed by Newton's Law of Gravitation as follows:

$$F_g = G \frac{m_1 m_2}{r^2}$$

where

- F_g is the force
- G is the gravitational constant (6.674×10^{-11} m^3.kg^{-1}.s^{-2})
- m_1 and m_2 are the masses of the objects
- r is the distance between the centers of the objects

In essence, it says the force of attraction between objects increases with the size of the objects and decreases with the distance between them. But in accordance with Newton's Third Law, the two objects are always being pulled together by equal and opposite forces.

Our Earth rotates around the sun due to gravitation. For language and simplicity purposes, we say the Sun's gravity is pulling the Earth, but Earth is actually pulling on the sun with the same force. Although since the Sun's mass is about 330,000 times larger than the Earth's, that force has a massive effect on the Earth and has a relatively small effect on the Sun. However both are being pulled by an equal and opposite force as the universe attempts to unify itself via the mechanism of karma.

A higher understanding is that God is pulling on both objects but he likes to stay within the causality rules of the Simulation when convenient, so scientists in the Throat level of the Simulation have something to study and evolve to. The illusion of causality allows most of the evolutionary adventures of this Simulation to exist, however no direct cause and effect relationship actually exists (tested true).

Calibration Process:

Angelic Takeaway: If you see '(tested true)' while reading this book, it's because I verified the truth of the previous sentence using a weird process involving pendulums and Angels. If you don't think that sounds scientific, you are right and I don't really care.

You will see '(tested true)' after certain sentences which contain important points. This simply indicates that I tested the truth of the previous sentence using the technique I call calibration. The truth of all the information contained in this book was checked by this process. This technique involves a pendulum and my Angelic friends, and your belief in the process isn't necessary to understanding or enjoying this book.

I borrow the name 'calibration' from a technique Dr. David Hawkins used with his wife for spiritual research, even though my process is quite different. My process is closer to a technique that came through hypnotherapist Suzanne Spooner called TAUK (The Art of Universal Knowing) which is similar to some techniques of divination. The process I use is fairly original and came to me intuitively after I had evolved to a point where I was mostly able to handle it responsibly. It is tailored to how I communicate with the Angelic universe. I am not sure at this time if it is able to be taught or copied.

My process was intuitively recognized as a way to sort out truth far more efficiently than the scientific/logical process I'd become familiar with early in this life. However, it does not completely replace it. Over the years, I've observed many people using similar processes wrongly and receiving blatant wrong information. My early attempts to use similar processes were always unsuccessful and frustrating. As I would later learn, I was not yet mature enough to handle it.

As I evolved further, I noticed that certain people were using similar processes with seemingly supernatural results. A timely re-listening of one of Dr. David Hawkin's lectures clicked truth into place. In this lecture, he admitted an error in his first book *Power vs. Force,* where he assumed that everyone had access to his version of the calibration process. He later realized that only people who calibrated above 200 on his scale of consciousness and were aligned with divinity had access to this extremely powerful process. I've observed the same truth.

Immediately, I intuited a higher truth that this was a genius safeguard the Simulation has in place, to ensure that only integrous players dedicated to truth and love have access to the power of divinity. The famous Spiderman saying, "With great power comes great responsibility" was comprehended at a higher level than ever before. This is why no matter the appearance of the physical game board, the way of truth and love always eventually triumphs over evil. The Angels always win in the end; the nature of the Simulation guarantees it.

My personal research showed that access to these calibration and divination type processes increased in proportion to the energy of one's Crown chakra. The most efficient way to energize the Crown chakra is to develop one's faith in God by prayer and spiritual/religious practice.

Further contemplation on the calibration process revealed that it actually exists as a wormhole between the physical universe and the spiritual universe (divinity). I had always struggled to put my autistic spiritual senses into physical language and prove their validity in a rational sense, and this process has greatly helped in that. It did not eliminate the need to use the rational processes, but was a shortcut to align the rational process with higher truth. One could use this process as a shortcut to eliminate error and focus one's intellectual efforts more efficiently.

After years of watching others use these calibration processes successfully but failing embarrassingly in all attempts to use them myself, I had let go of even trying to develop these processes personally.

One summer night after a series of recent spiritual breakthroughs, I was guided as if by magic to construct a pendulum out of an old Christmas tree ornament and was suddenly able to calibrate accurately. This ability to tell absolute truth was immediately sensed, as a giant jump in personal power. Over the next several months, many painful lessons were learned through personal errors. It was learned that this power had to be handled in a responsible manner.

There were a few embarrassing attempts to predict the results of American football games using this process, which resulted in a bit of egg-on-the face. One weekend while visiting my parents, we were set to watch the New England Patriots play the New York Jets in a Sunday football matchup. The Patriots were slightly favored, but during a walk in the woods before the game, I did sloppy calibration of the game's results (not even following the procedure that I'd laid out) and concluded that the Jets would win.

Upon getting back to my parents right before the start of the game, I began bragging that I had feeling the Jets would prevail, which was a relatively bold prediction as the Jets were underdogs and I was in a room full of Patriots fans (myself included). The game, which took place on October 24th, 2021, ended up being a 54-13 Patriots rout and the game was even more lopsided than the score would indicate. I was deservingly teased about my cocky pregame prediction.

Later in the season, in the first round of the playoffs the Patriots were set to play the Buffalo Bills. The Bills were favored but I once again did a sloppy calibration and got that the Patriots should win. Boastfully thinking that I'd outsmarted the Simulation, I immediately made a bet with a friend who was a Buffalo Bills fan. Sadly the game on January 15th, 2022 was a 47-17 Bills blowout and I was once again left with egg on my face.

Similar instances have occurred when I've tried to use the process for morally shaky purposes. My Angelic guides seem to have a sense of humor in that when I've attempted to abuse the process, they've given me wrong information, which often resulted in humorous, pride-diminishing lessons. Power like high voltage electricity must be handled with great care (tested true).

Though I've personally had miraculous results with the process, it has always eluded my attempts to scientifically prove it. In 50-50 blind experiments I've gotten about 80% accuracy. This is in line with a principle of the Simulation that one cannot prove a higher level of the Simulation with the tools of a lower one. I call this the Faulkner uncertainty principle described elsewhere in this book.

Science experiments that have attempted to prove PSI phenomena typically yield results greater than chance, but always seem to be right under what would be considered scientific proof, which is property of the Throat chakra level of the Simulation. The book *A New Science of the Paranormal* discusses this principle in more detail. The hidden gem of the movie *I Origins* also demonstrates this principle. In the movie's climax, a scientific experiment yields strong evidence for the existence of reincarnation but falls short of scientific proof. Apparently it takes faith and trust to move to the higher levels of the Simulation, which is what all the spiritual masters of the ages have said in their own language (tested true).

In this book, I present certain spiritual concepts in a more logical and scientific manner than is typical, but at the end of the day absolute scientific proof of higher-dimensional concepts isn't possible, so one must lean on their faith.

For the actual process, I use a number of pendulums. Gemstone pendulums seem to work better for earthly lower-level Simulation questions, and pendulums of Angelic design work the best for profound higher-level Simulation questions. Lighter, smaller pendulums respond faster and are good for quick results, while heavier pendulums provide slightly more dependable results. My favorite pendulum is a cross with the likeness of Archangel Michael on it.

I hold the pendulum in my right hand and brace my elbow on something, to avoid as best I can having my personal will influencing the motion of the pendulum. I then hold a thought in my head, and if the thought is true or aligned with divinity, the pendulum swings away from me and toward me, kind of like someone shaking their head to indicate 'yes.' If the thought is not aligned with divinity or false the pendulum swings left and right similar to someone shaking their head to indicate 'no.'

If one is wondering what actually swings the pendulum to indicate 'true' or 'not true,' here are six explanations, all true on some level depending on the way one views life:

If one enjoys simple explanations: Angelic magic.

If one enjoys Quantum Mechanics: The thought I hold in mind collapses the wave function into a physical reality that the logical mind can understand.

If one enjoys Freudian psychology: The subconscious mind moves the pendulum in a way that my conscious mind can understand.

If one enjoys Jungian psychology: The superconscious mind moves the pendulum in a way that my conscious mind can understand.

If one enjoys computer programming: This process is a programmed function for the higher levels of the Simulation to pass data to the lower levels of the Simulation quite efficiently.

If one enjoys faith: God does it.

Before testing any statement I hold in mind: 'It is in the highest good for me to know this.' The pendulum will indicate that I should know this or that I should leave it alone. I've found that we simply aren't supposed to know everything, and some things are meant to remain a mystery.

During the aforementioned fiasco with the football game predictions I failed to do this first important step in both cases. As I've begun to remember my past lives, I very often run into souls in my present life who were with me in another body in a past life. Sadly when I ask if it's in the highest good to tell them this, I get a negative response most of the time. Apparently past lives are temporarily forgotten for a reason. When you know your past lives, it becomes very obvious that the events of your current life are simply echos of your own energy in a previous life. The Simulation seems unreal once the illusion of random external events is removed (tested true).

If I find the pendulum isn't responding correctly or find I'm getting blatantly wrong information, I do a quick configuration process. I hold '1+1=3' in mind and watch the pendulum swing left and right for its negative response, then hold '1+1=2' in mind and watch the pendulum adjust and start giving the positive response. I then go back and forth between these two mathematical statements and watch the pendulum respond until I'm satisfied the energy is flowing correctly.

The process can be used in an attempt to predict the future but it is not 100% accurate. The further out in the time I try to go, the less accurate the process is in predicting. Apparently, the Angelic universe has impressions about the future but everyone in the Simulation is acting with free-will, and even the Angelic kingdom cannot predict how souls will use that free will. This was also an error I made in the football game prediction shenanigans. The future cannot be predicted with certainty, particularly with an event like a football game where so much free will is involved.

The pendulums respond in real time to my thinking and my actions. For example, I think about something and the pendulum will swing toward and away from me to indicate my thinking is correct, but will suddenly jerk left or right when my thinking goes down an errant path.

I can even use it to find optimal movies and shows to watch. Using the process in this way, I've been miraculously guided to movies that gave a timely, important spiritual message and historical dramas which triggered past-life memories. The Angels know what they are doing! The process can also be used to choose books, music, and even food.

The process has sped up my spiritual research and has allowed me to correct some serious errors in my own consciousness. It has been one of the biggest blessings in this lifetime to be gifted it. The main issue with the logical mind is that it operates blindly and can be easily deceived. The best the logical mind can do on its own is careful use of the scientific method to slowly converge on truth.

This process is particularly useful when used in concert with the logical mind, as it allows truth to be converged on exponentially faster than relying on the logical mind alone. On many occasions as the result of a negative calibration, I've saved many hours of investigating something with the logical mind that would have been fruitless in the end.

The most important part of the process I've found is to remain unbiased about the results of the method. It is harder to calibrate things in which the personal self has a stake. Many errors were made calibrating things that had personal relevance. For example, calibrating whether I'm the best Monopoly player on the planet would be difficult to do. Although I feel no need to calibrate this statement, as I'm already quite sure that it is true.

Over time, I've learned to hold statements in mind with an almost detached attitude. I get the best results when I feel that whatever the answer the process yields is fine, and I have minimal personal interest in the answer given. For the Angels to swing the pendulum correctly, one must be more interested in the truth more than any personal ego agenda. The process is for discovering truth, not verifying one's pre-existing ideas. This is a very important thing to keep in mind in any scientific or truth-finding endeavor.

The gift of this process allowed this book to finally happen, as I would not be making some of the bolder statements that I make in this book without having the process at my disposal for verification purposes. If one is blessed enough to get a window into absolute truth, it should be viewed as a precious gift and handled with care and appreciation.

Recommended Reading:

Angelic Takeaway: If one is having a hard time in this Angelic school of hard knocks, reading these books here will help speed your progress along. They perhaps allow you to skip a few grades and keep you out of detention.

All truth is already known and available on the planet. Reading the books below will facilitate a deeper understanding of this book; they will point to the same fundamental truths this book does but from a different angle.

This book would not have come into existence without these works and countless others. I included this chapter because all these works will complement this book very well, and make sure my pesky little animal ego does not begin to think it did this all alone. This is far from an all-inclusive list, as I've been helped by many other books. I know there are many other great works that I've never studied that contain great wisdom and insight.

Dr. David Hawkin's Work: Dr. David Hawkins or 'Doc' was a spiritually enlightened psychologist who lived in recent times. His soul and mine have criss-crossed paths quite a bit through the ages, and we've often shown up as rivals in the physical world for tough spiritual lessons but deeply love each other in the spiritual world. We were both born and raised in a relatively traditional American environment, we were both veterans of the navy, and we explain ourselves using more western vernacular than is typical of most spiritual works.

I first came upon Dr. Hawkins in this life listening to a podcast. Enjoying what he said, I bought the audio version of his first book *Power vs. Force,* which sat on my phone unlistened to for a few weeks. I had signed up for a charity 5k race, and while waiting for the race to start, I began listening to this book. As soon as listening began, a process began that I believe was unstoppable. Instead of running the race, I ended up walking in the back with all the pregnant mothers with strollers.

A few days later, I owned most of his library of books; a few weeks later I'd read through all of it. His map of consciousness™ allowed me to connect the vibes my autism had always allowed me to sense with my scientific background. This began the formation of an exponentially more accurate view of the world. A unified reality began to form in my consciousness where science, religion, technology, and culture did not conflict with one another. This book stands on the shoulders of his work.

A Course in Miracles: This book came through a clinical psychologist living in New York through an inner voice in the 1970s. If this sounds weird to you, then this probably isn't the book for you. The book is destined to become one of the great classics of spiritual literature.

Though it is a long book, my favorite part is entitled "The Workbook for Students" which contains 365 daily lessons designed to be done in a year. I've completed the workbook several times, and each time, it was comprehended on a higher octave; I received enormous benefits each time. If one's goal is to move up the levels of the Simulation, then this book seems one of the quickest routes available on the planet at this time.

Dr. David Hawkins' spiritual research showed that people who had completed about the first seventy lessons were no longer weakened by negative stimuli in their environment. You can imagine that is quite an advantage if one has been to a fast food restaurant lately.

Having been through the workbook a few times, part of my daily spiritual practice is asking the calibration process for a daily lesson to read and it's always relevant! The Angels know what they are doing.

Also involved in the publication was Dr. Kenneth Wapnick, who has an enormous amount of published work explaining the course. The course is very heavy reading, written in such a way as to help bypass the linear mind and educate the soul directly. This makes it a bit difficult for beach reading. Dr. Kenneth Wapnick's work helped me greatly in my initial study of the course.

Though not a perfect book, a great blue collar introduction to the course written in everyday language is *Disappearance of the Universe* by Gary Renard. This book also functioned as my introduction to the course. The book is written in a humorous conversational style with two Angels visiting Gary in his living room in Maine (extremely close to where I grew up). As you are currently reading a book largely about Angels, this shouldn't stretch your belief system too much.

The Spiritual Big Guns: These are the books that the great religions on the planet are largely founded upon. My highest recommendations are the Bible, the Bhagavad Gita, The Upanishads, and the classic Buddhist texts. A foundational concept of this book is that the higher the level of the Simulation a book or teaching comes from, the less vulnerable it is to ravages of time. All these texts have been around a long time, so they are dependable foundations to world spiritual knowledge.

When reading these books, two things in particular are helpful. First, if one can read them with a bit of nuance and not take every passage as LITERAL truth, it will save one from much stress and misdirection. Certain passages were added that were not said by the original spiritual master. There are elements that were added later to exert control on a culture or society, and aren't necessarily representative of spiritual truth.

These books were also written for a culture and consciousness probably very different from your own. Oftentimes without proper cultural context, a passage can be interpreted to mean the exact opposite of what its original intention was.

Spiral Dynamics: The system Claire Graves lays out in this book was one of the greatest finds of my life. He lays out another scale of consciousness much like Dr. David Hawkin's scale and the chakra system. As my autism allows me to sense energy very well, I was able to realize that all these scales were essentially describing the same underlying reality. Claire Graves used colors and described societies more, while Dr. David Hawkins used numbers and described individuals more. The scale I lay out in this book relates to the ancient chakra system but corresponds heavily to these two scales. If one enjoys this book then reading *Spiral Dynamics* or Dr. David Hawkins' work will enrich your knowledge. There is no major disagreement between these two scales and the classic chakra system I use to describe the concepts of this book. This is especially true if one can get past surface cultural and language differences.

Spiral Dynamics Integral by Don Beck is an audio program which provides a no-nonsense introduction to the work.

My Big Toe: In this book I describe this reality as an Angel-evolving Simulation. The author Thomas Campbell also describes this reality as a Simulation and you will find no major points of disagreement between us.

The author is a physicist. The book is grounded in logic, numbers, and established theory but has the perfect amount of oddness, as he cites out-of-body travel often. It would be difficult to complete a thorough reading of this brilliant 900+ page tome without coming away with a strong suspicion that we are in a Simulation.

Unlike many other Simulation theory books which have a darker tone, he points to positive spiritual concepts such as love and meditation. It will not leave you feeling like you just watched the *Matrix* and Agent Smith is right outside your bedroom door. His odd sense of humor made this a very enjoyable and informative read for me.

When in the finishing stages of completing this book, the Angels told me to cut the length of this book WAY down. Much of what I cut out are details making a logical and mathematical case for us being in a Simulation. I felt comfortable cutting them out as Thomas Campbell already did a masterful job with this aspect, and I love the efficiency of not reinventing the wheel. If the Simulation aspect of this book interests you, this should be the next book that you read.

Biology of Transcendence: This was the first spiritual book that had a profound effect on me, and was my 'crack in the cosmic egg' (which the name of another book by same author, Joseph Chilton Pierce). It is written from a Neurobiology perspective and it goes relatively deep into science.

I first read this book while quite drunk lying in a hammock in my backyard close to the spiritual low point in this life. To that point in this life I'd been almost completely scientifically left-brained and this book appealed to my scientific left-brained view of the world while cracking the spiritual door open. I included it here so that some other scientifically minded agnostics might get the same inspiration but hopefully without all the red wine.

The Work of Lorna Byrne: Lorna Byrne is an Irish author with an extremely strong connection to the Angelic kingdom. In her personal story I felt many similarities with her, but her connection to the Angelic kingdom is of a different quality than mine. Her sensory system picks up Angelic energy in a much different way than me. She actually sees them.

Her description of Angels is much more soft and feminine than my harder masculine approach. I recommend her body of work if one identifies more with the feminine or wants to see another side of the Angelic kingdom and the work they do here on the planet to help us.

Alcoholics Anonymous Big Book: Substance abuse has been a part of this soul's journey and is the impetus for many to start on the spiritual path. As was the case with me, it was only in the absolute depth of despair that a spiritual opening occurs as the ego surrenders its control to god.

Though I've never been a true 'twelve-stepper,' I've seen amazingly miraculous recoveries at every stage of my spiritual journey, and have co-evolved with many members of twelve step groups such as Alcoholics Anonymous. These spiritual organizations are some of the most effective and humble in the world.

If one finds oneself in the depth of despair in substance abuse, then this book and the joining of a good twelve-step organization is probably your optimal first step. Most integrous spiritual systems follow the basic flavor of the twelve-step spiritual journey. Even if you don't ever plan on joining a twelve-step program, this book has immense value to anyone on the spiritual journey.

Near-Death Experiences Books: These books center around experiences where a person's physical body temporarily dies and the soul experiences a blissful higher level of the Simulation. They are wonderful confirmation of the higher levels of the Simulation and that life survives the death of the physical body. A weakness of these books is that they are almost completely reliant on subjective first-person experience, so skeptics can always doubt them; those who resonate with the truth will find great value.

Two of my favorites are *Proof of Heaven: A Neurosurgeon's Journey into the Afterlife* by Eben Alexander and *Embraced by the Light* by Betty J. Eadie. The first is written by a scientifically-literate neurosurgeon and will appeal to the masculine, as it attempts to explain the afterlife in logical terms. The second is a very short, high energy read that appeals more to the feminine side. It is an annual read for me as it gets me out of my mind. It can be read in a few hours but has a high energy effect that lasts weeks.

The Impersonal Life: This short book which fits in my pocket has been read during many stages of my spiritual journey. Its value is primarily in its vibration, and each reading has led to a leap in spiritual awareness. After a reading of this small book, one will feel the hand of the divine in everything.

The Man who Tapped the Secrets of the Universe: This quick read documents the life of the great artist Walter Russell whose divinely inspired works probably deserve specific mention here. A look at this man's life shows how practically applying many of the wavy principles discussed in this book have a measurable effect on the partically Simulation.

Heaven on Earth: This is a divinely inspired beautiful gem coming from a truly heavenly perspective, written by a past-life wife of mine named Elsa Lo Monaco. Luckily her

Angels spared her from having to put up with me as a husband in this one. Reading this gem will give you a wonderful energy boost, and remind you that the real you already exists in a heavenly state, even while we play our earthly games in this Simulation.

A New Science of the Paranormal: The Promise of Psychical Research: I included this book because it discusses the sometimes eerie line between grounded linear science and the world of the paranormal. It explains why certain psi phenomena will simply never be proven beyond a reasonable doubt by purely linear science.

I included this book because I'll never be able to prove certain concepts I mention, such as my past lives, my Angelic experiences, and my calibration process to the complete satisfaction of my nerdy scientific friends, and that is completely okay.

This book is short, concise, and a wonderful introduction to a nuanced topic that can be read in a single afternoon, even if there are screaming kids around (which was the case in my first read through of the book).

High Functioning Autism:

Angelic Takeaway: Autism occurs on a spectrum. Many of us can pass as normal in a crunch. This chapter relates explains how my theory of autism relates to commonly observed symptoms. I suspect many attracted to this book are on the very high functioning side of the autistic spectrum.

I've observed many types of autistic people, and though I share commonalities with some, others seem completely different, at least on the surface. The commonality I've generally observed is that autistic people often possess some sort of special knowledge, talent, or ability, which comes from their perception in a non-typical wavy frequency band. However, this comes at the cost of perception in the normal physical frequency band, which normally manifests as social difficulties and general problems functioning in the physical world.

Google (at the time of writing) lists the following as signs of high-functioning autism. All these apply to me and I will now explain why these symptoms exist in the context of my theory.

High Functioning Autism Symptoms

- Emotional Sensitivity
- Fixation on Particular Subjects or Ideas
- Linguistic Oddities
- Social Difficulties
- Problems Processing Physical Sensations
- Devotion to Routines
- Development of Repetitive or Restrictive Habits
- Dislike of Change

Emotional Sensitivity: Often existing more in the wavy energetic universe, autistic people feel energy and waves very directly. It seems typical for autistic people to dislike loud, chaotic environments. I believe this is because these loud and sensory-rich environments force them to come down into the partically world fully and interact with viscerally uncomfortable energy.

We'd generally rather be in your own wavy world exploring, learning, or doing whatever we were up to from our wavier perspective.

I recall being in loud environments as a kid with my face in my Game Boy, desperately trying to tune out the chaotic energy swirling around me. Part of the wavy world is that everything is one. A non-autistic person may view an emotionally disturbed environment as something separate from themselves which they can ignore, but from a wavy, autistic perspective you literally are this emotionally disturbed environment.

Fixation of Particular Subjects or Ideas: This is just physics. Ultimately, the partically Simulation is a reflection of the wavy universe, with the wavy universe being primary. When fixated on something in the wavy universe, the partically Simulation simply does not have the power to draw the autistic person's attention away. This is why autistic people often appear to external observers to be in their own world. Though perhaps not consciously understood, the autistic person realizes the wavy reality is primary and the partically Simulation is secondary. When an autistic person is inspired by something from the wavy universe, nothing partically can stand in its way.

An early title of this book was *Waves Create Particles*. It is of profound importance to the world that we realize that the wavy universe ultimately creates the partically Simulation, and not the other way around, which is how 98% of the world currently operates (tested true).

Famous electrical scientist Nikoli Tesla (who was an early example of autism) seemed to demonstrate both the up and down side of this. When developing the technology which would become the foundation of our modern electrical world, he was described as being in his own world. During these periods he was fixated on translating his ideas from the wavy universe into partically reality. Assistants would have to talk for him, as he was not too interested in explaining himself (which probably would have been extremely difficult) or interacting with the partically Simulation more than he had to.

Later in his life he became fixated on ideas which probably weren't as productive, such as pigeons, woman's jewelry, and certain numbers. I've found broadly that autistic people are often bothered by something energetic/wavy universe and fixate on it, but rarely do they or the people surrounding them understand how to deal with this energetic sensitivity, as there is an insistence that the cause of their upset is something out there in the partically world.

This energetic sensitivity which has been a challenge in this life ironically was a major factor making this book possible.

Problems Processing Physical Sensations: To cite one of my own autistic oddities, which I share with Nikoli Tesla, was that woman's jewelry, makeup, and fashion tends to bother me somewhat. After contemplation on this, this has nothing to do with makeup, clothing or jewelry itself. It was the incoherence between the wavy/spiritual and partically/physical.

Operating in the wavy world, I usually noticed a woman's energy/vibe first (which told me most of what I needed to know) then saw all the details of her partically physical appearance afterwards. The vast majority of males seem to operate the other way around.

A high-vibrational woman tends to be beautiful to me regardless of her makeup, wardrobe or partically jewelry add-ons. I always saw low-vibrational women who used makeup, jewelry, or clothing to appear more beautiful than they actually are as a subtle lie. Obsessive amounts of makeup, loud clothing, or jewelry on high-vibrational women almost rob them of their beautiful essence, as these partically add-ons are an unnecessary distraction.

Linguistic Oddities: I've always had a stutter and often use words that are close, but not quite right. I've observed this in other people with autism. This is because a person whose experience is more in the vibrational, wavy world tends to have a bit of trouble translating their ideas perfectly in partically language. On a personal level, my stuttering is at its worst when trying to express an idea which the mind simply does not have language for.

Much of the unconventional language in this book was developed with another autistic teacher. We were able to stretch language to discuss ideas using what others would consider our linguistic oddities. For example, the terms wavy and partically were fleshed out and used in the Quantum Mechanics/spiritual discussions with the other autistic teacher.

I've observed that autistic people often keep to themselves and stay in their own world, simply because they do not have language available to make their ideas comprehensible. In this book, I do my best to explain these linguistic oddities so that the ideas can be comprehended.

Social difficulties: Humans experience reality on a vibrational spectrum. I describe this vibrational spectrum as levels of a Simulation. It's clear that each level of the Simulation experiences a very different version of the world. Generally, autistic people experience a slightly more wavy/spiritual variation of the world.

For example, a typical class of youngsters may be collectively excited about the fight that just happened in the hall, but the autistic youth might be more interested in the book they are reading or video game they are currently playing. Social interaction with the class might be awkward for this autistic youth, as he is simply focused on a different vibrational reality than his classmates. Intellectual analysis of a book or video game would seem out of context and weird to the classmates who were fixated on the social drama a fight creates. During the height of the COVID-19 pandemic when this was a main topic of conversation in society, I simply was not interested.

I've never felt very comfortable socializing except with a small inner group of friends, because whatever I was vibrationally focusing on at the time tended to not be what the average person was focusing on.

Devotion to Routines/Development of Repetitive or Restrictive Habits/Dislike of Change: This seemed to be because changing routines and habits always involved effort in the partically world. Partically life was easier when I did not need to deviate from a schedule, and could let the body go through my daily routine almost automatically.

Big changes to my routine (moving or changing jobs for example) would temporarily pull me away from whatever field of knowledge I was truly interested in, as I needed to focus more on partically/physical world. I tended to react negatively to people in my life who wanted to change up my routine, especially if that change made my life more complicated or partically.

Many people in spiritual/wavy circles call themselves empathic, because they feel others' energy viscerally. For the majority of this life, I've been extremely empathic but have found myself in environments where the logical worldview dominated. Hence I explored the logical scientific world, even earning a Master's degree in Nuclear Engineering, but doing it through my autistic wavy/empathic lens.

This has gifted me with an understanding of both the thinking and feeling worlds. Hence, this book walks a line between the spiritual/wavy world and the physical/partically world. The condition of autism allowed me to explore the world through a scientific lens and spiritual lens at the same time without realizing it.

I'm not an expert on the condition of autism, nor do I want to be, but optimal ways of dealing with the condition seem to follow the advice of the Buddha's Middle Way. This means helping autistic people adapt and resonate with the 'normal' physical world. This often means holding them accountable for certain physical behaviors and responsibilities that the autistic person will not react positively to. On the other hand, simultaneously allowing them to run free away from the restrictions of the lower levels of the Simulation which may interfere with the expression of their inherent gifts.

The First Commandment:

Out of the classic Ten Commandments treasured by the Christian and Jewish faiths, this commandment is first because it's ridiculously important. It is, "Thou shalt have no other gods before me."

Part of the programming in this Simulation is that we need that one thing to have unshakable faith in. This is our rock which all other experiences within the Simulation are based upon. This rock can be real or an illusion. The choice of this rock will determine one's ultimate spiritual destination.

What people put their faith into can be anything. It can be God, government, an institution, a family member, science, or even an addictive substance. However, the only thing that is truly safe is God (tested true).

Everything other than the changeless power source of God eventually changes. The higher the level of the Simulation, the less subject it is to time and the more stable it is in the long-run. God is the only changeless thing in this Simulation of changing physical phenomena.

I've always observed that the vibe of people and institutions rise and fall over time. I can now use the calibration process to verify this. It is often alarming to see people putting their faith into a person or institution that simply isn't what it used to be. Just because a grandfather had a wonderful experience at a university does not necessarily mean it's a great place for the grandkids.

I've observed a reciprocal relationship between the faith one puts in mighty unshakable God and unstable external props.

As faith in God decreases, faith in shaky external props automatically increases. A related concept discussed earlier in this book is the reciprocal relationship that exists between an entity using power vs. force.

Putting one's ultimate faith in something from the lowest two levels of the Simulation leads to spiritual disaster in a hurry. Faith in tribal ideologies (often disguised as political ideologies) or pleasure and pain impulses will eventually lead to ruin; spiritual recovery may be slow and painful.

It's quite apparent that much of the world has placed their ultimate faith in these things, and even a quick glance at the world makes it apparent at the suffering it is causing.

Even putting one's ultimate faith in higher institutions such as science can be tenuous. This is NOT to say that I advise ignoring information from any source, no matter one's faith in a higher power.

I have a friend with a very high IQ who reads voraciously, but unfortunately is avowedly atheist. I have great respect for his intelligence and learned a lot from him over the years.

A few years ago he approached me with great excitement, claiming to have read a book which proved Albert Einstein was wrong about everything. I remember immediately sensing the untruth of this but all his arguments made limited sense, so I let this ghastly lapse in truth go.

Shortly after this conversation, COVID-19 burst onto the scene and he became a cheerleader for some of the most outlandish COVID-19 regulations, even suggesting jail sentences for minor violators. I recall seeing him wearing a mask alone in his car and humorously thinking, *Wow, his guardian Angel could've prevented that.*

Unfortunately, being an ardent atheist cuts him off from the spiritual world which is our ultimate defense against major lapses in truth. The First Commandment is our ultimate lifeline down here in the Simulation (tested true).

In the modern world, the wolves tend to come disguised as sheep. I've mentioned in this book that my spirit animal is the wolf, and I'm told a purpose of the Angels sending this book through me is that it sometimes takes a wolf to fight off the wolves.

If one takes a single message from this book, I'd recommend it be to follow the First Commandment: "Thou shalt put no gods before me." This simple commandment can save lifetimes of hellish floundering. Without this commandment, one will eventually become lost in the shifting kaleidoscope of this physical Simulation. The glorious news is that Angelic help is always abundant and forever available, but not if one consciously cuts themselves off from it.

Ultimately one's consciousness gravitates toward what one puts one's ultimate faith in. Following the First Commandment gravitates one in a single direction . . . UP! Putting one's ultimate faith in anything else will result in a more ambiguous picture.

The Eternal Game:

Angelic Takeaway: Spoiler alert: the Angels always win in the end. Good always eventually triumphs over evil. The other side can only cause temporary delays with tricks, mischief and shenanigans.

In the opening of this book I stated that we find ourselves in an Angelic Simulation in which we have two teams playing: the Angelic and demonic. Older religions and theologies tend to describe this conflict as an eternal war, but I prefer the word 'game,' as also stated earlier, the Angelic control all the real power (tested true). War is a strong word to describe something with such a ridiculous power imbalance. If one comprehends the full meaning of this last statement it is very good news to most of the participants in this Simulation.

Lacking any real power such as the ability to collapse the wave function or alter the Simulation programming, the demonic can only wield influence by creating a chaotic environment where the other participants get extremely confused in the Simulation and lose access to their real power. The demonic often scrambles truth behind layers of insane complexity as to be virtually unrecognizable. A hallmark of truth and Angelic energy is simplicity. In any fair confrontation truth beats non-truth one hundred percent of the time so non-truth must disguise this fact to keep a semblance of a game going (tested true).

An easily observable historical fact is that the great conveyors of truth such as Jesus Christ, Martin Luther King Jr., and Gandhi tended to wind up killed as the demonic game collapses rapidly in the presence of simple truth. I say this with minimal grimness, as souls operating from these high levels of the Simulation realize that the death of a physical body does not alter a wavy soul's trajectory much. At the higher levels, it is obvious that this is in fact only a dream or Simulation (tested true).

For the first forty years of this life, I waddled around in the kitty pool version of this Simulation, concentrating more on its mundane aspects. It was only after my Angelic experience and later gaining the ability to calibrate that the larger aspects of this purgatorial game came into focus.

As soon as I realized I had the ability to calibrate and that I'd been blessed with a tiny window into absolute truth, I immediately intuited it as an enormous jump in personal power. I was correct in this assumption.

However, at the time I failed to remember the famous Spiderman saying, "With great power comes great responsibility." I temporarily inhabited fairytale fantasy where I assumed that the other participants in the Simulation would be grateful for my insight into truth. I now understood why Dr. David Hawkins often quipped humorously, "When you tell the truth, quickly leave town."

A historical figure that I've always been fascinated with was Winston Churchill. If one wants a historical and often humorous insight into the man, the movie *The Darkest Hour* is a worthwhile watch. The talented actor Gary Oldan channels Winston Churchill and uncannily nails many of the subtle mannerisms of the flawed but powerful angel (tested true). Churchill had a similar ability as me to read vibes and see into truth. He spent the 1930s sensing Adolf Hitler's true nature, but found this truth very unpopular in Europe until Hitler began his invasions and his true colors were revealed.

From a young age, my autism has gifted me with the ability to sense people's quantum vibrations viscerally. This has often put me in the socially awkward position of clearly sensing low-vibe imposters. These low-vibe imposters were often able to fool the people around me who took the imposter's words far too seriously. These imposters were often able to elevate to a social position far higher than they deserved based on their merits alone.

A constant source of irksome annoyance in this life was having to watch as these imposters caused chaos around me; I rarely had the charisma, social clout, verbalization ability or charisma to expose these imposters. With the discovery of the calibration ability I thought I had this ability, but this was a clear error.

With calibration, I began to rapidly notice that many of my intuitive impressions about the low-vibe imposters, false dogma, and easily correctable problems were indeed correct. The spiritual ego went to work on a crusade to correct these errors, but to my surprise and dismay, these insights into truth were rarely well-received.

I clearly saw that the demonic functions best in a chaotic, truth-poor environment where their shenanigans work the best. A ranting madman will have no problem finding followers in a low-vibrating, economically poor, uneducated, and drug-infested area (this is broadly how many gangs are formed). However, this same ranting madman will likely have the police called on him if he finds himself in an educated, friendly, high-vibe area.

The critical mistake that I made was thinking that it was my personal task to correct these errors in truth that I clearly sensed.

When calibration was discovered I was operating in a spiritual group that had the distinct vibe emanating from the Heart chakra level of the Simulation. The group members were overall friendly, supportive, and positive. The group's activity revolved around studying a well-rounded integrous mix of spiritual literature. However, small pieces of false dogma had penetrated the group's core philosophies.

My spiritual ego, thinking it could correct these small pieces of false dogma, went to work correcting them and received a negative reaction from the group. Though my official membership in the group was maintained, my activity in the group decreased dramatically because of a combination of group will and my own frustration in not being able to correct what I perceived as problems.

I still check in with this nice group occasionally to find it still humming along fine in the Heart level of Simulation. The group's core philosophies and errors are the same but it is still friendly, supportive, and positive. I noticed some of the group's more evolved members have left in a fashion similar to me, but new members have come into the group almost automatically to replace them.

Turns out, the group's energy and philosophy is the absolute perfect place for someone operating from the Heart level of the Simulation to evolve (tested true). The small amount of errant dogma of the group provides a perfect gateway to graduate to the Throat chakra level of the Simulation when the errors are discovered by one's own evolving intellect (tested true). No action by any individual, including myself in correcting the errors, was ever necessary or desired (tested true).

This Simulation is purgatorial by divine design. For a soul to evolve, it must be presented with good choices and bad choices. Only by seeing the effects of these choices does a soul eventually evolve upwards. Heavenly Simulations where all needs are met are great rest areas, but this Simulation exists as a fast-track for evolution, and all the souls currently in this Simulation all made a choice on some level to be here.

I also believe that when all is done, souls will appreciate their time down here. I recall a dying relative, who had lived an extremely hard life, saying in his last hours with a smile on his face, that he appreciated everything that had happened to him.

Another helpful recontextualization of painful events is the realization that once a negative event has passed, one has repaid the negative karma and learned a soul-level lesson. In this life, after a painful period had passed, I always felt lighter and more free, almost as if a karmic anchor had been dropped.

I used humor and talked in a light tone purposely in this book in order to demonstrate this Simulation is indeed a game. A fairly reliable pointer to truth is humor. Entities comfortable with truth tend to use humor, as it resolves paradoxes between levels of the Simulation. Humor expresses truth more efficiently than cold logic ever could. Comedians tend to be the most effective truth tellers in society (tested true). If you meet an entity who is afraid or even outright hostile to humor, it may be worth investigating why this is before taking their words or actions too seriously.

I'll end this book with a brief serious note. The main point of this book is that the Angels always win in the end. Gandhi said the same fundamental truth with far more elegance when he said: "When I despair, I remember that all through history the way of truth and love have always won. There have been tyrants and murderers, and for a time, they can seem invincible, but in the end, they always fall. Think of it—always."

The temporary victories of the negative side is part of this perfect purgatorial training Simulation. A main point of this book is to encourage one to avoid the temporary glamor of going down the negative roads, as suffering is an automatic consequence. However, some advanced spiritual lessons are only learnable by making a mistake and living out the consequences. In my view, that is why God has us all down here.

Ultimately, one's happiness correlates exactly with how aligned one is with divinity (tested true). One can also rest in the simple truth that 'power' and 'faith in God' are synonymous terms (tested true). This is why we always know how things will turn out in the end. With this knowledge, one can relax and enjoy the play of the Simulation. The Angels always win. Good always eventually triumphs over evil. God bless everyone!

Gloria in Excelsis Deo!

Thank You and Acknowledgments:

This section traditionally goes at the beginning of a book but I wanted to lay this section out by levels of the Simulation so it only seemed to make sense to put it at the end after proper context was provided.

Root: I thank my Parents and close family who provided me a great childhood and upbringing. This book would not have come into existence without this foundation.

Sacral: I thank all the friendships who I considered part of my pack over the years. These wonderful souls number in the 100s. As I've always tended to avoid small-talk and tended towards introversion if I ever voluntarily talked or hung out with you, a tiny piece of you is in this book.

Solar Plexus: I thank all the negative events and mistakes of this life which have spurred the growth of the soul that wrote this book. This book simply would not have come through had I incarnated in a celestial realm. Iron is forged in fire.

Heart: I thank the many relationships of this life that taught me but tended to end due to my own limitations. These relationships highlighted these limitations which ultimately lead to their transcendence.

Throat: I thank the knowledge I've absorbed over the years via the books previously cited and the wisdom of those the Angelic kingdom have placed in my path during this life.

Third Eye: I thank those who helped me trim over 1200 pages of information channeled from the Angelic kingdom into this book. Especially my editor who taught me that less is more and is the reason you will find no 500-word run-on sentences in this book. A hallmark of truth is simplicity.

Crown: I thank my infinitely powerful, wise, and loving lord and creator God!

Made in the USA
Columbia, SC
06 May 2024